AN END TO SUFFERING

Also by Pankaj Mishra

FICTION
The Romantics

NONFICTION
Butter Chicken in Ludhiana:
   Travels in Small Town India

AN END TO SUFFERING

THE BUDDHA IN THE WORLD

PANKAJ MISHRA

FARRAR, STRAUS AND GIROUX
NEW YORK

Farrar, Straus and Giroux
19 Union Square West, New York 10003

Distributed in Canada by Douglas & McIntyre Ltd.
Printed in the United States of America
Originally published in 2004 by Pan Macmillan Ltd, Great Britain
Published in the United States by Farrar, Straus and Giroux
First American edition, 2004

Grateful acknowledgment is made for permission to reprint
"Gridhakura Hill," from *Collected Poems* by Allen Ginsberg.
Copyright © 1984, 1995 by Allen Ginsberg. Reprinted by permission
of the Wylie Agency (UK) Ltd.

Library of Congress Cataloging-in-Publication Data
Mishra, Pankaj.
     An end to suffering : the Buddha in the world / Pankaj Mishra.—
  1st American ed.
       p.   cm.
     ISBN-13: 978-0-374-14836-2
     ISBN-10: 0-374-14836-8 (hardcover : alk. paper)
     1. Buddhism—Influence.   2. Gaurama Buddha—Influence.
  3. Mishra, Pankaj.   I. Title.
BQ4012.M57 2004

                                                        2004056266

Designed by Rafaela Romaya
Map designed by Raymond Turvey

www.fsgbooks.com

10 9 8 7 6 5 4 3 2 1

We need history, certainly, but we need it for reasons different from those for which the idler in the garden of knowledge needs it, even though he may look nobly down on our rough and charmless needs and requirements. We need it, that is to say, for the sake of life and action.

FRIEDRICH WILHELM NIETZSCHE

Contents

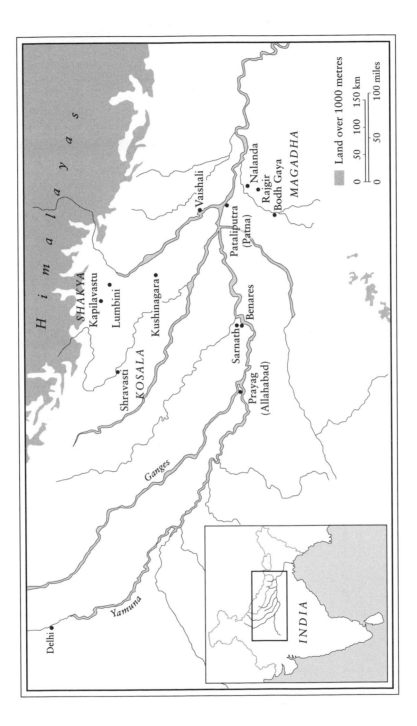

H i m a l a y a s

SHAKYA

Kapilavastu
Lumbini

Kushinagara

Shravasti

KOSALA

Vaishali

Pataliputra
(Patna)

MAGADHA

Nalanda
Rajgir
Bodh Gaya

Sarnath
Benares

Prayag
(Allahabad)

Ganges

Yamuna

Delhi

Land over 1000 metres

0   50   100   150 km
0   50   100 miles

INDIA

Prologue

IN 1992 I MOVED to a small Himalayan village called
Mashobra. Later that year, I began to travel to the inner
Himalayas, to the Buddhist-dominated regions of Kinnaur
and Spiti. These places were very far from Mashobra, but
travel to them was easy and cheap: rickety buses that originated in the nearby city of Simla went hundreds of miles,
across high mountains and deep valleys, to a town near
India's border with Tibet. I often went on these long journeys attracted by nothing more than a vague promise of
some great happiness awaiting me at the other end.

I remember my first trip. The monsoons had just ended,
with several dull weeks of fog and rain abruptly cancelled
out by a series of sharp clear days. On that chilly, bright
morning, the bus was late and crammed with nervous
Tibetan pilgrims, peasants and traders, its dusty and
dented tin sides already streaked with vomit.

Luck, and some pushing and shoving, managed to get
me a seat by the window; and then, after that bit of luxury, the crowd, the bad road and the dust seemed not to
matter. Everything I saw – the sun leaping across and
through dark pine forests, the orange corn cobs drying on

slate roofs of houses lost in immense valleys and, once, a tiny sunlit backyard with a pile of peanut shells on the cowdung-paved ground – seemed to be leading to an exhilarating revelation.

The day flew quickly past my window. But evening came cautiously, and the bus lost some of its cranky energy as it struggled up a narrow twisting road into the Sangla valley. Pink-white clouds blurred the snow peaks of the surrounding tall mountains as the river in the ravine below roared. The valley broadened at last. The mountains became even taller and more self-possessed. Long shadows crept down their rocky slopes and then over the green rice fields beside the river. Lights shone uncertainly through the haze ahead. Then, a long curve in the road brought them closer and revealed them as lanterns hanging from the elaborately carved and fringed balconies of double-storeyed wooden houses.

The bus began to climb again; the houses and the river-side fields receded. Boulders now littered the low barren slopes of the mountains where occasionally a glacier had petered out into muddy trails. Finally, at the end of the flinty snow-eroded road, the air growing thinner and thinner and Tibet only a few desolate miles ahead, there was a shadowy cluster of houses on a hill.

I was panting as I walked up a narrow cobblestone ramp. The bluish air trembled with temple bells. But the sound came from some other temple, for at this temple – shyly nestled under a giant oak and festooned with rows of tiny white prayer flags – there was only an old man hunched over an illustrated manuscript, a Tibetan, probably, judging by his face and the script on his manuscript, whose margins shone a deep red in the weak light from the lantern next to him on the platform.

The temple, though small, had a towering pagoda-like roof; the gable beams ended in dragon heads with open mouths. The carved wooden door was ajar and I could see through to the dark sanctum where, serene behind a fog of sweet-smelling incense, was a gold-plated idol of the Buddha: a Buddha without the Greek or Caucasian visage I was familiar with, a Buddha with a somewhat fuller, Mongoloid face, but with the same high brow, the broad slit eyes, the unusually long and fleshy ears, and the sublime expression that lacks both gentleness and passion and speaks instead of a freedom from suffering, hard won and irrevocable.

I had been standing there for a while before the old monk raised his head. Neither curiosity nor surprise registered in the narrow eyes that his bushy white eyebrows almost obscured.

We didn't speak; there seemed nothing to say. I was a stranger to him, and though he knew nothing of the world I came from he did not care. He had his own world, and he was complete in it.

He went back to his manuscript, wrapping his frayed shawl tightly around himself. Crickets chirped in the growing dark. A smell of fresh hay came from somewhere. Moths knocked softly against the oil-stained glass of the lantern.

I stood there for some time before being led away by the cold and my exhaustion and hunger. I found some food and a place to rest in the village. The long strange day ended flatly, its brief visions unresolved.

I spent a sleepless night in a farmer's low attic, with the

smell of old dust and dead spiders, and some slivers of moonlight. I was already up the next day when the roosters began to cry.

I went immediately to the temple, where there were worshippers – Buddhist or Hindu: I couldn't be sure – but the monk was nowhere to be seen. The morning arose from behind the snow-capped mountains. Then, suddenly, it overwhelmed the narrow valley with uncompromising light. Sharp knives glinted in the river. The village was bleached of its twilight mystery. The wooden chimneyless houses puffed thick blasts of smoke from open windows and doors. A long queue of mules carrying sacks of potatoes clattered down the cobblestone ramp. I was restless and wanted to leave. My return journey to Mashobra blended in my memory with other journeys I made to the Sangla valley in later years. But for many days afterwards, my mind rambled back to the temple, to that moment in the shadow of an oak before the Tibetan exile silently in tune with the vast emptiness around him, and I wondered about the long journey the monk had made, and thought, with an involuntary shiver, of the vacant years he had known.

It was around this time that I became interested in the Buddha. I began to look out for books on him. I even tried to meditate. Each morning I sat cross-legged on the dusty wooden floor of my balcony, facing the empty blue valley and remote mountain peaks in the north, which, I remember, turned white as that first autumn gave way to winter, and the apple and cherry trees around my house grew gaunt.

It seems odd now: that someone like myself, who knew so little of the world, and who longed, in one secret but tumultuous corner of his heart, for love, fame, travel, adventures in far-off lands, should also have been thinking of a figure who stood in such contrast to these desires: a man born two and a half millennia ago, who taught that everything in the world was impermanent and that happiness lay in seeing that the self, from which all longings emanated, was incoherent and a source of suffering and delusion.

I had little interest in Indian philosophy or spirituality, which, if I thought of them at all, seemed to me to belong to India's pointlessly long, sterile and largely unrecorded past. I didn't see how they could add to the store of knowledge – science and technology – and the spirit of rational enquiry and curiosity that had made the modern world.

My interest in the Buddha seems even stranger when I recall how enthralled I was then by Nietzsche, among other western writers and philosophers. Probably like many other impoverished and lonely young men I was much taken by the idea that one could overcome despair and win from the world, through sheer will, the identity and security it seemed reluctant to give.

I can't recall a spiritual crisis leading me to the Buddha. But then I didn't know myself well; the crisis may have occurred without my being aware of it. In my early twenties, I lived anxiously from one day to the next, hoping for a salvation I could not yet define.

Earlier that year I had left Delhi and moved with a few books and clothes to Mashobra. A Himalayan village was a strange choice for a young Indian man like myself, someone with little means and an uncertain future. But I hoped that in the silence and seclusion of the mountains I would finally be able to begin fulfilling an old and increasingly desperate ambition.

I had wanted to be a writer for as long as I could remember. I could not see myself being anything else. I had written little, however, apart from a few ill-considered reviews and essays during my three years at university in Delhi. I felt that I had wasted my time while most students worked hard to acquire a degree and find a job – the privileged gateway to the secure and stable life of marriage, children, paid holidays and pensions that the deprivations of our parents had prescribed for us.

Although I was eager to leave Delhi, I didn't want to stray too far from cities, to which I eventually saw myself returning. It seemed important for an aspiring writer not to isolate himself from society, the civilization from which all books, art and music seemed to emerge. A part of me was also vulnerable to the British-created romance of the 'hill station': the exclusive retreat in the mountains where life disarranged by the great heat of the plains could be recreated in miniature. It was why I had first gone to Mussoorie, a town in the Himalayan foothills, only to find it overrun by Christian missionaries and tourists from Delhi. It was why I had then gone on to Simla, which, in the nineteenth and early twentieth centuries, had been the summer capital of British India.

The British watched over their most valuable imperial possessions from this Himalayan town. They also played hard there: ballroom dances, polo, amateur theatre and scandals defined the self-enclosed world of Anglo-India that Rudyard Kipling first commemorated in *Plain Tales from the Hills*. There were few books on British India that did not attempt to evoke the pleasures of this most prestigious hill station. I had read these books attentively. In the spring of 1992, when I went looking for a cheap cottage in Simla, I was looking forward to promenades on the Mall, to spending brilliant snowy mornings in dimly lit coffeehouses, to browsing away the afternoons in dusty bookshops, and to the evenings that died silently on a neglected dirt path through the fir trees.

I was swiftly disabused. On the winding road to Simla from the railhead, Kalka – the road that revealed at every turn another vista of green hills against a blue sky – there were sandbagged checkpoints. In the adjoining state of Punjab, Sikh separatists had been fighting for over a decade for their own state. A violent insurgency had just broken out in nearby Muslim-majority Kashmir. From both states came the news of terrorist murders, bombings, extrajudicial execution and torture – the news from a world that had existed at my university only in the posters warning of bombs in public places but was now urgent in the faces and voices of the policemen, who, cradling automatic rifles, brought their fear into the cramped bus on that hill road as they ordered the passengers to open their baggage and shouted at those who were slow to respond.

On the narrow mountain road, these checkpoints seeded long traffic jams. The bus shuffled through black clouds of diesel fumes and a cacophony of truck and car horns. After many hours, there was Simla. Sighted from afar, from a sudden bend, it seemed a big heap of concrete-box buildings, less a picturesque hill station than an Indian small town recreated vertically amid green hills; and the view didn't improve much as we got closer.

The Indian economy had just begun to awaken from a four-decade-long socialist torpor. Cable TV, Häagen-Dazs ice cream and shopping vacations in Singapore were still some years away for an emerging middle class. For now, ambitious, mostly young men and women from the cities of Delhi and Chandigarh, savoured their growing wealth at the mock-Tudor shops and video-game parlours on the Mall Road. Their glowingly clear skin tones and brand-name jeans and sneakers, their emblems of class as well as caste, gave off an appearance of general well-being, of the kind the British probably had at the height of their power. They gave Simla a touch of glamour. But on the street just below the Mall, hectic with hunchbacked coolies in rags, the city began to deteriorate, packed alley by alley until it seethed at the very bottom of the hill in a favela-like squalor of low tin shacks and exposed stagnant drains.

The old wooden cottages of the kind I had seen myself living in (muslin curtains in the windows, rose beds in the backyard) were mostly gone, burnt to the ground – the rumours blamed arson – or demolished to make room for blocks of flats. There were hardly any places to rent cheaply. A lethargic estate agent showed me round a few of the new flats with damp cement walls that already spoke of decay and gloom; he then stopped returning my phone calls. I persevered for a few days, walking around the city, browsing through the two bookshops on the Mall Road, eating at expensive restaurants and worrying about money.

I remember the morning I took the bus to Mashobra, to what had been described as a 'nice picnic spot' in my guidebook. I was hoping only to kill some time before starting on the dreary journey back to Delhi.

The half-empty Himachal Roadways bus never stopped

groaning, even long after it moved out of the constriction of Simla and emerged into the broad open valley that slumbered peacefully in the pale sunshine. Soon, we were surrounded by damp cedars and didn't regain our freedom for some time. The harsh winter had lingered here in the form of miniature mountain ranges of snow that sat dirtily beside the rutted road. At tea shacks in dark little clearings, men in woollen rags hunched over pine-cone fires.

The bus left the highway, stuttered down a road between tottering houses of wood and tin, and then abruptly stopped. The driver killed the ailing engine, and everyone got out.

I was the last to leave. After the pungent warmth of the bus, the cold came as a shock. I saw that I was on a long ridge, facing a vast abyss filled with the purest blue air. The overall view, extending far to the east, was clear and spectacular: a craggy row of white mountain peaks rising above several tiers of hills and ridges, all of them supervising the deep wooded valley before me.

Wouldn't it be wonderful, I thought, to live here? I thought of asking someone about places to rent. But the bus had emptied fast – I had been the only tourist on it – and there was no one around. It was then that I noticed the red tin roof of a largish house, and the spiralling dirt path that seemed to lead towards it.

The house was indeed big and handsome, in an old-fashioned unostentatious way, with windows running round the balconies on its two floors – it had been built, I later learnt, in the early seventies, when timber from cedar trees was plentiful and cheap. I would come to know well the smell of old quilts and incense contained in its walls, the smells that overrode the change of seasons and evoked whole lives of virtuousness, regular habits and religious piety.

On that first morning, it stood confidently on a broad ridge, facing the mountains towards the east, its windows opaque in the sun. Baskets with peonies hung from the eaves. On the wide sunny porch some red chillies lay drying on a bright yellow sheet. A window on the second floor was open; so was the main door that opened, I could see, onto a wooden staircase.

I knocked and then heard the thump of bare feet on the floor. Someone appeared in the second-floor window: a thin boy. I tried to explain what I was looking for. He disappeared and then a little later Mr Sharma came down the stairs.

He was a tall man, and seemed even taller in his long woollen cap, giving off an air of sombre dignity. I told him – a bit awkwardly, his young nephew appraising me from the first floor – that I had been a student in Delhi, and was now looking for a place in the mountains where I could read and write for a few years.

Mr Sharma looked uncertainly at me for a moment, and then said that he would show me a cottage he had just built.

We walked through an orchard – I didn't know then that these were apple and cherry, peach and apricot trees – and came to a narrow spur at the corner of the hill. It was here that the small cottage stood, directly above a cow shed and what looked like storage rooms for fodder.

The cottage was functional: there were three rooms altogether, built in no particular order or design but placed next to each other; a bathroom and kitchen had been tacked on almost as an afterthought. The rooms still smelled of wood shavings – the aroma stayed for many months until pushed out in October that year by the fragrance of freshly picked apples stored underneath.

It was the balcony, however, that held me. Just beneath it was a small field of corn, barren and worked over by an old hunchbacked peasant. From the edge of the field, pine forests sloped down far into the valley, as far as the paddy fields and wooden houses with shiny slate roofs at the very bottom, in what seemed another season and climate. If I leaned to my left, I could see Mr Sharma's orchard. Looking up, I held the same view I had as I came off the bus – the valley, the snow-capped mountains and the sky that seemed locked in a trance so private that you could only watch and be still yourself. In my mind's eye, I could already see myself sitting on the balcony on long evenings and gazing at the darkening world.

To my surprise, Mr Sharma asked for a token rent: only 1000 Rupees per month. I was expecting more, and had even begun to wonder how I could afford the cottage. He said that he too had come to Mashobra many years ago, wanting to read and write. His father had set up the first Sanskrit college in Simla. Mr Sharma himself published a monthly magazine in Sanskrit from one of the rooms under my cottage. He said he hadn't built the cottage to make money; it was meant to host needy scholars like myself.

I felt uncomfortable being called a 'scholar'. I had been an indifferent student, originally of commerce, which I hoped would help me avoid the conventional role of doctor or engineer set out for not very well-off Indians like myself. I hadn't written much and had barely any idea of what I might write. But I didn't correct Mr Sharma; I did not wish to disappoint him. I had lived far more precariously in the hill station of Mussoorie, at a boarding house run by Christian missionaries who saw me as a potential convert, and who accosted me on my evening walks and wished to know the state of my soul. As I saw it, I was closer to being a scholar than a Christian.

And then it didn't really matter after I moved to Mashobra – a few days after my first visit – and, with my books and my absorption in them, began to look like a scholar of sorts.

It was very cold when I first arrived. For much of my life, I had longed for this kind of extreme cold. On the summer afternoons of my childhood, when a scorching *loo* raged just outside the darkened windows and doors, and while everyone in my family slept – the siesta being part of the obligatory surrender to the heat that emptied the streets of our small town – I sprawled half naked on the grainy stone floor and read and reread the *Mahabharata*, dreamily transplanting myself among the white peaks in the religious-kitsch calendars on the walls of our old railway bungalow. I imagined myself with the Pandava brothers in their self-imposed exile, and with the Hindu sages and seers shown meditating next to glaciers – men whose lengthy and bushy beards had seemed to the calendar artist a sign of wisdom and self-control.

And, now, I was in the Himalayas. But for many days I was far from exultant. I felt subdued by the pale-blue light that filled the valley, delicately shading the hollows of the distant mountains. I was oppressed by the silences, which were so fine that they could be broken by the apologetic cough of the hunchbacked peasant working somewhere invisibly in the orchard. Strange apprehensions seemed to lie in the damp shade of the pine forest I went walking through. The smell of the home fires drifting upwards from the valley inspired no memories of the many smoke-filled mornings and evenings of my small-town childhood; nothing, in fact, seemed to have any clear associations with my past.

It was as if the cold weather in a new place was forcing another side of me to emerge; as if I had grown too accustomed to living on the plains, where the same fierce white light fell from the sky all year long, enclosing everything – the self as well as the towns, fields and rivers – in a changeless substance.

I felt particularly restless in the evenings. The bare apple trees in the orchard looked beaten, and, as the lights of a hundred unseen homes began to twinkle on the distant hillsides, vivid fantasies of security and warmth arose in my mind. Cruel icy winds, the residue of snowstorms in the highest mountains, sometimes blew through the cracks in window and door frames and almost extinguished my kerosene lamp. I bought a locally made heater from one of the shops in the village. But the power supply was erratic, and the two rods barely had time to glow a weak orange before the light went out altogether. The hours spent huddled under the igloo of Mr Sharma's quilts and hot-water bottle did not finally relieve the viciousness of the tap water.

Occasionally, Mr Sharma dropped in, after supervising the milking of the cows and paying off the hunchbacked peasant. He brought fresh milk, or tea in steel tumblers which, because of the cold, always had a thick layer of cream over it, and was consumed in two or three quick sips. We sat wrapped in thick shawls in my room on facing wicker armchairs, Mr Sharma very erect in his.

We didn't always speak. In fact, the silences could lengthen considerably; they made me uneasy and I was the first to break them, often by asking Mr Sharma if the power supply was likely to become more regular, whether the plumbing in the bathroom could improve soon, if the large spiders I had seen around the house were poisonous, or – and I knew that this subject did interest him greatly – if it had snowed enough over the winter to help the apple trees.

Mr Sharma did not seem to notice either the silences or my questions. When he spoke in his slow measured way it was invariably about the depredations of modern civilization on nature. Even the supposedly eternal snows on the high Himalayan ranges were melting fast. The water in the river Sutlej that arose in Tibet and flowed not far from us was polluted. The hillsides were littered with plastic bags. The deforestation in the hills not only caused earthquakes but also terrible floods on the plains. Human beings had forgotten that they too were part of nature. They had been arrogant enough to think themselves masters of nature, and nature was now going to have its revenge on them.

I thought he talked to me of things he turned over in his mind but couldn't share with the people he lived with: his father, Panditji, a sprightly octogenarian with the appearance and robust self-absorption of a Hindu seer, who performed sacrificial rituals and made horoscopes; his affectionate mother who, like most women of her generation, had not received much formal education; or his sister, a woman of melancholy beauty who had been widowed some years previously and now worked at a government office in Simla.

The difference in our ages was great – he was then in his late fifties. Perhaps that's why he thought of me as primarily a listener, and responded frugally to my own curiosity about him. I wanted to know more about his past in Simla. He had first known the city when it was the summer capital of the largest portion of the British Empire, and perhaps subconsciously I wanted him to endow it with the glamour I had arrived too late to see.

But he said he disliked Simla. It appeared from various things he said at different times that his father's Sanskrit college had been of little use to him, and that he had to work at the missionary-run Bishop Cotton School in Simla, teaching Hindi to the children of rich local shopkeepers, people he might not have had much time for in the past. Mr Sharma seemed to me then to contain many unfulfilled aspirations, his over-formal manner being the defensive reflex of someone who saw the outside world as full of threats to his dignity.

The weather steadily improved. In the morning, there was a thin layer of frost on the ground. But the afternoons were warm. I often lay on the grass outside the house during the long hours of sunlight. My book remained unopened as I surrendered to idleness. I watched the clouds in the sky and smelled the grass and the soil beneath me; the fragrance summoned the silent overgrown gardens of my childhood, the places of retreat where I had once watched the industriousness of ants and snails and enacted scenes from the *Mahabharata*.

The rooms were cool and mysterious and aloof when I went inside. They had not yet insinuated themselves into my being as had the many provincial rooms I had lived in as a child, the rooms with their particular detail (the frayed wicker chair so hospitable to daydreams, the dry aroma of a cupboard, the pattern of cracks in the stone floor) from which separation was always painful.

I began to go on little walks, to the shops on the main road, and learnt more about Mashobra. Most of the village's two thousand inhabitants – farmers, low-level government employees, small shopkeepers – had little money. But there was no wretchedness of the kind found on the Indian plains. Its houses, opening out boldly on to the road, or hidden in cobbled alleys down the hill, were tall and large. The only ragged people on the road were out-of-work foreigners, Kashmiri and Nepalese porters, sullen, silent men wearing dusty ropes around their necks. The village seemed to belong to itself; and there were quiet Sunday mornings when the soft bells of the old English church could sound too insistent.

One day in the forest on the hill looming over the village, I came across a helipad and well-laid lawns, and then found myself surrounded by armed guards. I had strayed into the former retreat of the British viceroys, now assigned, like their much grander residence in Delhi, to the President of India, if hardly ever used by him. There were bigger and emptier houses on the road leading north from the village: old bungalows that hid behind tall hedges, and had, apart from the kind of melancholy gardens and arbours I had read about in Turgenev's novels and stories, dingy smoke-filled sheds for servants, where women with broad Mongoloid faces squatted around wood fires.

The road had more surprises as it cut through a pine forest, past a meadow and an old Kali temple and ended at a hilltop forest rest house, which the locals pronounced Carignano, and which turned out to be Craignano, the site of a mansion built in the late nineteenth century by an Italian confectioner from Turin.

Mr Sharma couldn't tell me what an Italian was doing in the Himalayas in the nineteenth century. But he did know that the wealthier British often escaped to Mashobra from hedonistic Simla. He had also heard of some of the Indians who now owned the bungalows. One of them was the descendant of a lecherous Maharajah whom the British had banned from entering Simla. One bungalow served as the hideout of a prince from Nepal. Three decades before, a famous film actress from Bombay had bought one of the best properties in Mashobra, but she had never been seen in the village. An industrial magnate from Delhi, someone fleeing private tragedy – the death of his young son – was the most faithful among the absentee owners of the bungalows, which were maintained largely by the servants, who were mostly migrant labourers from distant villages.

I felt slightly diminished by this new knowledge about Mashobra. On clear days, when I walked to the top of the hill with the presidential house and saw the snowy peaks on the horizon and felt a fresh cool breeze on my face, I could believe that a new life was beginning for me, in which I too would have a claim on the world's ample store of happiness. But the big houses made me fear that I was going to be as disappointed in Mashobra as I had been in Delhi.

*

I had taken to Delhi my provincial ability to be quickly impressed, and a hunger for new adventures, possibilities of growth. In well-protected enclaves, there were libraries and bookshops, cultural sections of foreign embassies, film festivals and book readings. There were even – if you had the money and the confidence – a dozen five-star hotels. But these excitements were temporary – best possessed at a high level of wealth and security, and maintained beyond the first few minutes only if, after the new European film, you were returning in an air-conditioned car to a house with high walls. For to emerge into a humid night from the cool auditorium of the British Council onto the broken pavement with the limbless beggars; to push and elbow one's way into the sweat, dirt and noise of a packed bus; then to watch with a foolish little twinge of privilege the stranded men at the bus stops, was to be robbed of the new and fragile sensations of the previous few hours; it was to have yet again a sense of the hollowness of the city's promise and the mean anonymity of the lives it contained; it was to know the city as a setting not of pleasure but of work and struggle.

I was somewhat relieved to find out that my association with the Sharmas gave me a certain status in the village. Strangers greeted me with 'Namaste' as they passed me on the road. The men in the cavernous shops, idle behind open sackfuls of kidney beans and chickpeas and rice, were attentive, eager to talk and offer gossip about local politics.

The Sharmas themselves lived quietly, except when a special occasion – a festival, a shradh (a death anniversary ritual) or a yagna (a fire sacrifice) – brought the scattered family together in a happy whirl of silk scarves, crying babies and sizzling puris (some of which came my way). Mr Sharma's sister left for her office in Simla early in the morning and returned just before dusk. Only Mr Sharma and his mother remained in the big house with the many windows, which looked deserted during the long afternoon. There were visitors, middle-class people in new cars whom the shopkeepers gazed at curiously. Mr Sharma's father, Panditji, who seemed to spend most of his day walking around the orchard or inspecting the cows while leaning on his stick, was, I discovered, very well known as a priest and astrologer. People from places as far off as Chandigarh visited him in order to know about, and improve, their prospects in this and the next life. He was also the personal priest of the former king of the nearby district of Rampur, whose political career he helped boost through elaborate fire sacrifices on his lawn.

Each month, Mr Sharma, working away unseen in his house, brought out his Sanskrit magazine, *Divyajyoti*, from an antique printing press kept in one of the dark rooms just below my cottage. Mr Sharma told me that it had a circulation of five hundred copies, and it went out to Sanskrit colleges and institutions in India and elsewhere. He wrote most of the magazine himself during the first half of the month. I did not ask him what he wrote about, but I imagined he pronounced on broad social and political issues of the kind he discussed with me. Some of the articles may have been commentaries on a fifth-century BC book of grammar Mr Sharma often held up proudly as proof of Sanskrit's divine origin and inspiration.

He brought the loose pages to the press, smiling awkwardly when I passed him on the narrow path through the orchard. For the second half of the month, Daulatram, the big round-faced jovial handy man, would laboriously typeset the longhand version, a solitary figure in a corner of the dark room messy with wooden galley trays and metal sticks: the tips of his fingers were stained black when he came up to my cottage to replace a fuse or to offer some freshly plucked fruit. A week before the fifteenth of each month, the issue would be printed. The press would begin to hum loudly as Daulatram turned on the power, and then, after an uncertain staccato start, ease into a regular beat, which was as peculiarly soothing as that of a train at night. Then, on the morning of the fifteenth, Daulatram would jauntily walk up the hill to the post office, holding the finished copies in a small bundle under his giant arm.

The days acquired a rhythm, began to pass. I was awakened very early in the morning, the sun bullying its way even through the thick coarse-textured blue curtains of my window. Shortly thereafter, I heard a knock on the door: it was Mr Sharma's young nephew with a plate of parathas and pickle. This was the gift of the women in Mr Sharma's household: his mother and his sister. The day stretched long and somewhat emptily after that, even though I went to bed babyishly early, at around nine o'clock, by which time the whole village was already asleep.

For years, I had felt a small thrill at the sight of the sentence, 'I read all morning'. The simple words spoke of the purest and most rewarding kind of leisure. It was what I did now: I read all morning, sitting out on the balcony, and then, early in the afternoon, with the sun roughly overhead, I walked up the hill, through a dappled pine wood, for lunch at a roadside food shack called Montu's dhaba.

Montu, a lumbering corpulent man with eyes perpetually red from drinking, ran the dhaba along with his wife.
They lived in two dark low-roofed rooms at the back, curtained off from the road-facing dhaba with a torn cotton
sari. At lunch I sat alone on the wooden bench, under the
outdated calendar with pictures of Shiva, and read the cen-
sorious articles in *Punjab Kesari*, a local Hindi daily, about
masturbation (bad for eyesight) and blue jeans (bad for
blood circulation), while Neeraj, the couple's polite young
son, brought warm chapattis on a small aluminium plate.

The food was unremarkable, the menu unchanging.
There was frequently a lot of something called 'mixed
dhal', which was all Montu said he could afford by way of
dhal in the days of post-socialist inflation. But his son
Neeraj asked hopefully each time if I had found the food
satisfactory, and I had to lie.

On the way back I stopped at the post office, a large
dusty room with a disused telephone booth and an old
damaged clock. There would often be a few men there –
mostly servants from the big empty houses – sending
money to the families they had left in remote Himalayan
villages. They would ask me to write a few cryptic mes-
sages on the small margins of their money-order forms.
'Everything is fine,' I usually wrote, 'use this money for
your medicines. I will send more soon.' Or: 'I am sorry
that I can't send more money. I have not heard from you
for a long time. I am very worried. I pray that you are well.
Please write and tell me so.'

There was rarely any mail for me, apart from an occasional letter from my parents and a cheque – payment for
one of the reviews I wrote to support myself. But the ageing postman was always grateful to give me some letters

for my landlord and save himself the steep walk to and from the house. I, in turn, would hand them to Mr Sharma's mother who sat knitting at the open second-floor window. She would sit there from late morning, all through the long drowsy afternoons until the sun disappeared behind the hills to the west, when the shadows, languid all day, swiftly stole across the orchard and the valley, and the soft golden peaks in the distance seemed to hold, briefly, all the light in the world.

Weeks passed. The summer was warm and long. Some exotically coloured birds cut slow lazy circles in the blue air all day. In the evenings, smoke arose in thin nervous columns from houses deep in the valley, where, late at night, the dogs would abruptly begin to bark.

The monsoons finally came in early July and pulled a thick veil of grey over everything; the rain was comforting at first, but then grew insistent and dreary. I began to long for clear days, and I think that it was soon after autumn set in, with the first of its long bejewelled afternoons, that I first went to the inner Himalayas.

The Invention of 'Buddhism'

THE DAYS WERE SHORTENING with intimations of winter when I returned from the inner Himalayas to Mashobra. When spring came, and the roads cleared, I began to travel to the Spiti and Pin valleys. There, in the lonely cold deserts, speckled wherever the snow melted into streams with green oases of pea and barley fields, and watched over by hilltop monasteries of sun-baked bricks, I saw many more images of the Buddha. I visited Tabo, and found the oldest monastery in the region still full of lamas, as jaunty in their maroon robes as the prayer flags fluttering from electric poles in the treeless expanses.

I came to recognize the colourful murals and to understand somewhat the symbolism of the mystical circular diagrams (*mandalas*) on the wall hangings. I could spot from afar the distinctive shape of the *gompas*, or Buddhist monasteries; and although I felt excluded by the faith they expressed, about which I knew little then, I came to value them for their solitude and distance from the known world.

I was intrigued, too, by the monks, their childlike simplicity, cheerfulness and serenity. I attributed these qualities to the plain and undemanding world the monks lived in, until I found out that some of them had travelled to, and spent time in, Europe and America. One of them had studied in a monastery near Lhasa for about twenty years; I was surprised to know that his subjects had been logic, epistemology, cosmology, psychology and ethics as expounded in Buddhist texts written in India as early as the second century AD.

I began to write a travel essay, in which I tried to record my surprise at finding traces of Buddhism in these remote Himalayan valleys. I wrote about the other kind of Indian Buddhists I had met before: they were Dalits, low-caste Hindus, millions of whom had converted to Buddhism since the 1950s in an attempt to escape an oppressively caste-ridden Hinduism. I tried to describe how these politically active Buddhists, who did not appear to take much interest in spiritual matters, differed from the monks in the Himalayan monasteries.

The small bookshop on the Mall in Simla was well stocked with books in English on Buddhism – in expectation, the owner told me, of the European and American tourists who came looking for writing on spiritual figures and themes, and often travelled from Simla to the hill town of Dharamshala, the home of the Dalai Lama and the Tibetan community in exile.

One of the books I found there was an English translation of the *Milindapanha* (*Questions of King Menander*), which I had seen mentioned as a basic text of Buddhist philosophy in an essay by the Argentinian writer Jorge Luis Borges. King Menander was a Greek who reigned in north-west India, now Pakistan, in the first or second century BC. He is said to be among the rulers of the time who embraced, or was at least familiar with, Buddhism. The book, which was preserved in Ceylon for centuries, consists of Menander's conversations with an elderly Buddhist monk called Nagasena.

Their dialogue on the individual self, which drew explicitly upon the Buddha's ideas, had particularly struck Borges. It begins with Menander asking Nagasena his name. Nagasena says that his name is 'only a generally understood term, a practical designation. There is no question of a permanent individual implied in the use of the word.'

Menander replies, 'If there is no permanent individuality, who gives you monks your robes and food, lodging and medicines? And who makes use of them? Who lives a life of righteousness, meditation and reaches *Nirvana*? Who destroys living beings, steals, fornicates, tells lies, or drinks spirits? . . . If your fellow monks call you Nagasena, what then is Nagasena? Would you say that your hair is Nagasena? Or your nails, teeth, skin, or other parts of your body, or the outward form, or sensation, or perception, or the psychic constructions, or consciousness? Are any of these Nagasena? Are all these taken together Nagasena? Or, anything other than they?'

Nagasena answers no to all of Menander's questions.

Menander says, 'Then for all my asking I find no Nagasena. Nagasena is a mere sound! Surely what your reverence has said is false!'

Nagasena now takes over the questioning. He asks Menander, 'Your Majesty, how did you come here – on foot, or in a vehicle?'

Menander replies, 'In a chariot.'

'Then tell me,' Nagasena asks, 'what is the chariot? Is the pole the chariot?'

'No, your reverence,' Menander replies.

'Or the axles, wheels, frame, reins, yoke, spokes, or goad?'

Menander replies that none of these things is the chariot.

'Then all these separate parts taken together are the chariot?'

Menander again says no.

'Then is the chariot something other than the separate parts?'

'No, your reverence,' Menander says.

'Then for all my asking, your Majesty,' Nagasena says, 'I can find no chariot. The chariot is a mere sound. What then is the chariot? Surely what your Majesty has said is false! There is no chariot!'

Menander protests that what he had said was not false. 'It is on account of all these various components, the pole, axle, wheels and so on, that the vehicle is called a chariot. It's just a generally understood term, a practical designation.'

'Well said, your Majesty!' Nagasena replies. 'You know what the word chariot means! And it's just the same with me. It's on account of the various components of my being that I am known by the generally understood term, the practical designation, Nagasena.'[1]

There were many such clear and simple exchanges in the book, illustrating the Buddhist view of individual identity as a construct, a composite of matter, form, perceptions,

ideas, instincts and consciousness, but without an unchanging unity or integrity.

'I think, therefore I am,' Descartes had said; and when
I first came across these famous words as an undergraduate they expressed all that then seemed holy to me:
individuality, the life of the mind. It was comforting to
believe that the human mind was capable of acting rationally, logically and freely upon the inert outside world. I
was attracted, too, by the idea of the authentic self, which
I had picked up from the French existentialist philosophers, who for some reason were very popular in India.
These descriptions of the self – as a discrete entity shaped
through rational thought and act – helped offset the uncertainties (financial, emotional, sexual) that I lived with then.

But the dialogue between the Greek king and the
Buddhist monk seemed to refute intellectually the Cartesian 'I', by implying that one cannot speak of a separate
self or mind thinking 'I think' inside the body, inasmuch as
this self is nothing but a series of thoughts. It suggested
that the 'I' was not a stable and autonomous entity and
indeed was no more than a convenient label for the provisional relations among its constantly changing physical
and mental parts. It also matched better my experience: of
finding incoherence where there was supposed to be a self,
of being led on by stray thoughts, memories and moods,
and thinking that nothing existed beyond that flux.

I read other books. I learned quickly that although
Buddhism often had the trappings of a formal religion –
rituals and superstitions – in the countries where it existed,
it was unlike other religions in that it was primarily a
rigorous therapy and cure for *duhkha*, the Sanskrit term

denoting pain, frustration and sorrow. The Buddha, which means 'the enlightened one', was not God, or His emissary on earth, but the individual who had managed to liberate himself from ordinary human suffering, and then, out of compassion, had shared his insights with others. He had placed no value on prayer or belief in a deity; he had not spoken of creation, original sin or the last judgement.

He had spoken instead of a suffering that was man-made and thus eradicable. He had confined himself to human beings living everyday lives with desire, attachment, pride, jealousy and hatred. He had analysed the workings of these emotions and asserted that they arise from a craving for and an attachment to a self that has no true existence. He had developed analytic and contemplative techniques which helped prove that neither the self nor the phenomenal world are solid, stable and discrete entities, and which attuned the human mind to 'things as they really are': interconnected and in a state of change.

The Buddha was, broadly speaking, an empiricist who denied that there are any fixed substances underlying appearances; this is true as much for what one feels to be one's inner self or ego as for the outer world. He claimed that experience, rather than speculative metaphysics, holds the key to wisdom. He assumed that the quality of all human experience depends on the mind and so had been concerned with analysing and transforming the individual mind. To see that one was neither identical with one's thoughts as they arose continuously and discursively in one's mind, generating desire, anxiety, fear and guilt, nor indeed limited by them, was to be aware of the possibility of controlling them and of moving towards a new kind of spiritual and intellectual freedom.

Clearly, the Buddha had been more of a trenchant thinker and psychologist than a religious figure. He, and later interpreters of his ideas, had investigated in detail the contents of human consciousness; they had located in it a quality of will which when strengthened through medita-tion can become an effective barrier against craving and suffering.

But, reading the often very abstract and difficult Buddhist treatises on the mind, I often wondered why the Buddha, ostensibly the founder of a religion, had con-cerned himself with this kind of close and dry analysis of the inner world of experience; why had he not extended his analysis to the external world, tried to establish clear, distinct and certain foundations for knowledge, and founded, like Descartes, a tradition of scientific enquiry? Certainly Buddhism with its rational outlook was immune to the kind of conflict between religion and science that defined modern western philosophy.

It seemed that the Buddha had had other priorities and that he had been concerned almost exclusively with the inescapable fact of suffering. But here, too, he seemed to differ radically from the intellectual fathers of the modern world, Rousseau, Hobbes and Marx. For he had presumed to offer a cure for human suffering that did not involve large-scale restructuring of state and society.

Mr Sharma, whom I told about my growing interest in the Buddha, couldn't say much about this. He had taken to dropping in more often than before, and he appeared to have loosened up a bit. He told me more about his life. He had grown up in a village near Simla, among apple and pear orchards. He had spent no time at all on the plains; he spoke with something like pride of how his few visits there had proved to be ordeals. When he spoke of the Himalayas as a place of exile and refuge, when he told me about the nearby regions which the Pandava brothers in the *Mahabharata* had visited thousands of years ago, he seemed to be speaking not so much of the myths of the race – the idea of the Indian plains with their relentless heat and dust as a trap – as of his own life.

He had never married; family life with its obligations was, he said, not for him. But he seemed not altogether at ease in his self-imposed solitude. I wondered if he sometimes resented it, and wished, like everyone else, that he could have had another, more active and fruitful life, far away from the small place where he had spent, and was now to end, his life.

He seemed a bit puzzled by my interest in the Buddha. He said that Dalits, low-caste Hindus, who had converted to Buddhism thinking it to be something opposed to Hinduism, had dragged the Buddha's name through mud. For the Buddha was actually the tenth incarnation of the Hindu God Vishnu, and had emerged from the mouth of Brahma, and therefore was part of rather than opposed to the Hindu tradition.

I told him that this was more myth than history. The Buddha may have emerged metaphorically from the mouth of Brahma, but the evidence collected by British scholars in the nineteenth century had proved that he had also been a flesh-and-blood being, a figure no less historical than Jesus and the Prophet Mohammed, and, furthermore, that he had lived and died not far from where we were. I also told Mr Sharma that I had been to the Buddha's birthplace in Nepal and seen the iron pillar erected there by Ashoka, the third-century BC Indian emperor.

*

The Buddha's birthplace is called Lumbini, and is just north of the vast Indian plain across which the great rivers of the subcontinent, the Ganges and the Yamuna, flow. The legends of the Buddha speak of it being close to the Himalayan foothills. This gives the place romance: tall mountains and waterfalls and pine forests as the backdrop to the Buddha's luxurious childhood.

But when you finally get there – after a long, arduous journey within either India or Nepal – the high mountains to the north are no more than a rumour; at best, an added chill in the winter breezes, and a faint swelling on the horizon on clear spring days. The feeling of being exposed in the vast flat land never leaves you, especially in the summer when, after weeks of blistering heat, whirlwinds of fine dust and dry leaves scatter across the exhausted rice fields and the huddled villages of mud and straw.

Occasionally, there are clusters of mango and tamarind trees and ponds: oases of shade and cool, where the physical world regains form and colour. The land that looks so parched grows quickly green after the first rains of the monsoons in late June or early July. Two months of monsoons impose an unruly lushness upon it. But the endless rain wearies; the prickly heat saps energy; and the rivers and streams often burst their banks, turning the earth into obdurate mud. It is only during the months from October to March that the weather stops being punitive. All day long a mellow light falls gently over the busy fields and the villages from a tenderly blue sky. The evenings are short, and the nights often chilly.

In 1985, when I visited Lumbini, I was sixteen years old. I had just left home for the first time and was living as a student in Allahabad, one of the emerging urban centres of the Buddha's time and now a decaying old provincial city in the Gangetic plain. I travelled cheaply and very slowly, on trains pulled by steam engines and country buses and, once, on a ferry over a dangerously swollen muddy river, passing through the places that the Buddha as a young scion called Siddhartha had dreamed of visiting.

I am not sure if you can travel much faster these days. Things don't change much in that impoverished part of North India; when I revisited Lumbini many years later I found myself wandering through the same empty land, past the same yellow fields of mustard and forgotten villages and small towns.

Lumbini itself has a few more buildings, mainly monasteries run by Buddhists from Japan, South Korea, Thailand and Myanmar. New monasteries are being built in the distinctive national styles of South-east Asia. Some miles away, there is an expensive hotel catering mostly to Japanese tourists, and a research institute with a grand but deserted library.

Very few Buddhists live in Lumbini or its environs and these are mostly monks from South-east Asia. There is a temple with a stone relief of Maya, the Buddha's mother, who was worshipped by local Hindus for centuries as a Hindu deity. The nearby towns – poor and squalid – are full of shrines to Hanuman, the Hindu monkey-god. Further into the countryside, the blue-tiled minarets of the mosques, looming out of the flat dusty land, proclaim the faith that originated in distant Arabia. On the whole, the Buddhist revival of our times, so concentrated now in the rich societies of the West, seems to have left Lumbini untouched.

Perhaps this is why when I first visited the place – on a melancholy spring evening, the light fading but still sharp and golden on the sugarcane and rice fields – it took me some time to realize where I was.

I hadn't imagined the birthplace of the Buddha to be a real, accessible place until Vinod, a fellow student at the university in Allahabad, told me about it; and although Vinod got the whole trip going with an invitation to his ancestral house, which was not far from the Indian border with Nepal, he wasn't much interested in visiting Lumbini, which he had already seen and had found very uninteresting.

He, like me, wanted to go to Nepal because it was the only foreign country we were, or so it seemed then, ever likely to visit. There were other students in Allahabad who went on tours to southern Nepal – tours that were more like sorties since after two days and nights of ramshackle country buses and cockroach-infested 'guest houses', you never really got much beyond the border. The mountains remained on the distant horizon; and most people returned trying to suppress the disappointment of having found Nepal as flat and dusty as the part of North India they themselves lived in.

Nevertheless, the visit to Nepal retained its glamour. The richer students bought themselves a Chinese-made Walkman, and almost all of us who managed to go returned from the trinket-selling shacks at the border with at least one garishly printed baseball cap which we wore gratefully for a year or two, trying to overcome, but more likely setting off, the shabbiness of our terylene pants and shirts.

Vinod might not have been much interested in the base-ball cap. It wouldn't have gone well with the embroidered Benares-silk kurtas and tight churidars he usually wore; it would have added an unnecessary frivolity to his serene good looks and quiet manner. Compared to the general run of students at the university – people from impoverished rural or semi-urban families in the Indo-Gangetic plain – he seemed well off. He was, I had heard, the only son of a rich landlord. He lived in a three-room house outside the campus while most of us lived – two or sometimes three to a room – in one of the dingy university hostels.

Most of us hired bicycles at 75 paise an hour to move around the city while Vinod had a rickshaw waiting outside his house at all times of the day and night, along with a driver, a low-caste boy in his early teens, who seemed to pedal with extra vigour when he brought prostitutes to Vinod's house, twisting and turning through the potholed alleys with such abandon that it was hard to distinguish the ringing of his bells from the jangling of the heavy silver bangles and anklets worn by the very young women he carried.

Vinod, who was much older than I, had a fully realized personal style – or so it seemed to someone as timid and inexperienced as myself, who had freshly emerged from a constricted life at home. I remember that I would visit him in the afternoons so as to catch a glimpse of the women. Often the boy resting on the rickshaw would stop me from going upstairs, and I would hang around the dusty deserted alley, the solemn tones of All India Radio news-readers leaking out of the shuttered windows, until the woman had emerged from the narrow staircase, freshly and clumsily lipsticked, blinking in the harsh sun.

All the forbidden deliciousness of sex lay in Vinod's dark bedroom when I went upstairs. It was present in the mixed smell of sandalwood incense and cheap lipstick, on his dimpled bed, the discarded strings of jasmine flowers, which were already wilting as Vinod, his handsome face perfectly composed, and still in his sleeveless vest, leaned over a small table and cut a guava into thin little slices.

'*Aaiye-ji, aaiye-ji*, come in, come in,' he would say, the 'ji' always an unaffected part of his courtesy. '*Paan layngay na, aap*? You will have some paan, no?' I rarely had any paan and did not much like chewing either the betel leaf or tobacco. The first couple of times I met him had been at a paan stall near the university, and he never lost the notion that I was an addict. He would walk up to the window, open it and then, instead of shouting for attention – for the boy below never seemed to take his eyes off the window – calmly place his order. Closing the window – the room made enigmatic again after the moment of drab light – he would turn to me and ask, 'What are you reading today?'

He himself was a fanatical reader. Like many students wishing to demonstrate a modern outlook and intellectual maturity, he possessed the Hindi translations of Sartre and Camus. But much of the shelf space in the rooms was taken up by the lectures of 'Osho' Rajneesh, the international guru of the 1970s and 80s, who exalted both sex and meditation, and whom Vinod thought of, he once told me, as a great philosopher. There were books by J. Krishnamurti and several pamphlets by Swami Vivekananda, the nineteenth-century monk and thinker, who in 1893 had introduced Hinduism to the West at the World Parliament of Religions in Chicago.

He also had different books on the various systems of Indian philosophy. But they had more to do with his course work as a postgraduate student, which he neglected, staying away from classes and living, from what I could see, a life of willed leisure: he read in the mornings; the women in the afternoons were followed by long sessions of body-building at an akhara; the women sometimes returned at night, with the boy driving more cautiously and the rickshaw hood up.

The question about my reading was how he attempted to respond to my fascinated interest in him. Otherwise, he asked me few questions about myself. He seemed self-contained, fully consumed by the present moment, and with none of the anxiety with which the rest of us – poor students with uncertain prospects – darkened the future.

On the map, Nepal seemed close to Allahabad, at the end of a short straight line to the north, just a few hours away. But Vinod and I left at dawn and travelled for much of the day, first by train and then by bus, under the empty sky, past townships of naked brick houses, the roadside shops with dirty glass jars full of sticky sweets, the buildings with the faded signs exhorting family planning, and the young men at auto-repair shops with dated hairstyles.

Late in the afternoon we reached the border. We waited here for a long time, as idle as the long queue of trucks waiting to get into Nepal, which lay just beyond the customs and immigration post: a small dark room before which uniformed police officials lay half sunk in their charpoys, and from which drivers with the necessary papers emerged every few minutes and strode back to their vehicles in a triumphant flurry.

Our own turn finally came, and then the disappointment that had been building up all day became sharper as we crossed the border and into a township. The signboards on top of the shacks selling cheap electronic goods and nylon T-shirts and baseball caps displayed a strange script. Some of the men in the crowds were short, and had Mongoloid features. But the rest of the scene – the heaps of roadside rubbish, the wandering diseased cows, the stalls with fried foods, the buses of abraded metal – seemed defiantly familiar.

The landscape became empty again as we left the border behind. There was little traffic, except for a few donkey carts hobbling over the rutted verge of the road. The bald brown mountains in the distance displayed patches of weak sunshine, but white bands of haze fenced in the mud villages and the rice fields, and scraps of white paper and plastic bags lay undisturbed on the ground before the shuttered roadside shops selling beer.

The half-empty bus meandered on narrow country roads for what seemed many hours. It was flagged down a few times, before the usual low shack selling cheap liquor and cigarettes. Vinod, sitting in the row just ahead of me, fell asleep, his head gently bumping against the sharp-edged frame of the window. Other passengers – mostly local villagers anxiously gripping cloth bundles and cheap cardboard suitcases to their chests – also nodded off, their heads gently uncertain on their shoulders. I too felt some of the soporific quality of that afternoon and I didn't at first bother opening my eyes when the bus stopped and the driver jumped out of his cockpit, shutting the door behind him with a loud thud.

I looked up to see a parking spot: a field of pure dust,

blackened in places by diesel oil where buses and trucks might have stood, and fenced by shop shacks of the kind we had passed. Vinod still seemed asleep. Some men got off to urinate. They waddled as they unfastened the strings on their floppy pyjamas and then stood rigid, legs apart. I joined the men, and it was as I stood there with them, forming a row of sorts, leaking water into a small beshram shrub, staring ahead somewhat embarrassedly, that I saw the monk, the trees, and the partially constructed buildings in the near distance.

He may have been from Korea or Japan – I couldn't tell the difference then, and the pagoda-shaped buildings he was walking towards were as hard to place as he was. He was walking away from us, indifferent to our presence, even to the cloud of dust which the worn tyres of the bus had kicked up towards him, and which enveloped him, settling quietly on his ochre robe and tonsured head.

I heard the driver say, 'Five minutes and then we leave.' I turned back to see Vinod emerging from the bus, his face still blurred with sleep. He staggered slightly as he walked towards me. He said, '*Dekhiye jo dekhna hi, yahi hai Lumbini*. See what you have to see, this is Lumbini.'

His voice held the disappointment of his own first visit. And perhaps it was hard not to expect more, and not to feel let down, at the sight of the birthplace of the founder of one of the world's greatest religions, preceded by only a field of dust and some incomplete buildings.

The bus would leave in five minutes. I hurried after the monk. I saw him enter the hedge-fenced compound of one of the odd-shaped buildings, and then I lost sight of him. Inside the compound there was a garden with a complicated design, through which ran a narrow cement path. I followed the path, past low shrubs and cactuses, and little pools of water holding slices of the sky.

And then, suddenly, the land cleared again, the sun low and hazy in the sky ahead of me, the light golden and still. Green rice fields stretched to the horizon, dabbed occasionally with peasant women in bright clothes and black buffaloes with gleaming sides.

I saw a strange hillock on my left – an archaeological mound. Immediately before me, in a seemingly perfect configuration, there was a rectangular tank, a large sal tree draped with handkerchief-sized prayer flags, and what at first seemed to be a low-roofed temple with a long pillared veranda.

I turned to hear soft chanting. It was coming from one of the buildings behind me – monasteries, I finally realized. Walking on, I saw the monk. He stood on the moss-grey steps of the tank, his hands folded, his head bent; the still greenish water before him held the interlaced branches of the surrounding sal tree.

He did not move as I passed him, on my way to the white pillar I had seen beyond the tank and the sal tree. Around the ugly iron railing, which enclosed it and which was festooned with prayer flags, were a few clay flowerless pots, with stubs of incense sticks protruding from their dry soil. The pillar was of stone, with many cracks running down its thick girth. At its base was an inscription in an unfamiliar script. A tiny metal board offered, in fading and chipped white paint, the translation and some other information.

It said that the pillar had been erected on orders of Ashoka, the great Indian emperor of the third century BC, who embraced the ideas of the Buddha and instituted non-violence as state policy.

The translation of the inscription read:

> Twenty years after his coronation, King Devanampiya Priyadarsi (beloved of the gods), visited this place in person and worshipped here because the Buddha, the sage of the Sakyas, was born here. He ordered a stone wall to be constructed around the place and erected this stone pillar to commemorate his visit. He declared the village of Lumbini free of taxes and required to pay only one-eighth of its produce as land revenue.[2]

Ashoka! Rarely a day had passed in my adult life without my encountering Ashoka's name or works in some form. The lions and wheels carved atop of his stone pillars were the crest of the government of India; they were featured on rupee notes, public hoardings, official stationery and in newspaper advertisements. But so unexpected was the pillar, so miraculous seemed Ashoka's presence and the surviving tokens of his generosity and goodness in the remote land of the Buddha's birth, that I had to read the translation again to confirm that I hadn't made a mistake.

Ashoka was among the great names I was taught to revere at school. My textbooks presented him as Buddhism's first imperial patron, and his life in the form of a religious legend. He was the particularly brutal conqueror who at the end of his genocidal invasion of eastern India converted to Buddhism, put the resources of his vast empire at its disposal, held an important council of Buddhist monks where the future shape of the *dharma*, or the Buddha's teachings, was determined, and sent out Buddhist missionaries to

Afghanistan and Central Asia. Ashoka's conversion to Buddhism, the textbooks implied, was the most significant event in the history of Asian culture.

I read about Harsha, the seventh-century AD Indian emperor whom the Chinese pilgrim Hiuen Tsang had described as a generous promoter of Buddhism. I was also told about the Chinese Buddhist pilgrim Hiuen Tsang himself, who had made an extraordinary journey to India also in the seventh century.³ The history textbooks contained a sketch of him, carrying what seemed to be a backpack and a parasol; they also emphasized the cosmopolitanism of the Buddhist university of Nalanda, where Hiuen Tsang had studied, and where young men were taught grammar, medicine, mechanics, ethics and philosophy.

In the millennium after Christ, the Buddha's ideas had travelled as far as China, Korea and Japan and many other Asian countries, and had assumed new forms there. In China, they had displaced even the powerful influences of the local sages, Confucius and Lao-Tzu. A ninth-century Chinese translation of the *Diamond Sutra*, an Indian Buddhist text, was the oldest-known printed book in the world. Buddhism was already the state religion of China by the seventh century, when Hiuen Tsang brought back rare manuscripts from India. Buddhism had been an equally powerful force in Japan and South-east Asia.

Obviously, the Buddha had been one of the great men, if not the greatest man, born in India. But I would have been hard pressed then to distinguish clearly between his ideas and those of, say, Mahatma Gandhi, Pandit Nehru or Rabindranath Tagore.

I had been quick to correct Mr Sharma when he claimed that the Buddha had emerged from the mouth of

Brahma. I had told him confidently about my visit to Lumbini, and about Ashoka's pillar, which I had not at all expected to find. I couldn't admit that for a long time I hadn't known much more about the Buddha than he had.

Growing up in North India in the 1970s and 80s I had come across a broad outline of the Buddha's life. He had been the young scion of a ruling clan called the Shakyas in a remote city-state in North India, leading a life of leisure and some luxury, when sudden exposure to old age, sickness and death led him first to doubt and introspection and then to the abandonment of his wife and son and a lonely search for wisdom. He had practised and grown disillusioned with extreme asceticism, before discovering one night 'the middle way' between self-mortification and the sensual life. He had given his first sermon near Benares, where he had also found his earliest disciples, and set up the *sangha*, the monastic order, which later spread his *dharma* around the world. He had then wandered through North India for the rest of his long life, speaking to both kings and commoners about the causes and cure of suffering, before achieving *nirvana*, or liberation from rebirth.

This well-worn story, lacking all specific detail, was one reason why for a long time I, like Mr Sharma and probably most other Hindus in India, thought of the Buddha as a Hindu god, an incarnation, along with Rama and Krishna, of Lord Vishnu, rather than a historical figure. I didn't know then it was precisely this notion of Buddhism as a branch of Hinduism that had been angrily rejected by the Dalit converts to Buddhism, who wished to liberate themselves from Hinduism and who publicly affirmed during their conversion ceremony that they 'do not believe that Lord Buddha was the incarnation of Vishnu'.

The Dalits were partly right. Much of what we now know as Hinduism – the cults of the gods Vishnu and Shiva, the *Bhagavadagita* – took shape only after the time of the Buddha, and was not called Hinduism until the nineteenth century. But it was true that the Buddha had broken with the religious orthodoxy of his time, which consisted mainly of rituals aimed at appeasing the gods of nature and so allowed the hereditary elite of priests who performed them, the Brahmins, to claim a higher estate (*varna*) than the warriors (*kshatriya*), the merchants (*vaishya*) and the servants (*shudra*). He had done so no less radically than Mohammed and Christ had spurned the religious systems of their time. But he had not offered an exclusive new God, or a theory of creation as replacement for previous beliefs. Although he attracted followers he had not called himself their leader and refused to appoint a successor to take over after his death. Nor had he demanded mass allegiance, like many other founders of religions.

He had rejected the abstract speculation popular then among Brahmin philosophers about the nature of reality and soul. He had spoken instead of ordinary human experience: of how neither the individual self nor the world is stable, how our desire for things innately impermanent makes for frustration, turning life into perpetual discontentment, and how human individuals could achieve liberation, *nirvana*, by freeing themselves from greed, hatred and delusion. He had traced suffering to the human belief in the solidity of the self and the phenomenal world. He had claimed that individuals could avoid suffering through an awareness, heightened by meditation, of the self as primarily made up of, and kept on the boil by, desire, disappointment, fear and resentment.

The Buddha had upheld release from suffering as the only worthwhile spiritual aim, and in emphasizing rigorous and regular practice, not complacent belief, Buddhism had opened itself to people from all faiths, classes and castes. This distinguished the Buddha clearly from the cult of deities and sacrifice and the upholding of social hierarchy that Brahminical religion and ideology then and later mainly consisted of.[4]

The Buddha did not directly attack Brahmins or their world view. But he warned individuals that rituals were of no use to them, and he had tried to make them self-aware and responsible for their own salvation. He insisted that virtue and salvation were open to people from all estates. It is why, according to one scholarly conjecture, insecure Brahmins attacked and undermined Buddhism in India, even before Turkish invaders in the twelfth century sacked the few remaining Buddhist monasteries there.

But one needs history to make informed speculations. It wasn't just Buddhism, but also the religion I was born into – Hinduism – that appeared to have no history. Unlike Islam and Christianity, it had neither a founder nor a church; there was no conceivable date from which it could be said to have begun, and it appeared not to have produced, during its long existence, personalities or institutions influential enough to enter the historical record. So it was that early in my childhood, myth and legend had become my guide to the world.

Living in a small town that had no bookshop or library, almost the only thing I read was the classical Indian literature I found at home. But even if I had looked for

histories of the Buddha I would have found mostly legends. There were few archaeological and textual records
about ancient India, particularly about the sixth and fifth
centuries BC, the centuries when the Buddha is supposed to
have lived. Even the life of Jesus is better known than the
life of the Buddha. Not only is the historicity of the Buddha not clearer than that of Jesus, there had been no Paul
among the Buddha's followers to institutionalize and give
an evangelical edge to his teachings.

The Buddha's own view was that individuals had to
realize within themselves the truth of what he said. It was
why he appointed no successors and did not seek to institutionalize his teachings. In his retreats during the rainy
season, he answered specific questions from and gave
discourses and sermons to laymen and monks; he had
dialogues with them of the kind that Socrates is supposed
to have had. He left no writings; it is not even certain that
he was literate. The followers of the Buddha, many of
them monks or *bhikshus*, held a council soon after his
death in order to recite and authenticate his teachings.
There was another council a century later, but the teachings were not written down on palm leaves for at least
another century; and when they were they appeared in
Pali, a variant of Sanskrit that the Buddha had not used.

The collection of these Pali texts called *Tripitika* (The
Three Baskets) contains the Buddha's discourses and his
prescriptions for monastic discipline. But they offer only a
disjointed narrative of his life. As Buddhism spread across
Asia, many different movements and schools emerged,
each claiming to possess the original and definitive version
of the Buddha's life and teachings. The movement known
as Mahayana (The Great Vehicle), which emerged in

north-west India around the second century AD and travelled to Tibet, Central Asia, China, Korea and Japan,
produced its own extensive canon, which it claimed was
superior to the canon found in the older Theravada (Way
of the Elders) movement of Sri Lanka, Thailand, Cambodia and Burma. A comparative study of these canons does
not go very far. The Tibetan and Chinese traditions of
Mahayana have, confusingly, different versions of even
the main events in the Buddha's life. It is not even certain
in some of them if the Buddha was called Siddhartha
Gautama by members of his clan, the Shakyas. Certainly,
none of them makes for easy reading.

The first known biography, or hagiography, was apparently produced in the second century BC. *Buddhacarita*, a
more detailed and literary version by a Sanskrit poet called
Asvaghosha, was written as late as the second century AD,
and is considered a masterpiece of Sanskrit poetry.[5] It was
also around the second century that the *Jatakas*, a collection of stories in the Pali canon about the Buddha's
previous lives, was compiled in verse. These embellished
versions of the Buddha's life encouraged sculptors and
painters to portray the Buddha, most memorably in the
cave paintings of Ajanta, western India, in the third,
fourth and fifth centuries AD; previously, he had been represented through footsteps, a tree, a wheel or an empty
throne, as in the bas-reliefs at the great *stupa* (sacred reli-
quary mound) of Sanchi in central India.

The life of the Buddha was never as important to
Buddhists as the biographies of Jesus and Mohammed
have been to Christians and Muslims. For some of the
earliest Buddhists, the man known by his family name
of Siddhartha Gautama, or Shakyamuni (the Sage of the

Shakyas), was only the latest of the thousands of incarnations of Buddhas, or the fully realized version of the Bodhisattvas (Buddhas-to-be) he had been in previous lives; and his teaching, his *dharma*, was deemed more important than his life or personality, which in any case was inaccessible.

In the newer books on Buddhism I saw at the bookshop when I was living in Simla years later, scholars still worried, and argued, about whether we could know for sure the Buddha's year of birth, conventionally noted as 566 BC, or whether he, or his disciples, said the things attributed to him in the Buddhist texts compiled long after his death. The books also told me that the Buddha's vision – of the impermanence of phenomena and the illusoriness of the self – found larger acceptance only two centuries after his death; and that, until then, he had been only one of many new thinkers to emerge in North India in the sixth and fifth centuries BC.

The books on the Buddha I read in Mashobra were almost all written in Europe or America. In the nineteenth century, western scholars had discovered the Buddha through the new disciplines of history and philology. It was an immense achievement. For the West had known almost nothing at all of Buddhism during its own evolution from the Greek colonies in Asia Minor, where its first philosophers emerged, also in the sixth century BC, to the industrial and political revolutions that drastically reshaped the world in the nineteenth century.

Without the clarifying light of western scholars, the Buddha for me would have remained only one of India's many sages, with some dated, possibly dubious, wisdom to offer. He would have stayed sunk in myth and legend, a measure of what I considered India's intellectual backwardness, her inability to deal rationally with her past, which seemed no less damaging than her economic and political underdevelopment. And perhaps I wouldn't have got too far with my interest in the Buddha had I not known about his renewal by the West in the nineteenth century, or how many of the European and American writers I admired had praised him.

Indeed, the Buddha appeared to have inspired something of a cult in nineteenth- and early twentieth-century Europe and America, especially among artists and intellectuals. Schopenhauer spoke often and admiringly of Buddhism towards the end of his life and even claimed that he and his followers were the first European Buddhists. Wagner planned to write an opera about the Buddha. In America, Henry David Thoreau translated a French version of the Buddhist text, the *Lotus Sutra*, into English. The German writer Hermann Hesse wrote *Siddhartha* (1922), a novel about the renunciation of the young Buddha, which was embraced in the 1960s by young Europeans and Americans disenchanted with what they saw as the aggressive materialism of their societies.

In his last books, Nietzsche renewed his attack on Christianity by comparing it to Buddhism, which he thought was a subtle product of old and exhausted civilizations. Rainer Maria Rilke carried a small bust of the Buddha with him.

It was not just poets and philosophers but scientists and ethnologists who had spoken well of the Buddha. Albert Einstein had called Buddhism the religion of the future since it was compatible with modern science. The

French anthropologist Claude Lévi-Strauss had ended his memoir, *Tristes Tropiques* (1955), with extraordinary praise of the Buddha: 'What else, indeed,' he wrote, 'have I learned from the masters who taught me, the philosophers I have read, the societies I have visited and even from that science which is the pride of the West, apart from a few scraps of wisdom which, when laid end to end, coincide with the meditation of the Sage at the foot of the tree?'[6]

Not everyone found wisdom or redemption in the Buddha. He was often seen as someone fundamentally opposed to western values of individuality and rationality. Nietzsche admired the Buddha but saw him as a dangerous temptation to nineteenth-century Europeans who he thought were confronted with a meaningless world after denying God and traditional morality, and were likely to find refuge in the 'passive nihilism' of Buddha.

In 1922, when he was thirty-one years old, the Russian poet Osip Mandelstam published an essay in which he deplored what he saw as widespread Buddhist influence on European culture in the nineteenth century. He denounced 'the cradle of *Nirvana*' since it did not 'permit even a single ray of active cognition'.[7] He saw Buddhism as forming the 'metaphysical masts' of the nineteenth-century 'bourgeois religion of progress'.

To inert, anti-intellectual Buddhism, Mandelstam opposed the 'schematic intellect' and the 'spirit of expediency' that he found in the philosophers of the French Enlightenment. He hoped that the twentieth century would leave behind the aberrations of the nineteenth century and return to the robust intellectual rationality of the eighteenth century, to the values of the Enlightenment.

However, Mandelstam's sources of information about Buddhism were inevitably limited and unreliable in the 1920s. Most Europeans of the period were far more familiar with their own bourgeois religion of progress, which was to take revolutionary form in Russia, than about the religions and philosophies of the East. It was only in the early nineteenth century that scholars based in Europe began to collate the religious practices European visitors claimed to have seen in China, Korea, Thailand, Burma, Sri Lanka and other Asian countries. Around 1820, they invented the word 'Buddhism' in an attempt to categorize what seemed to be widespread reverence for a figure called the Buddha. In 1844, Eugène Burnouf, an academic at the Collège de France, published *Introduction à l'histoire du bouddhisme indien*, the first comprehensive attempt to explain the Buddha's teachings available in the West.

The book moved quickly around the world. It was excerpted the same year in *The Dial*, the journal started by Emerson and Thoreau in New England. It inspired, among others, Schopenhauer, whose overly pessimistic and largely misleading take on the Buddha influenced Nietzsche in turn and helped associate Buddhism with such vaguely ominous words as 'nothingness', 'void' and 'extinction'.

These words appear to have influenced the young Argentinian reader of Schopenhauer, Jorge Luis Borges. In 1922 in one of his earliest essays, called 'The Nothingness of Personality', Borges wrote about Buddhism. Borges, who was then twenty-three years old, attacked the nineteenth century in Europe for its 'romantic ego-worship and loudmouthed individualism' and quoted approvingly a German book on Buddhism to support the assertion, much repeated in the essay, that 'there was no whole self'.[8]

Borges disowned his precocious essay when he later wrote more knowledgeably about Buddhism. Both Borges and Mandelstam probably relied upon their youthful notions of Buddhism as an irrational and nihilistic religion to counteract the then prevailing European prejudices in favour of what was rational and life affirming.

It is also true that Mandelstam and Borges were unlikely to have met many Buddhists in the St Petersburg and Buenos Aires of the 1920s, when there were hardly any actual Buddhists in Western Europe or America, apart from some Zen Buddhists from Japan. It was only after THE SECOND WORLD WAR that Tibetan refugees and American and Japanese practitioners of Zen stimulated a new, deeper interest in Buddhism as a possible way beyond the excesses of rationality and individualism.

When I first came across them, these remarks of Mandelstam, Borges and others did not give me much sense of the Buddha or Buddhism. It was much later that I saw them as part of the intellectual introspection that had followed the great material success of the West in the nineteenth century, the self-questioning that intensified after the means to that success – nationalism, imperial expansion, technological advances – were seen as having led to the catastrophe of the First World War.

Nevertheless, I was fascinated then by the fact that some of the greatest writers and intellectuals of the West had not only engaged with but also appreciated the ideas expressed two and half a millennia ago supposedly by an obscure Indian sage under a tree.

It was around this time, in an idle daydream, that I first thought of writing a book about the Buddha: a historical novel. Although a part of me balked at the likely difficulty of the task, I was stirred by the imaginative journey a book on the Buddha seemed to require: the readings in old philosophies, the remembrance of empires and conquerors, the more enduring things great men in unknown times had done or said. I thought, in my mood of optimism, that my research for the novel would help me fill a large gap in my own knowledge of India's past, and give me the historical sense I felt I lacked.

I saw myself leisurely reading and writing in Mashobra for a few years. I couldn't have known then that it would be impossible to understand the Buddha or his teachings from books alone, and that I would have to leave Mashobra and enter the larger world, travel to places as different as America and Kashmir, England and Afghanistan, learn to see differently the western writers and intellectuals I idolized, before I could begin to understand the Buddha, his teachings, and their special relevance in these troubled, bewildering times from which his own age seemed, superficially at least, so remote.

I had never been religious-minded, at least never as much as my parents, or Mr Sharma who spent much of his morning in elaborate obeisance before idols and calendars of various gods and goddesses. I didn't feel I could enter religion and ritual in the same way an older Indian generation had done, while living a simple rural life. But although I didn't think that mystical self-absorption was the best way to approach an objective historical reality, I began to meditate, thinking that it might somehow help me understand the Buddha.

*

My attempts at meditation didn't last long. I managed to concentrate on my breathing and block all thoughts from entering my mind for up to two minutes before the dam broke. I was more absorbed by the books I found in Simla, the many reprints of nineteenth-century European accounts of India: letters, memoirs, travelogues and expository essays. Most of them reflected the nineteenth-century British discovery of India, when colonial officials, working largely on their own and in isolated parts of the country, first revealed to a worldwide audience the art, religion and philosophy of ancient India. From their old-fashioned fonts and starched prose I discerned the English or Scottish amateur in his sola topi supervising an excavation in the middle of an exposed plain, or poring over, in fading light, an unfamiliar script in the bougainvillea-festooned veranda of a bungalow.

Among the greatest discoveries these amateur archaeologists and scholars had made was of the Buddha's origins in India. It is understandable that Europe misinterpreted, or remained unaware of, the Buddha. The more startling fact was the almost total disappearance of Buddhism from India.[9]

It wasn't clear what had happened. In ninth-century China, the disgruntled followers of Confucius and Lao-Tzu had finally succeeded in driving Buddhism out from official favour. Scholars speculated similarly about India, where they claimed to see a fierce backlash from the Brahmins against the growing influence of Buddhism. There were reliable records of rulers in Kashmir and Bengal destroying Buddhist temples and monasteries. The nomadic people called the Huns had sacked monasteries in

north-west India as early as the fifth century. And then
Turkish invaders had brought their own iconoclastic zeal
to India in the twelfth and thirteenth centuries.

The Buddha's ideas had been the dominant influence
over the philosophy, literature, art and architecture of
ancient India for over fifteen hundred years after his death.
But the evidence of Buddhist civilization in India –
thousands of inscriptions, *stupas*, rock-cut sanctuaries,
monasteries, not to mention countless paintings, statues
and emblems – still awaited discovery and identification in
the early nineteenth century. Although Buddhist treatises
on logic could be found in Mongolia and Siberia, not a
single text of Buddhism had been preserved in any Indian
language. As I discovered slowly, the only Indian places
where Buddhism had survived the last millennium, and
was still honoured, were in the mountains close to Tibet
that I saw daily from my balcony in Mashobra.

I wished then that I had known this earlier. But
although I lived among them, I still could not associate the
Himalayas with real men and events of the past. They
belonged exclusively to the semi-mythical events of the
Mahabharata. Even the Buddhist monasteries, which
swarmed with old and young lamas and were clearly the
work of men inspired by faith, seemed part of the natural
scenery of the Indo-Tibetan Himalayas. I had never asked
myself how they had sprung up in those inhospitable
regions. I had the relevant dates and some broad facts:
that, for instance, the monastery at Tabo was established
in AD 996. But I was unable to connect such information
to anything else.

It was the travel books about the Buddhist Himalayas
that made me realize that the places I considered remote,

even half fantastical, had been visited, and their mysteries – the once puzzling mysteries of the Buddha and Buddhism – revealed almost two centuries ago by Europeans.

Among the earliest of these visitors in the nineteenth century was Victor Jacquemont, a young botanist from Paris investigating the natural history of India. One day in Simla, I found two volumes of his letters, many of them written by him from the Indian Himalayas to his relatives in France. I had then just returned from one of my first trips to the Buddhist regions bordering Tibet, and I was fascinated by Jacquemont's references to his travels in the same parts and to Simla, which he had visited soon after it was founded in 1820.

Many of Jacquemont's letters from India resemble the travel writing of a later age. They are reports of the exotic, designed to give pleasure to, and provoke envy among, people who feel themselves trapped in much less exciting places; Jacquemont probably exaggerated the gap he felt between the life he had left behind in Paris and his time in India among Maharajahs and dancing girls. He frequently lapses into snobbery; there was much in India that did not meet his need for beauty, refinement and rationality. He seems to have talked only to the grandest Indians, Maharajahs and Brahmins. But his intelligence and curiosity redeem even his occasionally petulant outbursts – and made him popular among the stolid British imperialists he met in distant places, and impressed Ranjit Singh, the powerful Sikh Maharajah of Punjab, enough for him to offer Jacquemont the viceroyalty of Kashmir.

Travellers from Europe had previously been scarce in India.[10] Early in the fourth century BC, the Greek colony of Bactria in what is now Afghanistan had sent out an ambassador called Megesthenes to the Indian city of Pataliputra, near which the Buddha had once lived. During his time in Pataliputra, Megesthenes had compiled the first western account of India, fragments of which survived and made their way into the writings of such Roman historians and geographers as Arrian and Strabo.

Rome traded extensively with India, particularly in the first three centuries after Christ. Ideas travelled along the Silk Road and other routes to and from India: Christianity and Islam to the East, and Indian sciences and philosophies to the West. The Buddha himself reached the West in the form of a garbled story of two Christian saints, Barlaam and Josaphat, the original source for which was probably Asvaghosha's popular biography of the Buddha, *Buddhacarita*.

The Christian polemicist Clement of Alexandria is said to have met in the second century AD some Indian traders who identified their religious practice in ways that now make them seem like followers of the Buddha. Mani, the third-century Persian founder of Manicheism, which influenced the young St Augustine and lingered on among the Cathars of medieval Provence, spent time in India and is supposed to have absorbed Buddhist influences. But there was little contact between India and the West for several centuries as, first, the Roman Empire disintegrated, and then the Arabs came to rule both India and parts of Europe.

During the Middle Ages, there was the odd traveller to Asia, such as Marco Polo, who served at the court of Kublai Khan, the most Buddhist of Mongol emperors. The traffic to India grew only after Europeans discovered in the sixteenth century the sea route to Asia and inaugurated their great age of exploration and conquest. Traders and diplomats set up trading centres, followed by missionaries of the Counter-Reformation who hoped to compensate for the Catholic losses to Protestant Europe by converting India and China to their faith. A few Jesuits managed to reach Tibet in the seventeenth century and reported coming across Buddhist notions about the self.

There had been a few French travellers in India in the centuries before Jacquemont's visit. In his *Essay on the Manners and Spirits of Nations* (1754), Voltaire relied upon the testimony of two intrepid French travellers, Jean-Baptiste Tavernier and François Bernier, both of whom had attempted ambitious accounts of the last days of the Mughal Empire in India. Bernier had even gone up to Kashmir, a place few Europeans then knew of. He gave not just France but also Europe its first authoritative, if only partly accurate, image of Asia: as a place of ageless Oriental Despotism, where the ruler owned everything in his realm.

Jacquemont, whose father was a philosopher in the mould freshly created by the French Enlightenment, could not but be different from Bernier and other previous travellers. The Orient Jacquemont travelled to may have been ageless or torpid, but the Europe he was travelling from had changed after its political and industrial revolutions, and was changing more radically and speedily than at any other time in the past two millennia.

In less than a century, France had experienced the Enlightenment, the Revolution and then Napoleon's empire. It had seen the rise of a bourgeois class whose aspirations for social and intellectual mobility were suddenly no longer restrained by religion, ancestry or any other traditional force. Members of this ambitious class wished to throw off the yoke of the clergy, nobility and monarchy. Their great thinkers and ideologues spoke of the rights of man; they asserted that man, far from being sinful, as Christianity had supposed, was essentially good; and that he no longer needed to believe in, or aspire towards, a transcendent order. For, with reason and science on his side, he had the capacity to change the world he lived in.

It was this new religion of rationality and progress – the belief in the human potential to work the kind of wonders which once only God could have performed – that the armies of Napoleon Bonaparte rapidly exported across Europe and, later, to many other parts of the world, making the French Revolution the first truly universal event in history. Three decades before Jacquemont arrived in India, Napoleon had invaded Egypt along with a team of scientists and commissioned a gigantic research project, which resulted in the twenty-four-volume *Description de l'Egypte*. Jacquemont himself was one of the men in the early nineteenth century sent around the world by the Jardin des Plantes in Paris to collect samples of flora and fauna then unknown to western science.

This energetic European engagement with the world, for which Descartes had provided the intellectual scaffolding, produced knowledge and buttressed European power. It eventually led Western Europe in the nineteenth century to the conquest of Asia and Africa and to empires much greater than those the Romans could conceive of. Even Marx was moved to describe rhapsodically the accomplishments of the European bourgeoisie while prophesying –

wrongly – its overthrow. In a small but important way, Jacquemont embodied the swiftly growing confidence of the European bourgeoisie that the future of the world belonged to them.

Jacquemont seemed to represent the strong-willed young men of French literature that I tried to identify with – the Nietzschean characters who always managed, against all odds, to seize the day and control their destiny. In his twenties, he had already had an affair with a famous opera singer, and had travelled to both Haiti and North America. He was not yet thirty when early in 1828 he set off for India, the country that France's traditional rivals, the British, had just managed to subjugate politically. Arriving in Calcutta, the chief city of British-ruled India, he found elegant riverside mansions full of bored British colonials.

Many of these men had left Britain in order to make a career or easy fortune in India. Before trade came under government control in the nineteenth century, British commerce in India had been much like robbery. Most of the colonizers were anxious to make their pile and return, as quickly as possible, before the onset of tropical disease, to a comfortable house in the British countryside. Yet Jacquemont found on the whole that 'perfidious Albion' was better behaved in India than in Europe. 'I certainly see,' he reported to Prosper Mérimée, another of his literary friends, 'the English, for the most part, in a more advantageous light than they exhibited themselves to you'.[11]

In Calcutta he learnt Hindustani from a Benares Brahmin and befriended Lord Bentinck, the reform-minded Governor-General of India, whose piety and rectitude reminded Jacquemont of Pennsylvanian Quakers, and to whom he talked of religion with his usual 'scepticism and incredulity'. In the late autumn of 1829, he left Calcutta with a retinue of servants and a sheaf of introductions to various British officials across India. He travelled through the North Indian plains, passing through the cities of Benares, Agra, Delhi and Dehradun, on his way to the Himalayas, where he told his father he hoped to live for four months, at the 'height of nine or ten thousand feet above the level of the sea, in a country where the summers are like those of Hungary, and the winters like those of Lapland'.[12]

In June 1830, Jacquemont reached Simla. 'Do you not see Semla on your map?' he wrote to his father. 'A little to the north of the 31 degree of latitude, a little to the east of the 77 degree of longitude, some leagues from the Sutlej. Is it not curious to dine in silk stockings at such a place, and to drink a bottle of hock and another of champagne every evening – delicious Mocha coffee – and to receive the Calcutta journals every morning?'[13]

It *was* curious: the appearance of what Jacquemont called the 'abundance, luxury, and riches of European civilization' at more than two thousand metres in the Himalayas. Arriving in Simla almost two centuries after Jacquemont, and almost fifty years after the departure of the British from India, I saw only traces of Europe. The takeover by the erstwhile natives, the Indian middle class, appeared complete. There remained something piquantly incongruous in the toy-like shops with Tudor fronts, the theatre called 'Gaiety', the hotels called Chapslee and Sherwood, and the promenade on the Mall that warned of steep fines for Indians spitting betel-juice on the cleanest road in the city.

Much of Simla's fairyland appearance owed its origin to Jacquemont's host C. P. Kennedy, an artillery captain, who then guarded British strategic interests in a region at the extremity of British territory in India.[14] As Jacquemont described him to Prosper Mérimée, Kennedy enjoyed unlimited power over a vast region and was 'more of a king of kings than Agamemnon himself, without any Achilles to oppose him among the petty mountain-rajahs, his vassals'.

Kennedy had chanced upon the site of Simla soon after the British wrested the region from the Gurkhas of Nepal in the Anglo-Nepalese war of 1814–1816. He immediately saw its possibilities. The views were wonderful, the summer months pleasant and the autumn cool. In 1822, Kennedy enlisted hundreds of coolies who felled the cedars and oaks and built a gabled cottage on a wide ridge facing the snowy peaks: it was the first house in Simla. Other British officers quickly emulated him. In 1827, Lord Bentinck became the first of the many British rulers of India to spend a summer in Simla. With him came the official machinery of British India. The town of Simla arose, 'as it were,' Jacquemont wrote, 'by enchantment'.

Jacquemont did not fail to enjoy its rare pleasures to the full. There were other British officials with Captain Kennedy, lonely bachelors, pleased to have a new and friendly European with them. Attended by his generous hosts, Jacquemont busily consumed 'elegant and recherché breakfasts', Périgord truffles and Rhine wine and champagne while claiming in letters to France that he was only relaxing for a bit before throwing himself into months of hard lonely work in the inner Himalayas.

Jacquemont left Simla 'restored', he wrote to his father,

to his 'accustomed vigour', and planning to go up to the
borders of Tibet. A cook, a steward and scores of Gurkha
soldiers accompanied him. At Sarahan, he was received in
the middle of a hurricane by the King of Bushair and presented with a bag of musk. A few days later, he crossed the
Sutlej, on his way to the less inhabited, Buddhist parts
of Kinnaur, and to one of the more improbable encounters in which the nineteenth century – the age of European
exploration – abounded.

'Buddha, here,' Jacquemont reported to his father from
Kinnaur, 'begins to steal the clouds of incense of which
Brahma has the exclusive right on the Indian side of the
Himalaya.'[15] Jacquemont did not say what made him think
so. Things have changed so little in Kinnaur that he may
have seen what I saw more than a hundred and fifty years
later: an old lama stooped over an old manuscript in a
temple that seemed Hindu but was in fact Buddhist. Or, he
may have spent a night in a dark mountain-top monastery
and awakened the next morning to the echoes of a gong
and gone down to low-roofed halls filled with incense
smoke and the soft chanting of the monks.

Jacquemont's casual reference to the Buddhist
Himalayas almost obscures the fact that in 1830 the
Buddha was still one of the many mysteries of India. In the
early nineteenth century much of India's pre-Islamic past –
the stone pillars and Buddhist *stupas* of the Buddhist
emperor Ashoka, the Indo-Greek sculpture of Afghanistan, the erotic temples at Khajuraho – still lay buried deep
in jungles or in the earth. There were only a few clues to
their existence. Jacquemont told his father that he had 'no
doubt in my own mind that the Brahmins possessed much

information to which they are now strangers', and that, 'in this respect India resembles Egypt'.

He wasn't alone in thinking this. A country out of touch with its past: that's how India was also seen by its British conquerors, who took it upon themselves to repossess its religions and cultures, and whose achievements were commemorated in the books I found in Simla. In 1784, a judge called William Jones had set up the Asiatic Society of Bengal in Calcutta. Jones, who learnt a total of twenty-eight languages, confirmed the similarity between Sanskrit and Greek. James Prinsep, an architect, deciphered the ancient Indian script of *Brahmi*, the ancestor of most Indian scripts, that the British had found on pillars and rock faces across South Asia, and threw the first clear light on Ashoka, the first great patron of Buddhism; and later in the nineteenth century Alexander Cunningham, an army officer, excavated the site near Benares where the Buddha had preached his first sermon.

Most of the explorers worked for the British administration in India and weren't usually trained scholars. Some of them were philistines and vandals, who did more damage to existing or recently dug-up monuments than had been done by centuries of decay and neglect. The best among them, such as Jones and Prinsep, were motivated by the possibility that the strange country they had come to rule might once have had a civilization as distinguished as those of Greece and Rome.

They worked with intuition and premises that were often shaky. Very little was known about ancient India; even when they chanced upon monuments and texts they often lacked the experience or knowledge to make the right connections. When in 1820 a British army captain

called E. Fell discovered the great Buddhist *stupa* of Sanchi
in the jungles of central India, he wasn't at first sure which
religion it belonged to. It was too old to be Muslim. His
suspicion that it was Buddhist was not helped by the fact
there were no Buddhists to be seen in India. It wasn't even
clear then that the faiths followed in Thailand, Burma and
Ceylon were versions of the same religion. The British
scholars at the Asiatic Society in Calcutta still thought that
the Buddha had been Egyptian or Ethiopian, or perhaps
was another name for the Norse god Woden.

The clues to an Indian origin of the Buddha were many
but confusing. In the last decade of the eighteenth century,
a British naturalist and surveyor called Francis Buchanan
had visited Burma where he met Buddhists who told him
that the Buddha was from India. He found evidence for
this a few years later, when his work took him to the
ancient town of Bodh Gaya in the eastern Indian state of
Bihar. Buddhists no longer lived among the centuries-old
ruins he saw. Hindus worshipped the statues of the
Buddha, who by then had long been part of the Hindu
pantheon, but Brahmins were in charge of prayers at the
pyramidal temple that looked to him Buddhist in origin
and inspiration.

The locals told Buchanan of strange pilgrims to the
ruins from far-off lands who revered a god called Gautama. Buchanan realized that Gautama was the Buddha,
and recognized that the pilgrims were from Burma. But he
still didn't know that Bodh Gaya was where the Buddha
had achieved enlightenment while sitting under a pipal
(Indian fig) tree.

Buchanan probably would not have used the word
'enlightenment' to define the Buddha's revelation: the

word by then had different connotations for Europeans, and was associated not so much with religion as with its rejection in favour of a rational, materialist outlook. The growing British interest in Buddhism was very rarely fed by a feeling for religion, or by the discontent with existing conditions and desire for salvation that had set ancient peoples on their philosophical and spiritual quests. Brian Houghton Hodgson, the British official who contributed more than anyone else to the western discovery of Buddhism, ended his days in Britain, as a country gentleman, riding to hounds.

Hodgson was barely eighteen when he arrived in India in 1818 to serve as an administrator. Ill-health forced him to spend much of his time in the cool climate of the Himalayas. As the sole British representative in Nepal, which was partly Buddhist, Hodgson turned, perhaps out of boredom, to collecting Sanskrit and Tibetan manuscripts and interpreting them with the help of a local Buddhist he met in Kathmandu. He was struck by the fact that Buddhism still existed as a religion and culture; also by the fact that all the place names in the accounts of the Buddha's life appeared to be Indian. But he couldn't take his researches very far, partly because he was not supported by British institutions of learning, and partly because he felt contempt for what he found in the texts: what he called the 'interminable sheer absurdities of the Bauddha religion or philosophy'.

This is why Hodgson's importance today lies not in the essays he wrote in the 1820s on Buddhist doctrine, but in the manuscripts he collected and sent by the truckload to Europe, where they formed, particularly at the Collège de France in Paris, the first scholarly source of western knowledge about Buddhism. A scholar at the Collège de France called Eugène Burnouf received most of Hodgson's largesse, which he used in his book, *Introduction à l'histoire du bouddhisme indien.*[16]

Hodgson's solitary scholarship, the general British indifference and his own complacent attitude towards the subject of his researches contrast sharply with the great intellectual energy that marked the early transmission of Buddhism to peoples outside India. When in the first century AD the first Buddhist scholars from India reached China, they were soon met by translation teams. With its literary and philosophical traditions, China was well equipped to absorb and disseminate Buddhism. The Chinese eagerness to distribute Buddhist texts was what gave birth to both paper and printing. Not surprisingly, it was a particularly Chinese form of Buddhism, nourished by contact with India, which travelled to Korea and Japan in the fourth and sixth centuries respectively.

Unlike Hodgson, the first scholars of Buddhism weren't dilettantes. Nagarjuna, the South Indian thinker, whose many philosophical works in Sanskrit led to the rise of the Mahayana movement in the second century AD, was also a monk. So were the philosophers Asanga and Vasubhandhu, who lived near what is now the city of Peshawar in Pakistan, and Dignaga, who is considered the founder of the Indian system of logic. The Buddha had rejected the notion of a divinely inspired or sacred language; and so, unlike the Bible, which was not fully translated into European vernaculars until the sixteenth century, Buddhist texts in Sanskrit, particularly from the Mahayana tradition, attracted translators from the time they were first compiled.

In the fourth century AD, Kumarajiva, a central Asian monk, was invited by the Chinese emperor to translate Sanskrit texts into Chinese; he translated, among others, the *Lotus Sutra*, of which as we have seen Thoreau in nineteenth-century America produced an English version. Around the same time, the Indian scholar Buddhaghosa travelled to Sri Lanka and put together a compendium of the Buddha's teachings called *Vishuddhimagga* (*Path of Purification*). The western Indian monk Paramartha, travelled to China by sea in AD 546 and spent the rest of his life producing translations of Mahayana texts. The eighth-century monk Santarakhshita from north-western India became a major figure in Tibetan Buddhism through his translations into Tibetan. Hiuen Tsang was only one of the Chinese and Korean travellers during the seventh and eighth centuries AD who spent many years in Indian monasteries and universities, studying Buddhists texts and translating them.[17]

Hodgson seems to have been like Jacquemont, who distrusted traditional religion and worshipped the nineteenth-century god of reason and science. These attitudes were fairly conventional then. Many utilitarian thinkers and rational philosophers in Britain scorned Indian religion and philosophy and demanded that India's British rulers force the natives to embrace European ways. The most famous among these was the historian Thomas Babington Macaulay, who argued decisively during a crucial British debate on education in India that Indian civilization and culture were barbaric, and the best way forward for Indians was to abandon them and to adopt English civilization, whose superiority was self-evident.[18]

Jacquemont grew contemptuous of the fading British attempt to understand India through learning its classical languages. 'The Sanskrit will lead to nothing but Sanskrit,' he kept insisting in his letters to France. 'It has served only for the manufacture of theology, metaphysics, history intermixed with theology and other stuff of the same kind: triple nonsense for the makers and the consumers; and for foreign consumers especially.'[19]

Jacquemont had a low opinion of Oriental philosophy and literature in general. In a letter to his father, he mocked the 'insipid and tiresome poems' of the Persians Hafiz and Saadi, which had greatly inspired Goethe, and judged futile the efforts of August Wilhelm von Schlegel, the German philosopher and critic, who at the very time Jacquemont was collecting natural history specimens in India was setting up a Sanskrit printing press in Bonn and publishing translations of the *Bhagavadagita* and the *Ramayana*. Schlegel's efforts in Bonn greatly encouraged Sanskrit studies in Europe. He followed his brother, Friedrich Schlegel, and Novalis among the German Romantics who looked towards India for spiritual relief from a Europe that by adopting the bourgeois religion of progress was losing its soul.[20] He hoped that the study of classical India would bring about a new Renaissance on the same scale as the one based on Greek and Roman antiquity that had apparently lifted much of Western Europe out of the Middle Ages.

Jacquemont was not impressed. 'Have not the absurd at Benares and those in Germany a family likeness?' he asked. 'We adopt in Europe,' he wrote to a friend in Paris, a completely false notion of the real intellectual habits of the Indian nations. We generally suppose them inclined to an ascetic and contemplative life; and upon the faith of Pythagoras, we continue to look upon them as extremely occupied with the metamorphosis of their souls after death. I assure you, sir, that the metempsychosis is the last of their cares; they plough, sow, and water their fields, reap and recommence the same round of labours; they work, eat, smoke, and sleep without having either the wish or the leisure to attend to such idle nonsense, which would only make them more wretched, and the very name of which is unknown to the greater number of them.[21]

This was the blunt commonsensical appraisal of the traveller who felt he couldn't be fooled. Jacquemont was at least partly right. Whether or not they worried about salvation in this or the next world, most Indians then knew nothing or very little of the hymns, invocations and liturgical formulae of the four *Vedas* or the philosophical idealism of the *Upanishads* that people in Europe took to be the very essence of Indian civilization. These texts had long been monopolized by an elite minority of Brahmins who zealously guarded their knowledge of Sanskrit. Some of these Brahmins educated the British amateur scholars, who earnestly studied the canon of what they supposed to be ancient Indian tradition and managed to remain mostly unaware of the more numerous non-textual, syncretic religious and philosophical traditions of India – for example, the popular devotional cults, Sufi shrines, festivals, rites and legends that varied across India and formed the world view of a majority of Indians.

Jacquemont claimed to have a better idea of what actual knowledge consisted of. It certainly did not lie in the distant past, or in the kind of abstract speculation ancient Indians had indulged in. It consisted of facts verifiable by observation and experiment: of science.

'My father,' Jacquemont wrote towards the end of his visit, 'will perhaps be somewhat displeased with my not bringing him back some very profound system of Indian metaphysics, but I have at present upon the Ganges a boat which descends from Delhi to Calcutta, laden with things much more real than the *real essences*: they are the archives of the physical and natural history of the countries I have hitherto visited.'[22]

Jacquemont never lost his exalted sense of himself and the new Europe he represented. In March 1832, he was on his way to Bombay. From there he hoped to catch a ship to France, when he ran into Governor-General Bentinck and his wife. Though they met deep in the desert of Rajasthan, they were attended by 'all the luxuries and refinements of Europe'. Jacquemont and Bentinck dined together and talked of England and its 'probable destinies'. They talked also of Europe, and concluded by exclaiming, as Jacquemont reported,

> how strange was our meeting there, and talking there of such things. He, a man from England, one of the crowd there; here the absolute ruler of Asia: I, quietly engaged in my philosophical researches amidst barbarous tribes. We smiled at the idea of deeply-laid combinations to bring in such extraordinary circumstances, which have arisen chiefly from chance and necessity. How little understood is this political phenomenon in Europe.[23]

His most extraordinary encounter in India occurred in a village called Kanum, close to Kinnaur's border with

Tibet, not long after he left Captain Kennedy's luxurious resort in Simla in order to spend a few months in the inner Himalayas. He knew partly what to expect as he crossed the Sutlej river into the Buddhist parts of Kinnaur. 'At Kanum,' he wrote to his father, 'I shall soon see that incredible Hungarian original, M. Alexander de Körös, of whom you have no doubt heard: he has been living for four years under the very modest name of Secunder Beg, that is to say, Alexander the Great, dressed in the Oriental style.'

Captain Kennedy had already warned Jacquemont about the Hungarian eccentric who had allegedly walked on foot from Europe to India. De Körös had shown up in Simla three years previously, dressed in rags and looking like a Russian spy. Kennedy had had to detain him until he could check his credentials with his bosses in Calcutta. De Körös spent a few resentful months among the bohemian bachelors of Simla before he was finally allowed to leave.

In Simla, he stayed with James Gerard, a British army doctor, who later met de Körös in the village of Kanum and reported that he was studying Tibetan texts, living 'like the sages of antiquity, and taking no interest in any object around him except his literary avocations', and 'highly pleased with the prospects of unfolding to the world those vast mines of literary riches'. Such austerity did not impress Jacquemont whose attitude towards de Körös reflected the refined Parisian's disdain for the rustic East European. But de Körös's obsessions belonged as much to the Europe of his time as Jacquemont's did.

He was born in 1784 in a small village at the foot of the Hungarian Carpathians, a cold windswept place, probably not very different from the villages of the inner Himalayas where he spent much of his later life. Legend traced his ancestors, the Szekeleys, to the Huns, the still obscure nomadic people who invaded Europe in the fourth century AD. But de Körös's Hungary was subject to the Habsburg empire and its educated classes were only beginning to feel, around the time of de Körös's birth, the rebellious nationalism that had already fired the French and American revolutions and was about to remake Europe as a whole. By the time de Körös began his education, Hungarian culture and language, both conspicuously different from the European cultures around them, were attracting a new kind of attention from the Hungarian elite. The question – who are the Hungarians? – was now urgent.

The Hungarians who wished to separate themselves from imperial Austria and claim a unique identity for themselves preferred to think that their ancestors had come from somewhere in Central Asia. The notion that Hungarians were proud horsemen of the Central Asian steppes agreed with de Körös's own cherished sense of being linked to Attila the Hun, whose raiding armies seriously damaged the already frail Roman Empire by the fifth century.

As an ascetic young scholar, de Körös vowed to dedicate his life to discovering 'the obscure origins of our homeland'. At university in Göttingen, the Orientalist scholar Johann Eichhorn encouraged him to study the Central Asian peoples. He picked up several languages at Göttingen – he was to know seventeen altogether – and became even more determined to travel to Central Asia and find the intellectual glue for Hungarian patriotism.

When he finally set out for Asia in late 1819, at the age of thirty-three, he aimed wide. His final destination was what we now know as the Central Asian Republics and westernmost China. He intended to travel first to the Ottoman capital Constantinople and study the texts of medieval Arab geographers there. But the news of an epidemic in the city made him travel instead to Alexandria, from where he moved, in slow stages, to Aleppo in modern-day Syria.

At Aleppo he changed into Asiatic dress, invented a new name for himself – Secunder Beg, the Persian version of Alexander the Great – described himself as an Armenian and joined a caravan moving towards Baghdad. In the autumn of 1820, he reached Tehran, where he spent a few months learning Persian and convincing himself through his study of Arabic texts that his ancestral homeland was to be found in either Bukhara, now in Uzbekistan, or Yarkand in the Tarim Basin, an area just north of the Tibetan plateau and now part of the Chinese province of Xinjiang.

But his travels were repeatedly thwarted by rumours of Russian armies, which were then rapidly advancing across Central Asia. In 1822, he was in Kashmir, failing to persuade anyone to take him through Tibet to Yarkand, when he met William Moorcroft, in another of the auspicious encounters of nineteenth-century India.

Moorcroft was the first qualified veterinarian in England. A disastrous financial speculation had forced him to India, where he managed the East India Company's stud farm, and later became the first great explorer of the western Himalayan ranges. At the time he met de Körös, he had spent two years shuttling between the valley of Kashmir and the northern plateau of Ladakh, trying to get to Yarkand and Bukhara. He claimed that he was concerned about the declining quality of horses in India and wanted to find a superior breed in Central Asia, of the kind he thought Attila the Hun and his army might have used. Like de Körös, he was thwarted by the Chinese ban on western travellers in Tibet. But the Kashmiri traders probably had their own reasons for refusing to help him. For Moorcroft was an intriguer, an early player of what came to be known as the 'Great Game' of Central Asia, involving the ambitions of the British, the Ottoman and the Russian empires.

He was obsessed with the Russian Empire, particularly the possibility that Russian ambitions in the region would undermine British power. He suspected that the Sikh Maharajah of Punjab, Ranjit Singh, who then controlled Kashmir, was conspiring with the Russians against the British. He later tried on his own initiative and failed to get Ladakh to pay tribute to the British rather than to Ranjit Singh. The effort earned him a reprimand from his British superiors who did not wish to annoy the Sikh Maharajah.

But Moorcroft persisted. He immediately saw opportunities in the raggedly dressed Hungarian who claimed to be an Armenian. He invited de Körös to join his entourage. They travelled together for nearly eight months, spending time in both Kashmir and Ladakh. Early in their acquaintance, Moorcroft gave de Körös his copy of a book on Tibet, the *Alphabetum Tibetanum*, which was then the only book in a European language on Tibet. A collection of facts and fables, based on missionary records, it had been published by a Catholic priest in Rome in 1762. Most of it was a hit-and-miss affair: among other significant errors, it identified the religion of Tibet as Manicheism, the long-forgotten religion of pre-Islamic Persia that was supposedly influenced by Buddhism.

De Körös studied *Alphabetum Tibetanum* during his months in Kashmir, between picking up basic Tibetan from a Persian-speaking Ladakhi, and translating letters in Russian that Moorcroft managed to intercept. Moorcroft encouraged de Körös to abandon his idea of travelling to Central Asia and instead to add to his scholarly skills by learning Tibetan in the Indian Himalayan country adjoining Tibet. He told de Körös of the immense favour he could do for Europe by compiling the first accurate dictionary and grammar of the Tibetan language.

Moorcroft doubtless wished to flatter de Körös. But he probably also realized that the British needed more than a cursory knowledge of Tibetan as a first step towards preventing the country from falling into Russian hands. He gave de Körös money to carry out his research, wrote him introductions to Ladakhi and British officials, and also appealed for financial assistance to the Asiatic Society of Bengal.

Moorcroft was so persuasive that de Körös even managed to convince himself that Tibetan texts might contain something about the origins of the Hungarian peoples. In May 1823, de Körös left Srinagar for Leh, from where he travelled on foot for nine days to a monastery in Zanskar, the most remote part of Ladakh, where the cold kept villagers indoors for much of the year. Here, in an unheated cell, de Körös spent sixteen months with the local lama, Phuntsog, a learned authority on Tibetan Buddhism. Sitting huddled together under sheepskin cloaks, de Körös and Phuntsog took turns uncovering their hands to turn the pages of the Tibetan manuscripts.[24]

De Körös probably didn't know that he was only beginning to read the greatest collection of Buddhist literature, comprising around a hundred volumes, most of which were translations from the Sanskrit of texts that had been lost in India itself. Buddhism had reached Tibet from India only in the seventh century, long after its arrival in East Asia. From the beginning, it had taken a distinctive form, influenced by the form of Buddhism called Vajrayana (diamond vehicle), which arose in India about the time it was adopted by many of the Indian monks who brought Buddhism to Tibet.

It dealt in magic, symbolism, esoteric ritual, and even used sexual desire as a means to enlightenment. It considered crucial the role of the guru, or teacher, in spiritual practice, and did not much exalt the *bhikshu* (monk) over the *upasak* (layman). Tibetans revered many different types of Buddhas and images of such *Bodhisattvas* as Manjusri and Avalokiteshvara. They deployed *mandalas* and mantras as aid to meditation. It was this form of Buddhism which later made Tibet appear the land of magic and mystery to foreign visitors.

In October 1824, de Körös decided he couldn't endure another winter in Zanskar and left for the Kulu valley in the south, hoping that Phuntsog would join him there to continue his education. But the lama never showed up. The snow closed the passes from Zanskar; and de Körös, now at a loose end, found himself travelling to the British outpost at Simla, where he expected to make use of Moorcroft's introductions.

It was in this way that Jacquemont's host in Simla, Captain Kennedy, received the strange solitary traveller from Hungary one day in late 1824. De Körös expected to be welcomed as a prodigal scholar from Europe, working to advance the knowledge of barbarous tribes; he wished to be acknowledged in the role Moorcroft had created for him. He had little idea of how implausible his story seemed to the British: the Hungarian scholar seeking his national origins in Central Asia and hoping to learn Tibetan, a language few outsiders had heard of. Also, Moorcroft by then had been away from India for years and his sponsorship of de Körös looked to the British as ill-considered as his anti-Russian intrigues in Ladakh. Kennedy released de Körös from informal house arrest only after five months, the time it took him to establish the Hungarian's credentials in distant Calcutta.

By then de Körös was tired of the high-spirited bachelors of Simla and eager to get back to his studies in Tibetan language and literature. He set off for Ladakh again, this time armed with a small stipend from the Royal Asiatic Society. But he floundered for the next year, first failing to meet Phuntsog, and then finding him less than cooperative. In the meantime, the British in Calcutta heard of the publication of a Tibetan dictionary compiled by a Baptist missionary, decided that de Körös's labours had been pre-empted and cancelled his stipend. De Körös, back in Simla, protested that the dictionary was worthless and that his efforts were still needed. Other scholars in Calcutta unexpectedly proved him right, and in 1827 the British resumed de Körös's stipend.

In 1825, de Körös had visited Kanum, a village on the river Sutlej close to the border with Tibet, with a view to learning Tibetan there. The local monastery called Kangyur, which had been established in the eleventh century, had plenty of manuscripts, but de Körös found the lamas disappointingly Hindu in their outlook, and with little knowledge of Tibetan. Nevertheless, he returned to Kanum in 1827 after regaining his stipend, and spent the next three years there. This time Phuntsog was with him, and the working conditions were better than what he had endured in Zanskar. He had his own cottage. The landscape was less harsh, even tinged with the green of pine forests and apricot trees.

One afternoon in the autumn of 1993, I walked up to Kanum. From the banks of the fast-flowing river, the grey mud houses on the hill appeared to be collapsing upon each other. From up close, the cluster of low-roofed buildings with tiny windows spoke of strong winds. Children with cold red faces peered from apparently bare rooms. The monastery with the pagoda-shaped roof smelled of rancid butter, and the Tibetan refugees there appeared strangely merry in sunglasses.

It was here that Jacquemont met de Körös in the summer of 1830. He knew of de Körös's prickliness from Captain Kennedy and others at Simla. Accordingly, he first wrote to de Körös, informing him of his arrival and requesting a meeting. De Körös, who was probably lonely, appeared almost instantly at his camp, looking, Jacquemont reported, like a 'Tartar shepherd'. Moreover, he revealed an eccentricity that he had developed in his great solitude by refusing to sit down in Jacquemont's presence.

He didn't think, he said, that he was the Frenchman's equal. Jacquemont failed to assure him to the contrary. The next day, Jacquemont visited de Körös at his cottage and found him transcribing Tibetan on a low wooden desk, surrounded by books and papers. De Körös once again insisted on standing up. Jacquemont, who was much taller than de Körös, had to bow his head in order to avoid bumping it against the low ceiling of the cottage. He finally gave up and sat down even as the Hungarian remained standing before him.

Later, de Körös showed him round the monastery, whose manuscripts were part of the large Tibetan Buddhist canon. Jacquemont reported scornfully on their contents. 'It's enough to put you to sleep standing up,' he wrote to his father. 'There are about 20 chapters on the kind of shoes that lamas should wear . . . learned dissertations on the properties of the flesh of gryphons, dragons, unicorns, and on the admirable virtues of the horn of the winged horse.'

But de Körös's nine years of monastic seclusion in the Himalayas weren't entirely fruitless. The Buddha's connection with India was not to be established definitively for several years, but de Körös was able to prove that Tibetan Buddhism, like all other Buddhisms in the world, had originated in India and that much of the Tibetan canon, called Kangyur, consisted of translations from Sanskrit texts. This was a considerable achievement when Tibet was as much a mystery as the Buddha.

Two years after meeting de Körös, Jacquemont travelled to Bombay in order to board a ship to France. He chose to walk across the Indian plains he had often described as melancholy and desolate. It was high summer, a time of disease, and at some point Jacquemont caught a fever. Later, he developed an abscess on his liver. He couldn't sleep for days on end. While trying to recuperate in the western Indian city of Pune, he wrote that 'a traveller in my line has several ways of making what the Italians terms a fiasco, but the most complete fiasco of all is to die on the road'.

Jacquemont knew then that he would not see France again. But it was unlike him to mourn or panic. His last letters are full of graceful farewells. He tried to assure his family that he was being looked after by considerate Englishmen. 'The cruellest pang,' he wrote in his final letter to his brother, 'for those we love, is, that when dying in a far distant land, they imagine that in the last hours of our existence we are deserted and unnoticed.'

Jacquemont was lucky, in death as in life. Moorcroft suffered a grimmer fate. He had set off for Bukhara via Afghanistan in 1824, shortly after setting de Körös off in the direction of the Buddhist Himalayas. He was arrested in Kunduz by the local chieftain and spent six uncomfortable months in prison and had to bribe his way out of an even longer confinement. He finally reached Bukhara, where he was the first European visitor in two hundred years. He even reportedly procured the high quality horses he had originally set out for. But on the way back to India later that year, he disappeared. There were rumours of death by fever and poisoning. Later travellers following the route of this greatest early explorer of the Himalayas encountered many different stories. But no one ever saw Moorcroft again. His prescient plans of opening up new trade routes through Ladakh and thwarting the Russians remained unfulfilled for decades.

His protégé, de Körös, lived longer. When Jacquemont saw him in Kanum, de Körös was at the end of his long penitence in the Himalayas. A few months later, he left Kanum, carrying with him boxes of manuscripts and printed Tibetan texts. He went directly to Calcutta, where for the next eleven years he supervised the production of a new grammar and dictionary of the Tibetan language, learnt new languages, and catalogued Tibetan and Sanskrit texts that arrived from the British representative, Hodgson, in Kathmandu, Nepal.

He lived in Calcutta as he had in the Himalayas: like a hermit, subsisting on tea and boiled rice. In 1842, when he was fifty-eight, he finally set out again on his original quest, which Moorcroft had interrupted two decades earlier. He wanted now to get to Lhasa where he thought all would be made clear about the origins of the Hungarian peoples. But he caught malarial fever a few hundred miles out of Calcutta and died in the hill resort of Darjeeling.

De Körös is unlikely to have found much trace of Hungary in Lhasa or Yarkand. European scholars were saying even when he was alive – and they turned out to be right – that the Hungarians were closer linguistically and ethnically to the Finns than to the Central Asians. He wasn't even the first European to learn Tibetan or to travel in the Tibetan Himalayas. The Jesuits had established a mission in Tibet as early as 1628. And when in 1904 the memoirs of a Jesuit from Tuscany called Ippolito Desideri were published in Italy, it became clear that he had visited Lhasa in

1716, more than a century before de Körös managed to get to the borderlands of Kinnaur and Ladakh. Desideri spent five years in Tibet, studying Tibetan texts and what he called the 'false religion' of 'Bod', particularly the key Buddhist doctrine of emptiness.

At around the same time, an emissary of Peter the Great, who had been sent east to discover gold, came across bronze statues of the Buddha, and loose-leaf pages in Tibetan, in a Buddhist temple in Siberia. The pages in Tibetan made their way to St Petersburg from where a baffled Peter forwarded one of them to a German scholar for translation. The pages finally reached a scholar in Paris, who was then busy cataloguing thousands of Chinese texts sent by Jesuit missionaries. The page was translated into Latin with the help of a Tibetan-Latin dictionary compiled by a Capuchin missionary in Tibet and sent back in 1724 to Peter. The page was then forwarded to Siberia where it was translated into Mongolian. On its return to St Petersburg, it was translated into Russian, and then back into Latin. In 1767, it was translated again by a Catholic priest in Rome who included it in his *Alphabetum Tibetanum*: the book Moorcroft was carrying when he met de Körös, which became the latter's introduction to Tibet.

Such was the wide, complicated web of learning described by the books I read during my first autumn in Mashobra, books written out of Europe's new thirst for knowledge and conquest. This scholarly work had not only touched but had been spun around my own world. A Hungarian searching for the intellectual basis of a hopeful nationalism; an English veterinarian looking for horses and seeking also to advance British imperialist aims; a French botanist collecting specimens on behalf of a prestigious European institution – a few unlikely men with diverse, not very Buddhistic, motives had once met and played themselves out in the mountains I saw from my balcony, and helped create the first western views of the Buddha.

The World of the Buddha

THE WESTERN IDEA OF history can be so seductive, with its promise of adding an extra emotional and spiritual dimension and validation to our limited life; with its ability to brighten the future and the past. It is especially attractive when you imagine yourself to be on its right side, and see yourself, in the way Jacquemont, Moorcroft and de Körös did, as part of an onward march of progress. To have faith in one's history is to infuse hope into the most inert landscape and a glimmer of possibility into even the most adverse circumstances.

Reading about these European travellers, I envied their ability to insert their personal being into the impersonal flow of events. Many years later, I would stand on a hill in civil-war-ravaged Afghanistan, where modern-day fundamentalists of the Taliban had vented their political rage on statues of the Buddha. I tried to imagine the Greek colony of Bactria, as this place had once been called, where Buddhist monks had set up their monasteries and universities, from where the Buddha's ideas of detachment and compassion had travelled westwards.

I thought then that one needed only the right historical

information in order to see both forwards and backwards in time. But there are places on which history has worked for too long, and neither the future nor the past can be seen clearly in their ruins or emptiness.

Returning from Lumbini that evening, from my first, brief and almost inadvertent visit to the Buddha's birthplace, the bus broke down, in the irreparable way it had always threatened to, just a few miles from the town where the baseball caps, along with smuggled goods from China, were sold. Vinod was among the passengers who got out and stood watching the driver tinker under the bonnet. Some of the male passengers waded into the roadside sugar-cane field, driven to theft by boredom; others began to walk more purposefully towards what seemed, from the smoke rising above the land, a small village in a grove of banyan trees beyond the rice fields to the north.

A bullock cart passed us slowly, driven by an old man in a white turban, with women in short veils squatting at the back in a silent semi-circle. The road remained deserted after that. The sun declined quietly in the clear sky and then very quickly night fell over the flat land.

We had to wait beside the road for a couple of hours before a truck came by and took us to the next township. Untouched by these distractions, my mind remained struck on Ashoka's pillar, the temple and the big tree in Lumbini. Silently, it kept repeating, 'The Buddha was born here, and Ashoka came visiting once'. But the empty dark land seemed to have absorbed into itself these famous men as placidly as it had the villages and the fields.

It was hard to imagine that dense forests once grew where the rice fields and a few trees now stood; that these forests guarded the banks of the small rivers that emerged from Himalayan glaciers and travelled across the plains before joining either the Ganges or the Yamuna.

Yet the histories of ancient India state that much of the Indo-Gangetic plain was covered with monsoon forests, and the image they bring to mind is of the Amazonian rain forests. It is not clear who lived in these forests. India then contained a number of ethnic and linguistic groups, Dravidian, Sino-Tibetan, Austro-Asiatic, etc. The people in the forest were probably hunters and gatherers, unable to move or see a way forward, until they encountered the nomads and pastoralists from the west who settled the Indo-Gangetic plains in the first millennium BC.

The new arrivals are supposed to have come from the steppes to the north and east of the Caspian Sea, from where they also fanned out to Persia and even further west. They spoke an earlier form of Sanskrit, which has been identified as one among the Indo-Aryan family that includes languages spoken in India, Iran and Europe. The name, Aryan, is derived from the Sanskrit word *Arya* (noble), and came to be used for them.

They were going beyond the simple life of food gathering and domesticating livestock and learning to use iron and bronze when, in the second millennium BC, they began to move in large numbers into parts of what is now Pakistan and Afghanistan. They probably encountered in those parts, alongside the river Indus, the traces or ruins of a civilization which flourished in the third millennium BC and then became extinct, in ways still unknown, by the beginning of the second millennium.

The surviving architecture and art reveals the Indus civilization to have been as sophisticated as the nearly

contemporaneous civilizations of Egypt and Mesopotamia. Perhaps, the Aryan migrants interacted with these
people of the Indus plains. Armed with horses, bows and
arrows and chariots, they might even have conquered their
well-planned cities and enslaved them. The Aryans certainly appear to have been involved in conflicts with the
indigenous inhabitants of the Indian subcontinent. Whatever the case, their own distinctive civilization – cities,
political and economic systems, art and literature – came
much later, long after they had penetrated eastwards into
the Indo-Gangetic plains.

Most of our knowledge of these Aryans comes from the
earliest of Indian scriptures, the *Vedas*, which consist of
hymns, spells, liturgical formulae and theological argument. First composed around 1500 BC, they reached their
final form a millennium later, around the time of the Buddha's birth.[1]

The word 'veda' refers to sacred knowledge – the
knowledge of ultimate reality, which is not revealed, as in
Islam or Christianity, but has always been. It is supposedly
eternal and has been heard by great sages, mostly Brahmins, who first emerged as the privileged class of men
dedicated to memorizing the *Vedas* and transmitting them
orally, and who later became the ultimate authority on
spiritual and religious matters.

The earliest of the *Vedas* was the *Rig Veda*. It hints that
the early Aryans may have settled first in a region spanned
by eastern Afghanistan and the Indo-Gangetic watershed,
and that they may have been both pastoralists and agri-
culturalists. Their deities were natural phenomena
personified, such as Agni (the god of fire), Varun (water),
Vayu (wind), Surya (sun) and Yama (death). Their chief

god and hero seems to have been Indra, a rowdy lecherous warlord, who corresponds to the Greek god Zeus. Indra is described as using a thunderbolt to kill the demons and releasing the waters they had imprisoned – this is perhaps an account of a conflict that occurred between the Aryans and the local inhabitants in the drought-stricken lands of north-west India. Indra may also have led the Vedic Aryans in the destruction of the walled cities and citadels of the remaining higher cultures they encountered at the sites of the Indus civilization. Later Rigvedic hymns speak of the Aryans winning battles against, and also mingling with, darker-skinned indigenous people called Dasyus.

These early Indians slaughtered cattle both for food and the elaborate sacrificial rituals prescribed by the *Vedas*. They also ate beef on special occasions. The cow, which is now considered holy in India, couldn't have been so to nomads and pastoralists. It is only after they settled down and turned to agriculture that they began to put a slightly higher value upon the cow, which produced milk, ghee, yoghurt and manure and could be used for ploughing and transport as well.

The hymns of the later *Vedas* also stress how metals and agriculture, particularly rice cultivation, became increasingly important: in the prayers contained in the *Yajurveda*, the Aryans asked the gods for milk, sap, butter, honey, rice, barley, sesame, kidney beans, vetches, wheat, lentils, bronze, lead, tin, iron and copper; above all, they prayed for freedom from hunger.

Much of Vedic religion was about sacrifice and magic. It was built around the simple idea of appeasement: the ritual giving of things – mostly food – in expectation of greater gifts. But it was also based on a profound assumption of interdependence, of a cosmos where life circulates in ever-renewed forms – what the *Vedas* called *rta*, the course of nature, the basis of all life and the world.

For the Aryans, the rivers flowed and the sun, the moon and the stars followed their course due to the principle of *rta* – the concept similar to the one implied by Pythagoras when he called the world a *kosmos* – and sacrifice to the gods was meant to affirm the unity and consistency of this cosmic order.

There were domestic rituals – most houses had a hearth or a small altar – but also big public events. The intermediaries were Brahmins, who alone possessed the correct verbal formulas with which to petition the gods for more cattle, food and prosperity – the early Indians, faced with problems of subsistence, couldn't but be materialists. Their specialized knowledge gave the Brahmins their power as an indispensable priestly class – a power that was to survive for centuries, and give to Indian society its most influential and enduring class and ideology.

Agni, or fire, was as crucial in the ritual sacrifice as the correct recital of mantras. It was the mediator between the beseecher and the beseeched, carrying the sacrificed things to the gods above.[2] The veneration for Agni also symbolized the Aryan ability to destroy and settle forests, and their evolution from the primitive existence they had led in their Central Asian homelands.

When the Vedic Aryans pushed eastwards at around 850 BC to the rain-fed regions of the Indo-Gangetic plain, they faced new challenges. The forests could be burnt down and the animals which inhabited them slaughtered – the repeated triumphs of human needs over ecology are

celebrated in the epic *Mahabharata*. But the social organization needed to settle the land cleared of forests was as
yet unavailable to a tribal people.

The origin of the caste system has been attributed to
this period.[3] It may have begun as a simple division of
labour, necessitated by the complex needs of a tribal
people during their transition from nomadism and pas-
toralism to a settled life. But the Brahmins, while trying
to secure for themselves a permanently high status, sought
to create a strict social hierarchy, and even contrived divine sanction for it in the sacred texts they controlled.
The *Rig Veda* spoke of the four-fold division of society:
the four estates (*varnas*) had apparently originated from the
four limbs of the divine primordial body.

Birth determined one's place in the ideal society of the
Brahmins – a self-serving, if powerful, vision which over
centuries was partly realized by the Indian reality of caste
(*jati*) and may have gained strength during the Buddha's
time. The lowest social group was of the *shudras*, the
darker-skinned aborigines or mixed breed, who belonged
to the tribal system but were little better than helots without the membership rights of the three higher castes: the
kshatriyas, who provided the rulers and warriors, the
brahmins, who were priests, thinkers and law-givers, and
the *vaishyas*, who were landowners, merchants, money-
lenders and who later produced the food surplus that
enabled Aryan society to move away from its tribal
origins.

The system naturally benefited the three upper *varnas*,
particularly the Brahmins, who guarded their specialist
profession zealously. For centuries they did not write
down the hymns of the *Veda* but transmitted them orally

only to other Brahmins in order to prevent non-Brahmins from learning them. They also gained in wealth and power from the increasingly elaborate nature of their ceremonies and rituals.

The longer a nomadic people stayed in one place the greater the need they felt for new and stable relationships among themselves. One of the earliest political systems in India can be seen in the new arrangements the sedentary Aryans arrived at as they attempted to govern and defend themselves. A ruling family or a confederacy of ruling families belonging to the same clan sought new forms of stability and identity after prolonged presence in a particular region; they formalized their possession of territory by naming it after themselves, and they set up basic administrative structures of tax collection and social welfare. This was how the small Gana Sangha, tribal republics, and the first large kingdoms of North India came into being.

This still wasn't a particularly complex or layered world, and it remained at an unvarying level for hundreds of years until new towns and cities began to develop around the sixth century. In contrast to the *Vedas*, which describe a primarily rural society, the Buddhist texts reveal that it was an urban civilization that the Buddha was born in. By the time of his birth in the sixth century, many of the forests that had covered the plain had been cleared and replaced with farms and lands for pasture. Some of the settlements had grown into large towns and even cities, for whose inhabitants the nomadic life of their Aryan ancestors must already have been the stuff of legend and myth.

This second wave of urbanization in North India after the Indus civilization was confined mostly to the territories east of the Indus, and close to the Ganges and Yamuna rivers and their tributaries. The reasons that it came about are common to the rise of urban civilization everywhere else: the growth of agricultural surplus.

At some point, the agricultural yield of the rich plain watered by the Ganges and the Yamuna began to be greater than what was needed by the local population, much in excess of what the primitive life of the past had required. Iron deposits were probably discovered in eastern parts of the Indo-Gangetic plains. The surplus produced with the help of such innovations as iron ploughshares and irrigation techniques could be invested in trade and commerce.

Large urban centres emerged initially as market towns. They were where money was first used as a unit of exchange in North India. Some places seem to have acquired size and importance by virtue of being sacred sites. Cities such as Benares may have owed their rise to their position on the river route through North India. Many of these cities, such as Hastinapur, the site of present-day Delhi, were villages that expanded after becoming political or administrative centres.

People in these towns had different backgrounds and followed diverse occupations. The later *Vedas* refer to jewellers, goldsmiths, metalworkers, basket makers, weavers, dyers, carpenters and potters. The Buddhist texts, which are our main source of information about the urbanization of the Indo-Gangetic plain, list about twenty-five skills.

The Brahmin-imposed hierarchy of *varna*, which had defined the human world for so long, lost its authority in the towns. In the agrarian society of the past, it had proposed itself as a complete explanation not only for what human beings did but also what they were. So, for instance, a Brahmin was not just a priest because he performed rituals; he was innately blessed with virtue, learning and wisdom. A servant wasn't just someone who performed menial tasks; his very essence was poverty and weakness.

But in the towns, where money was the new measure of value and merchants enjoyed an unprecedented power, a warrior could simply be someone who had been paid to fight. As one of the Buddhist discourses put it, the king of a state had to judge a criminal according to the nature of his crime regardless of his *varna*. A high-born Brahmin could be employed by a low-born merchant. The rise of an urban economy brought about dramatic changes in that it exposed the old social hierarchy as man-made, and forced human beings to define themselves afresh. It later allowed the Buddha to address a broad audience, not just one *varna* or other, and to speak of a basic human nature separate from social or religious roles, which could, with the right effort, achieve wisdom and goodness.

The broadening range of what human beings could do was matched by a growth in size and complexity of the communities in which they lived. Political and social conditions in what Buddhist texts called the Middle Country, or the Central Gangetic plain, had evolved fast just before the Buddha's birth.[4] There were four major kingdoms, and among them there were independent tribal republics and small city-states in the Middle Country, usually ruled by members of the kshatriya *varna* forming an oligarchy or a council of elders, and named after them.

There were more cities – centres of cosmopolitanism and, as it turned out, fertile ground for the growth of Buddhism – in the kingdoms. The capital of Kosala was

Shravasti, where the Buddha would later spend many monsoons in a mango grove donated to him by a rich merchant. The other important cities in the kingdom were Saket and Benares. Its eastern neighbour and rival was the iron-ore-rich kingdom of Magadha, in whose capital, Rajagriha, the Buddha also spent many years, and which became in his lifetime the first big empire in India. One of the smaller kingdoms was Vamsa, which contained the cities of Kosambi and Prayag (Allahabad). Further east, there was Avanti, which the Buddha does not seem to have visited.

By the time the Buddha came of age, power had begun to shift from the tribal republics and independent city-states to the centralized monarchies. Unlike their counterparts in Greece, the Indian city-states did not have geography on their side. In the Buddha's lifetime, the two major kingdoms around the Ganges swallowed most of the smaller city-states and tribal republics. Just before his death, the kingdom of Kosala, which lay north-east of the Ganges, conquered his own people, the Shakyas.

The end of smaller political units and the growing subjection of human beings to the remote authority of the bureaucratic state – these changes were as momentous in India as the end of the city-states in Greece. The Buddha accepted that large monarchies and centralized states were inevitable and formulated the ideal of a 'universal moral ruler'. But he never ceased to uphold the small republic, such as the one he had lived in, as a model of direct democracy, and even modelled the *sangha*, his monastic order, on it.

*

The Buddha was born as Gautama Siddhartha, which means 'he who fulfils his purpose', in one such republic. His clan, the Shakyas, who were kshatriyas, controlled what are now the borderlands of India and Nepal, a region of 2000 square kilometres. The Shakyas were at the northernmost edge of the fast-developing civilization around the Ganges, and by the time of the Buddha's birth they were not as self-contained and independent as before. They paid tribute to the kingdom of Kosala, and were dependent on trade with the cities in the south.

Their capital city was Kapilavastu. It is still not clear where it was. The Chinese pilgrims Fa Hien and Hiuen Tsang claim to have visited it in the fifth and seventh centuries AD respectively. They reported seeing a desolate place with a few monks and some ruins, one of which they identified ambitiously as the palace of the Buddha's father. The European explorers and archaeologists who traced the route taken by the Chinese pilgrims ended up digging at two different sites, one in India, the other in Nepal. The excavations at both sites produced compelling evidence in favour of each. Archaeologists from India and Nepal still wrangle over the exact location of Kapilavastu.

If Kapilavastu was like other Indian cities of the sixth century BC, then it was probably rectangular in shape and defended by a moat and mud ramparts. The king's palace stood in the centre of a network of streets and was two or three storeys high. The council hall where the eminent citizens of the town assembled stood opposite the palace. The walls of the town also included a site for ritual sacrifices, and the residences of the Brahmins. The shops and the workshops of the trades stood separately. Each trade had its own street: rice sellers in one, ivory carvers in another. Buddhist texts mention the presence in each city of powerful courtesans, who were artistically gifted and responsible for the sentimental and cultural education of many rich young men. Far away from the centre of the town, in clay and bamboo huts, lived the workers and servants: masons, carpenters, washermen, butchers, etc. The poorest of men lived in the parks just outside the town walls, where homeless people, various mendicants and other travelling ascetics hung out.

The city was separated from the Himalayan foothills to the north by wild jungles teeming with tigers and elephants. The young Buddha might have seen a faint outline of the great Himalayan peaks on exceptionally clear days. In the west lay the city of Shravasti, the capital of the powerful kingdom of Kosala. It was approached by a path that Buddhist texts call the Uttarpatha (northern route) on which caravans of ox carts loaded with goods and escorted by soldiers of the king of Kosala travelled for most of the year.

The caravans did not always halt at a relatively small place like Kapilavastu, but went on to the cities and towns in the east and crossed the Ganges to Rajagriha. The Buddha had heard, when he was a young man in Kapilavastu, that boats sailed down the Ganges to the cities of Benares and Prayag (Allahabad); and he had dreamed of travel to what to him then seemed impossibly distant places.

The Buddha's father was Suddhodhana. Later legends call him a great raja, or king, but he was probably a member of the kshatriya class who ruled the Shakyas by rotation or election: a head or chief of a tribe rather than a king, with a small territory under his control and with not much administrative structure.

His son's daydreams of travel amused him. He told Siddhartha that kshatriyas like him, members of the ruling class, did not wander around the world like a *parivrajaka* (renouncer), or oxherds and merchants. He expected his son to tend the family's farm and grow skilled in the use of arms, so that he too could be elected chief and come into his real inheritance; and saying this, Siddhartha's father would point to the city of Kapilavastu with its cluster of clay houses and bamboo huts and to the rice fields stretching in both directions.

Suddhodhana, who had two sisters as wives, Maya and Mahaprajapati, was protective of his son. In later life, the Buddha told his disciples about his upbringing:

> I was delicate, extremely delicate, too delicate. They laid out three lotus ponds for me in my father's house: blue lotuses in one, red in another, white in the third. I wouldn't use sandalwood that did not come from Benares, my clothes – my tunic, my robe, my cloak – were made of Benares cloths. Night and day I was protected by a white parasol to keep me from the cold and heat and dust and weeds and dew. I had three palaces, one for the cold season, one for the hot season, one for the rainy season. During the rainy months, I would shut myself high up in the top of the palace and never come downstairs. The only people around me were minstrel girls. I didn't even think of leaving the palace. And while in other houses people offer a broth of rice husks to slaves and labourers, in my father's house we gave the slaves and labourers bowls full of rice and meat.[5]

Some of Suddhodhana's anxiety about his son may

have had to do with the circumstances of his son's birth. The story in several biographical traditions of the Buddha is that his mother, Maya, had a dream in which she saw an elephant enter her side as she lay sleeping. The Brahmin experts Suddhodhana consulted about this predicted that she would give birth to a son who would either live the life of a householder or retire from the world and remove its veil of illusions. Shortly afterwards, Maya became pregnant.

According to the *Nidanakatha*, the introduction to the *Jatakas*, she was forty years old, and ten months pregnant, when she left Kapilavastu to be with her parents at the nearby town of Devadaha. Suddhodhana is supposed to have paved the road to Devadaha for the occasion; it must have been a bumpy ride on horse or ox cart for Maya even so. She hadn't travelled far when she saw the garden of Lumbini and told her attendants to stop. She bathed in a tank and then while she was standing under a sal tree her labour pains began. She remained standing and delivered a baby boy, from, according to legend, her right side. Maya returned considerably weakened to Kapilavastu, where she died seven days later, leaving her sister, Mahaprajapati, to look after the future Buddha.[6]

The stone relief inside the temple at Lumbini shows Maya clasping the branch of a sal tree with her right hand. At the bottom of the relief, there is a smaller figure of the young Buddha with his right arm raised and right leg thrust forward. It looks like a Hindu image, and on my second visit to Lumbini, I saw Hindus from India worshipping it. The stone figures were daubed with vermilion powder, of the kind you see on idols of Hindu gods; and there were marigold flowers at the feet of the Buddha.

This reflected an older tradition of worship. The syncretic nature of Indian religion had allowed Hindus to absorb even the Buddha into their pantheon. Just as the first British visitors to Bodh Gaya, the site of the Buddha's enlightenment and of an old temple, had found it overrun by Brahmins, so the first archaeologists arriving at Lumbini in the closing years of the nineteenth century found that the idols inside were revered by local Hindus, who referred to the relief of Maya as 'Rummendei', which turned out to be the name of a local deity. The temple had also been used for the un-Buddhist practice of sacrifice.

The earliest Indian religions created by nomads and pastoralists both preceded and outlasted Buddhism by several centuries. And, perhaps, what's most remarkable about them is not so much their sophistication as the fact of their survival into even modern times. The first verses I was taught in childhood were the Gayatri mantra, which dates back to the second millennium BC, although I remembered 'Baa Baa, Black Sheep' much better. I remember the feasts in strange homes, where after a yagna commemorating a funeral, I sat in a row with other young and available Brahmins and was served ghee-rich food in brass plates. The Brahmin priest, who was usually corpulent, sat at the farthest end, and ate greedily and loudly.

I remember, too, the yagnas on the Sunday mornings of my childhood, when my father, freshly bathed and bare chested, sat on the floor in the living room and while chanting Sanskrit hymns poured ghee into a small fire in a kund.

I am not sure what he asked the gods for. But sweet-smelling smoke filled the house for hours afterwards, along with an oddly disturbing sense that something sacred and primordial had been reaffirmed within its walls; and my father appeared familiar and accessible only the next morning when he changed back into his western-style work clothes and went out to inspect the railway tracks.

Living in a railway town, amid a landscape of iron and steel, we had moved far from the world of the Vedic seers, and their feeling of uncertainty, their anguish of living pre-cariously in a big, unknown universe. But we too still needed to affirm the sense of a profoundly interdependent world, its cyclical rhythms of birth and death, rise and fall, integration and disintegration.

These ritual propitiations of the gods were practised dur-ing the Buddha's time as well. But they had grown complicated, and the officiating Brahmins had become more demanding and arrogant. They and their ceremonies had begun to lose their appeal for many people, who now lived in towns and cities, in conditions much different from those in which the early Aryans had formed their compact with nature.

To many of them, language, which was previously the preserve of Brahmins, had become freshly available as a resource for intellectual activity. In one of Plato's dia-logues, *Cratylus*, Socrates discusses whether the name of a thing comes attached as its natural part or is arbitrarily imposed by human beings. The discussion makes no sense to us until we take into account the ways of thinking of pre-modern peoples: their inability to separate names from things.

When pressed by Socrates, Cratylus comes up with a supernatural explanation: 'Some power greater than human laid down the first names for things, so that they must inevitably be the right ones.'

This was also how ancient Indians saw it. For them, in the beginning was the word, or the *Vedas*, but only a few great sages had been privileged enough to receive it. Since the *Vedas* were eternal and uncreated and had existed prior to the world they referred to, their language was the very essence of reality, part of the overall unity of life. It created no distance from the world; and none perhaps was needed.

In fact, the word had a different kind of power in an oral culture. Just as the Bible was not translated and made available to a wider public by the Catholic Church, so the *Vedas* remained the exclusive possession of the priests, the Brahmins, whose high status rested on the fact that they alone could correctly recite Vedic hymns and charms and spells and thereby establish a link with the gods.

Where previously human beings, dependent upon nature, were not separate enough from the world to be able to analyse it or enumerate its properties, they had become, in their new urban setting, partly the maker of the world. Sacrifices didn't provide answers to the new troubling questions they now faced: how did the world come into being? Is there a soul? Who am I? What is a self?

There is a hymn even in the earliest *Veda*, the *Rig Veda*. Called the 'Creation Hymn', it speculates about the origins of creation, about the god that precedes all the deified

forms of nature, and concludes with this eloquent statement of doubt:

> But, after all, who knows and who can say
> Whence it all came and how creation happened?
> The gods themselves are later than creation,
> So who knows truly whence it has arisen?

> He from whom all this great creation came,
> He, whether he fashioned it or whether he did not,
> He, who surveys it all from highest heaven,
> He knows – or maybe even he does not know.[7]

The Greeks living in the prosperous cities of Ionia on
the coast of Asia Minor had raised the same simple
question – 'What is the stuff of life?' – and come up with
a variety of answers. For Thales, it was water; for Anaxi-
mander, air. In India, it was the thinkers of the
Upanishads, a series of expositions, who attempted to
move beyond the visible world, and thus marked the
beginning of Indian philosophy.

A dialogue between a father and his son in the *Chandogya Upanishad*, which was complete before the
Buddha's birth, hints at the new kind of abstract speculation that flourished at this time:

> 'Fetch me a fruit of the banyan tree.'
> 'Here is one, sir.'
> 'Break it.'
> 'I have broken it, sir.'
> 'What do you see?'
> 'Very tiny seeds, sir.'
> 'Break one.'
> 'I have broken it, sir.'
> 'Now what do you see?'

'Nothing, sir.'

'My son,' the father said, 'what you do not perceive is the essence and in that essence the mighty banyan tree exists. Believe me, my son, in that essence is the self of all that is. That is the True, that is the self. And you are that self.'[8]

The *Upanishads* attempted to explain the multiplicity of the world by relating it to an underlying ultimate reality, to which they gave the name of *brahman*, and which they thought pervaded everything. For them, the human subject has a soul, the *atman*, which survives even after the body where it temporarily resides perishes – the idea of rebirth first makes its appearance in India in the *Upanishads*. But *atman* is not an individual entity, although it may appear so; it is present in all things. The famous formula is *tat tvam asi* (thou art that). Liberation, or *moksha*, consists in recognizing that *atman* is identical with *brahman*, the ultimate reality. To know *brahman*, the essential unity of all appearance, is to be liberated.

This is remarkably similar to what Pythagoras in south Italy thought in the early sixth century BC. He believed in the immortality of the human soul, which he claimed travelled through a series of incarnations in human and non-human bodies. Man was mortal, but his soul was a part of the eternal and divine cosmos; and his proper aim in life was to purify himself and become part of the cosmic harmony from which he had been sundered.[9]

Religious Indians were inclined to achieve this union through a form of rigorous self-discipline broadly called *yoga*.[10] Meditation was one of the methods used to gain control over one's emotions and passions. Sitting still in a secluded place, the yogi attempted to disengage his perennially distracted mind and force it to dwell upon itself. The other method was mortification of the flesh: the body was exposed to extremes of heat and cold, and even subjected to severe pain – the Buddha was to practise, and then grow disillusioned with, this form of asceticism.

The most important idea that emerged in the *Upanishads* was of rebirth. The *Rig Veda* depicts men as living only once; the afterlife was seen, as in Islam and Christianity, in simple terms of punishment and reward. But the *Upanishads* speak clearly for the first time about the transmigration of souls, that most important of Indian religious assumptions, according to which death destroys only the body and not the soul, which reappears in another body.

The theory of rebirth seeded that of *karma* (literally 'action'), which the Buddha was to rework in radical ways.[11] According to this, desire moves men to act. Their actions cannot but have certain results. But the results cannot all be apparent in one lifetime. They are revealed in the next life and others beyond, just as this life manifests the results of actions undertaken in previous lives.

Initially, the theory claimed no more than that happiness and sorrow were caused by one's conduct in previous lives. The earliest of the *Upanishads*, the *Brhadaranyaka*, asserts:

> What a man turns out to be depends on how he acts and on how he conducts himself. If his actions are good, he will turn into something good. If his actions are bad, he will turn into something bad . . . And so people say: 'A person here consists simply of desire.' A man resolves in accordance with his resolves, and turns out to be in accordance with his action.[12]

The implications of this world view extended into every sphere of human activity in classical India. Sanskrit poetics assume that the individual reading and responding sensitively to a poem brings into play the experiences of his past lives, and that an unresponsive reading on his part can be put down to insufficiently refined previous experience.

This law of *karma* may have been the first widely acceptable explanation for human suffering; it remains popular around the world. In India it was rarely detached from social and religious obligations. The Brahmins enjoined all men to follow their caste duties and obey social hierarchies. In this rigid world view, it was the carpenter's job to work with wood and that of a Brahmin to officiate at sacrifices. The roles weren't interchangeable, and only staying within the prescribed boundaries could bring promotion. As the *Chandogya Upanishad* put it,

> Now people here whose behaviour is pleasant can expect to enter a pleasant womb, like that of a woman of the Brahmin, the Kshatriya, or the Vaishya class. But people of foul behaviour can expect to enter a foul womb, like that of a dog, a pig, or an outcaste woman.[13]

The Brahmins later proposed that life should be lived in four different phases, or *asramas*: the chaste student had to marry, become a householder, start a family, then gradually retire into religious contemplation before becoming a wandering ascetic. The Brahmins were especially keen on householders, for their own livelihood depended on men desiring and acting, producing and reproducing, within society.

Once fortified with Brahminical ideology, the theory of

karma not only offered men no escape from the world but also bound them more firmly to its never-ending cycle of action and consequences. It promised no clearer way to salvation than the realization of the essential unity of the universe. Not surprisingly, there were men who sought to reject altogether the idea of *karma*, along with the Brahmin-defined social order. These were the *sramanas*, the homeless wanderers and spiritual seekers produced by the new urban civilization. The Buddha was the greatest of these *sramanas*, who were to bring about something of a revolution of ideas in North India.

Unlike the wandering Sophists of Greece, whom they resemble superficially, these seekers offered no practical guidance on how to live and succeed in the world. Rather, they stressed renunciation of the active life: it was the best way out of the trap of *karma*, of endless life and suffering. The basis of sacrificial religion had been desire for the world. But the world, with its social and economic upheavals, its wars and rivalries, had proved to be an unsettling place.

The eighth-century Greek poet Hesiod evoked such a world full of two kinds of strife in his *Works and Days*:

> Strife is no only child. Upon the earth
> Two strifes exist; the one is praised by those
> Who come to know her, and the other blamed.
> Their natures differ; for the cruel one
> Makes battles thrive, and war; she wins no love
> But men are forced, by the immortal's will,
> To pay the grievous goddess due respect.
> The other, first-born child of the blackest Night
> Was set by Zeus, who lives on high,
> Set in the roots of earth, an aid to men.

She urges even lazy men to work;
A man grows eager, seeing another rich
From ploughing, planting, ordering his house;
So neighbour vies with neighbour in the rush
For wealth: this strife is good for mortal men –
Potter hates potter; carpenters compete,
And beggar strives with beggar, bard with bard.[14]

Hesiod found desire, envy and conflict as part of the natural order of things. In the sixth century BC, the philosopher Heraclitus mocked those who looked for stability and permanence in the world. Everything, he claimed, was in constant flux. War was the father of all and strife was justice. Good and evil were one, and whatever lived did so by the destruction of something else.

The Indian ascetic wanderers who saw their stable ritual-based society crack under the pressures of new ways of living were no less radical and comfortless. Many of them were solitaries, living deep in forests. Others were self-torturers – exhibitionists like those still seen in religious fairs in India, lying on a bed of nails, or walking barefoot on hot coals. Most of them sought power – the kind of magic power no longer available through sacrifices. But some also sought knowledge.[15]

The Buddhist text *Digha Nikaya* mentions six of the post-*Upanishad* radical thinkers, who around the time of the Buddha's birth wandered conspicuously through North India, inciting debate and discussion with their provocative views. The most radical among them was a materialist called Ajita Kesakambala, a contemporary of the Buddha, who denied even transmigration, declaring flatly:

There is no [merit in] almsgiving, sacrifice, or offering, no result or ripening of good or evil deeds. There is no passing from this world to the next . . . There is no afterlife . . . Man is formed of four elements: when he dies earth returns to the aggregate of the earth, water to water, fire to fire, and air to air, while the senses vanish into space. Four men take up the corpse; they gossip [about the dead man] as far as the burning ground, where his bones turn the colour of a dove's wing and his sacrifice ends in ashes.

Makkhali Gosala, the leader of the sect of Ajivikas, which preceded the Buddha and survived for close to two thousand years, claimed that the *niyati*, or fate, controlled everything:

All beings, all that have breath, all that are born, all that have life, are without power, strength, or virtue, but are developed by destiny, chance and nature . . . There is no question of bringing unripe karma to fruition, nor of exhausting karma already ripened, by virtuous conduct, by vows, by penitence, or by chastity . . . Just as a ball of thread will, when thrown, unwind to its full length, so fool and wise alike will take their course, and make an end of sorrow.

There was even an atomist called Pakudha Kaccayana, a precursor of the Greek Democritus, who asserted that there were seven elementary categories, the bodies of earth, water, fire, air, joy, sorrow and life, which were 'neither made nor ordered, neither caused nor constructed' and were 'eternal as a mountain peak, as stable as a stone pillar'. He went on to declare that even if 'someone cuts off another's head with a sharp sword, he does not deprive anyone of life. A sword just intervenes between the seven aggregates.'

A more uncompromisingly anti-Brahmin teacher, Purana Kassapa, claimed that there was no such thing as sin or virtuous conduct. As he put it, 'Even if with a razor-sharp discus a man were to reduce all the life on earth to a single heap of flesh he would commit no sin, neither would sin approach him.'

The most famous among these men was Mahavira, also a contemporary of the Buddha, who also left his family at a young age to become a wandering ascetic. Mahavira rejected the authority of the Brahmins and stressed that a balanced life, based upon the principles of non-violence and frugality, was the only release from the cycle of rebirths. His followers, called Jains, came to be known for their large presence in trade and commerce; they remain among India's most successful and philanthropic businessmen.

These new spiritual teachers did not challenge Brahmin orthodoxy through abstract speculation alone. They formed sects, and prescribed their own mental and spiritual exercises. The Brahmins had made renunciation the last phase of their four-phase life, thinking it appropriate for the old and unproductive members of society. But the unorthodox thinkers stressed the importance of relinquishing home, family and possessions early in life, and embracing celibacy and poverty. They repeated that each individual had to realize the truth personally, through long practice of asceticism or meditation.[16]

Many of those who followed the new gurus and left home and family became wandering *sadhus*, or mendicants, indifferent to weather, dirt or pain – they are the first known example of organized asceticism in history. Impressed by their renunciation and dedication, the general population fed and sheltered them. This tradition of hospitality to spiritual seekers continues in rural India today. In North India in 326 BC, Alexander the Great apparently met some of these ascetics, whom he called *gymnosophists* (naked men of knowledge). Millions of them can still be found at Hindu festivals and fairs in the cities of Hardwar, Allahabad and Ujjain. Their presence was large enough for a Greek emissary to India in the third century to note that the two important philosophical sects in India were of the Brahmins and the *sramanas*.

These homeless philosophers travelled across North India, occasionally coming together in the groves and parks outside the big Indian cities of the time. Here, they debated with each other in a relaxed, democratic way that must have been a clear contrast to the sterile formality of a Brahmin-supervised ritual. Large audiences gathered around the *sramanas*. The young Siddhartha would often be among the crowds in the park outside Kapilavastu, receiving and absorbing the ideas he would later modify.

The Death of God

THIS WAS THE VIGOROUS counterculture that emerged in India in the sixth century BC – the troubled times in which the Buddha appeared. Like the Beats and hippies of a recent era, people left their homes and professions, dissatisfied with their regimented lives of work, and moved from one *sramana* sect to another, from one guru to the next. The men who led them were India's first cosmopolitan thinkers, unhindered by caste boundaries or other parochial considerations, who became aware that human beings are united by certain shared dilemmas. These early dissenters both rejected and refined what we now know as the characteristic features of Indian religion: transmigration, non-violence, organized asceticism and mysticism. They began the process, which the Buddha advanced greatly, of taking Indian thought from the speculative – the *Vedas* and the *Upanishads* – to the ethical level.

This was perhaps inevitable. The Vedic Aryans had lived in a simple world. Like all primitive peoples living off the land, they had known a special proximity to nature, in which they found their deities and laws. Sacrifice helped maintain their compact with nature, and guaranteed the preservation of *rta*, the cosmic order. But as they expanded into North India and incorporated the language and ways of life of the non-Aryan peoples they encountered, the magic charms and spells contained in the *Vedas* turned out to provide few answers to the new problems of living together. Sacrifice had worked for a static and homogeneous society; it couldn't respond to change and diversity. It came to look redundant as the communal morality of the older closer-knit societies cracked. The Brahmins, who were thinkers as well as priests, responded to their changing condition by proposing *karma* as an explanation for social inequalities and the suffering they caused. Those people who found themselves gradually on their own in a hostile world and felt the first melancholy stirrings of individuality were offered the consolation of seeing themselves part of a larger reality, the *brahman*.

But for many people this kind of salvation was clearly not enough. And *karma* seemed too much like a prop for a social structure that was supposedly part of the cosmic order but was actually an elite's attempt to rationalize oppression and injustice.

In the new urban centres, where the vaishyas, or merchants, seemed more powerful than the Brahmin or the kshatriyas, the old social structure itself was under threat. Here, the unity and morality of rural Aryan society could only be a memory. People were lonelier, and could not control their lives by following moral laws that appeared to be without divine sanction. In one of the *Upanishads*, a king speaks thus of the tumultuous changes: '[Great heroes and mighty kings] have had to give up their glory; we have seen the deaths of [demigods and demons]; the oceans have dried up; mountains have crumbled; the Pole

Star is shaken; the Earth founders; the gods perish. I am like a frog in a dry well.'

It was in this context of widespread insecurity that the radical thinkers, the *sramanas*, emerged, denying *karma*, denouncing ritual, breaking flamboyantly from tradition and preaching what the Brahmins at least might have perceived as dangerous nihilism:

> When, finally, all the observances and customs upon which the power of the gods and of the priests and redeemers depends will have been abolished, when, that is to say, morality in the old sense will have died, then there will come – well, what will come then?[1]

Writing in 1881, Nietzsche claimed that Europe was, after its long history, only reaching the tragic lucidity about human affairs at which India had arrived before the Buddha. In his view of India's spiritual history, the Brahmin priests who started out as mediators with the gods had ended up replacing them. But then the gods and the mediators themselves had been thrown aside, and the world of transcendent values abolished, by the time the Buddha arrived to preach a 'religion of self-redemption'.

Nietzsche treated the Buddha very sympathetically, in contrast to his brusque, even brutal, dismissal of some of the great figures of European philosophy: Socrates, Augustine, Kant and Hegel. He was particularly keen to distinguish Buddhism from Christianity:

> It is a hundred times more realistic than Christianity – it has the heritage of a cool and objective posing of problems of its composition, it arrives after a philosophical movement lasting hundreds of years; the concept 'God' is

already abolished by the time it arrives . . . it no longer speaks of the 'struggle against *sin*; but quite in accordance with actuality, the struggle against *suffering*. It already has – and this distinguishes it profoundly from Christianity – the self-deception of moral concepts behind it – it stands, in my language, *beyond* good and evil.[2]

Nietzsche saw his position in Europe as akin to that of the Buddha in India. He claimed to stand at the end of two millennia of European delusions, when philosophers, no less than ordinary people, had exalted an imaginary other world at the expense of their life on earth. As he saw it, Europeans had lost the art of living in the world without positing life in the eternal as good and life on earth as evil, without demonizing passions and instincts and exalting abstract knowledge, without, in fact, making any moral judgements at all. They were far from living as naturally as he thought the ancient Greeks had once lived, in the world of endless change and strife that Hesiod and Heraclitus had celebrated.

Instead, for centuries men in Europe had tried to give meaning to their lives and the world they lived in by positing such concepts as God, soul, moral law, aim, being and unity. Christianity for Nietzsche was one of the greatest such man-made delusions:

Nothing but imaginary *causes* ('God,' 'soul,' 'ego,' 'spirit,' 'free will' – or 'unfree will'): nothing but imaginary effects ('sin,' 'redemption,' 'grace,' 'punishment,' 'forgiveness of sins').[3]

Christianity had helped men place the good and real in another world and stigmatize their natural desires and passions on earth as unreal and evil. This error had finally been exposed, partly by men who through the course of centuries pursued truth into the real world and found, through their growing use of science and reason, that 'the apparent world is the only one' and that 'the so-called "real" world has only been lyingly added'. As Nietzsche saw it, the self-deception could no longer be sustained in the political and social conditions of the nineteenth century, amid the prodigious advances of science and industry, of empires and nation states:

> Looking at nature as if it were proof of the goodness and care of a god; interpreting history in honour of some divine reason, as a continual testimony of a moral world order and ultimate moral purpose; interpreting one's experiences as pious people have long interpreted theirs, as if everything were providential, a hint, designed and ordained for the sake of the salvation of the soul – that is over now.[4]

Here, Nietzsche spoke partly from his own experience. Born in 1844, the son of a Lutheran pastor, he had come into a world swiftly and ruthlessly transformed by the bourgeoisie of Western Europe under the aegis of science and reason. This was becoming a world marked by steam engines, factories, railroads, industrial zones, teeming cities with slums, newspapers, telegraphs, telephones, mass media, new nation states, multinational capital, mass social movement and a growing world market.

Natural sciences were revealing the world in terms of laws of mechanics and energy. Men did not so much seek the meaning of the world as how it functioned so that they could turn it to their advantage. Charles Darwin had helped replace God with the ape as the subject of human enquiry. History offered its own secular explanation of how human societies had come into being.

Amid these changes, Europeans found it hard to remain honest Christians – just as the Brahmins had once struggled to remain Brahmins in the new urban centres of North India:

> What is it that Christianity calls 'the world'? To be a soldier, a judge, a patriot; to defend oneself; to look to one's honour; to seek one's advantage; *to be proud*: every practice of every moment, every instinct and every valuation translated into actions is today anti-Christian.

Such were the conditions of modern life, defined by the conflict of individuals seeking their self-interest, which to Nietzsche revealed the fragile human, not divine, sources of Christian morality. These conditions turned human beings into nihilists despite themselves. It wasn't that God did not exist – Nietzsche wasn't interested in making theological arguments against God. It was that men by their own actions had rendered God superfluous.

In *The Gay Science*, Nietzsche described the madman who runs into a marketplace, looking for God, and is met with laughter. 'Where is God?' he cries. 'Well, I will tell you. *We have killed him* – you and I.'

But for Nietzsche, 'many new gods are still possible'. As he saw it, new secular illusions were at hand in the nineteenth century to replace the superseded religious goals and values and to exploit the spiritual vulnerability of Europeans. These included religions of science, socialism and egalitarianism. They asked for another kind of blind faith, this time in the ideals of free trade, progress, democracy, socialism, justice and equality – all of which

Nietzsche denounced as disguised and degraded ideals of Christianity.

For him, they were wholly inadequate responses to what he saw as the seemingly insurmountable problem of nihilism. Men pursuing truth had found themselves robbed of their most ancient illusions – those values, aims, convictions stemming from faith in a so-called 'true world', which gave them a purpose and meaning on earth, and which they had used to create political and moral order. They were now faced with a terrifying meaningless-ness. Nietzsche feared that the spirit of nihilistic despair and destruction was likely to blight Europe after the death of its old moral certainties.

'The story I have to tell,' he wrote, 'is the history of the next two centuries . . . For a long time now our whole civilization has been driving, with a tortured intensity growing from decade to decade, as if towards a catas-trophe: restlessly, violently, tempestuously, like a mighty river desiring the end of its journey, without pausing to reflect, indeed fearful of reflection.'⁵ He claimed that the world was entering an 'era of monstrous wars, upheavals, explosions' and that 'there will be wars such as have never been waged on earth' – one of his extravagant and vivid visions of disaster that were realized in the twentieth century.

Much of the prophetic aspect of Nietzsche was hidden from me when I first read him as an undergraduate in Allahabad. I wasn't aware then of his reputation as an adolescent favourite in Europe and America – indeed, few students around me at the university in Allahabad would have known who Nietzsche was. I found his short aphorisms about art, death and boredom easier to grasp than the elaborately conceived attacks on Socrates, Christianity and Kant, or his frequent if cautious praise of the Buddha.

I was held by the inner drama he frequently confessed to – the loneliness, the urge for self-knowledge and self-overcoming – the drama that culminated in his mental collapse twelve years before his death. One statement particularly stood out. He had written it one bright winter in Genoa, after a period of pain and sickness: 'No, life has not disappointed me. Rather, I find it truer, more desirable and mysterious every year – ever since the day the great liberator overcame me: the thought that life could be an experiment for the knowledge-seeker.'[6]

Vinod asked me often about him. He had become curious after reading about him in a book by the self-styled God, 'Osho' Rajneesh. He was much taken by an aphorism I once read out to him. 'Life', Nietzsche had written, 'is essentially appropriation, injury, overpowering of what is alien and weaker; suppression, hardness, imposition of one's own forms, incorporation, at least, at its mildest, exploitation'.

Vinod immediately copied the lines down in a small notebook he carried in the pocket of his kurta. But when he asked me to explain more about Nietzsche's philosophy, I floundered. I was too ashamed to tell him that I didn't understand most of what I read in Nietzsche, or that I had the greatest trouble with the word he appeared to use most often: nihilism.

Nietzsche often implied that a belief in historical progress and modern science – articles of faith for me, and for educated Indians like myself – was a form of nihilism.

This was as puzzling as the character Bazarov in Turgenev's novel *Fathers and Sons*, who was defined as a nihilist not despite but because of his belief in progress and science.

More than what he wrote about, it was the image Nietzsche presented – the solitary thinker, struggling with what Thomas Mann in *Death in Venice* had described as the 'tasks imposed upon him by his own ego and the European soul' – that was initially attractive. He was part of my high idea of Europe and the West in general – the idea which Vinod also had, and from which he drew his conclusions about the role of people like the Buddha and Gandhi in India.

Years later, while I was living in London, this romantic image of Nietzsche began to dissolve. I knew more about Europe's nineteenth century: how it had shaped much of the world, and thus my own circumstances. The physical and emotional landscape Nietzsche had moved through became more vivid. I began to see what he had meant when he compared his position in modern times to the Buddha's in classical India: how both of them had lived at a time of tumultuous change, and confronted, in different ways, the phenomenon of nihilism.

The significance of what Vinod said to me late one evening up on the roof of his parents' house also came back to me. It was his own experience of nihilism, which I was too young to understand then, but which stayed in my memory for a long time afterwards.

That evening, after our bus had broken down, we had waited for a couple of hours before being rescued by a passing truck. It was not until late the next morning that we reached the town where the smuggled goods from China were sold. There, I bought a red baseball cap while Vinod looked on slightly mockingly. We then travelled to the border, from where another bus took us deeper into India, on increasingly narrow and broken country roads. It stopped just where late monsoon rains had washed away a bridge over what was usually a narrow river. An improvised ferry took us across the brown silt-laden waters of the river. A tonga stood on the other side.

It had rained early that afternoon. The thatch-roofed huts of the villages looked battered, the ponds under the clump of mango trees were full and muddy, and deceptively shallow pools had gathered on the ruts and potholes of the road, in which the tonga's large wheels plunged with a terrible crunching sound. The driver cracked his whip then, and the horse swayed angrily to one side and swished his tail, spraying us with water.

The few pedestrians walked very slowly, prodding the ground with large tattered black umbrellas, carefully raising their dhotis with one hand. Naked children floated paper boats in the larger potholes on the road; mud draped their brown legs as cleanly as breeches. They looked appraisingly at us as we approached – in what was in those parts a rich man's vehicle – and their furtive eyes seemed fearful as we drew close.

The power had failed and lamps were being lit at Vinod's house when the tonga finally drew up outside it. I dimly saw the outline of a rectangular double-storeyed white-painted building with a flat roof, standing in the middle of a large treeless compound.

Vinod shouted a few names into the darkness, and servants – silent white-clothed apparitions – abruptly emerged to take our bags. In the first room we entered, a man sat on a low wicker chair, his long thin shadow splayed across the wall by the lantern kept next to him. He got up as soon as he saw Vinod.

Vinod's father was tall, with an unexpected shock of white hair and a lined face that suggested a great and tormented old age, although he couldn't have been more than fifty. The gesture he made towards his son was one of respect and deference. Vinod made as if to touch his feet, but then walked past without saying anything. I had taken off my new cap as soon as I saw Vinod's father. I now followed Vinod somewhat embarrassedly, past his father and into the inner courtyard.

On the parapet of a well tiny candles fluttered bravely, outlining a large tulsi plant and making the abraded plaster on the whitewashed walls of the house look like a gigantic scab. Each room opening out into the courtyard seemed to contain its own small glow and flickering shadows. In the room I was shown to, bare except for a string cot with a rolled-up mattress, a candle rested along with incense sticks on a rack under the framed and garlanded picture of a young woman. The garland was of plastic; the light under the photo exposed the dusty cracks in the flowers. The beauty of the dead woman, her large liquid eyes and full lips, seemed to dominate the room.

The woman was Vinod's sister. He had a smaller framed photo of her hanging in his room in Allahabad. I had noticed that Vinod kept it face down on a table while he was with a prostitute. I had once asked him about her, and Vinod had seemed not to have heard my question. It was obviously something he did not want to talk about.

Vinod and I bathed in the open courtyard, next to the well from which a servant drew pails of cold refreshing water. Vinod's father came out and watched us as we dried ourselves, with an expression of tender solicitude on his face. Here, too, Vinod barely acknowledged his presence.

We later ate in the long narrow kitchen, sitting on low stools on the stone floor. In the far corner, an old man turned rotis over a wood fire, his brown skin glistening with perspiration. Vinod's mother sat before us, in a posture suggesting both resignation and ease, one hand supporting her head and the other slowly twirling a coir fan. She asked us questions about our journey, about life in Allahabad. Vinod barely said a word. I found myself replying to her, slightly disconcerted by her resemblance to her dead daughter.

Later, we went up to the roof. The clouds had vanished, and the night sky glittered indifferently over us. Strange noises kept erupting in the undergrowth, dogs howled in the far distance, and then it was quiet and the only sound was of the water dripping off the roof to the wet ground.

I felt a shiver of loneliness, and in that feeling was blended the strangeness of the evening in the large gloomy house in the middle of nowhere, the doting parents and their silent son. And, perhaps, it was the setting and mood it engendered that made me ask Vinod what I wouldn't have dared to ask at any other time about the woman whose photo hung in my room.

He was silent. And then when he began to speak, he didn't stop and spoke much more frankly than he ever had. He didn't wait for my response, but I don't think I could have said much anyway.

He said, 'I know you have asked me this before. What

can I tell you about that photo? It is of Sujata, my sister who was married to a businessman in Bombay. She was harassed by her in-laws and husband for not bringing sufficient dowry, although my parents had given them a car, several hundred thousands rupees in cash, and then one day, a year after her marriage, they poured kerosene over her and burnt her alive. There was a police case, but the in-laws claimed that she had committed suicide. They bribed the coroner. Her husband remarried.

'But I don't want to shock or upset you. That's why I didn't tell you before. And also because I came to feel that there is nothing shocking about her murder. It happens every day. It is part of our world. And there is nothing we can do about it.

'I have many friends in Allahabad who ask me the same question about the photo. I have never brought them here. I know they will ask me the same question and I know that they won't understand why we couldn't do anything either to save her life or to punish the husband. Some of them think it is a question of family honour, which you can settle with a gun. But this is primitive feudal thinking, which brought us to this pass in the first place.

'Perhaps you will understand what I mean. You will understand what I mean when I say that all of us are born with certain advantages and disadvantages, and then it's up to you to make something of them. I didn't lack much where I was born. You see this land, this house that my forefathers built. For you who have seen other places, big cities like Delhi, it may seem nothing, but for people here, these things mean wealth and achievement. You saw how people looked at us when we were travelling on the tonga.

They knew who I was, who my father was. This is the kind of reputation my family has had.

'When I was growing up, I took our power for granted. I went to school in a nearby village. The master used to take his class under a big pipal tree; we used to sit before him on the ground with our chalks and slates. He used to beat the other students with a beshram stick at the slightest provocation, but he was always sycophantic towards me, always trying to please me. The tehsildar brought boxes of sweets to the house on Diwali and Holi. The local MP and MLA came asking for money during elections and touched my father's feet. The peasants in the field trembled at my father's approach. My uncle kidnapped the daughters and sisters of his farm workers and raped them. He murdered two low-caste peasants who had dared to attack his friend, an upper-caste landlord. The police registered a case, the people in the murdered men's village went to Lucknow to complain to the chief minister of Uttar Pradesh, but no one could do anything.

'Times may change fast in the cities, but life in these parts stays more or less the same. Even today the position of my father is unchanged. The local MP and MLA still pay him tribute; ask him for donations and votes. I could have stayed here and inherited all this power. I know people in this region who have built upon their fathers' position, who are now in politics, in crime, who are running big smuggler mafias. But for little accidents of fate, I too could have stayed here, lived that kind of life, picked up the pretty girls in the fields and raped them.

'I think it was my cousins from the big town who first gave me a sense of where I was. They used to come during school summer holidays from Gorakhpur. They used to love doing all the things that bored me: swimming in the nearby canal on warm evenings, throwing stones at the mango and tamarind trees in the morning when it wasn't very hot.

'But they also had things I envied. They wore ready-made clothes and bought shoes from the Bata shop instead of having them stitched by the local mochi. All we had by way of entertainment was a radio, but they went to the cinema once a month and spoke intimately of heroes and heroines I knew only by name. I wanted to be like them. I think it was during those holidays when I began to think of the world outside and grow dissatisfied with the place I had grown up in.

'What did I see when I looked around? I saw all this land and the workers on it, the servants, and my family's authority that had been maintained for decades for no other reason than that no one had challenged it. I left this compound and what did I see? I saw those half-naked boys and those wretched huts we saw on our way in. I went inside those huts and they are crammed with children that no one knows what to do with. There is not much to eat, so they die fast, but more are born each week.

'There is no one to tell their parents what to do. There is a family planning centre not far from here but it is closed for much of the month. The man in charge of the centre collects his salary and pays a commission to his boss, and no one says anything. So the poor go on reproducing and suffer malnutrition and disease, and then if they manage to grow up, they suffer cruelty and injustice.

'This is not what they taught me at school. This is what I learnt to see later. I saw that I went to school but my sister stayed at home and learnt to cook in that little kitchen

A pandit had taught her to read the Hindi alpha-
[t]hat was all she could do. She had girlfriends in a
[vi]llage who knew no more than she did. She grew
up a simple girl, with no knowledge of anything outside
her home, and then one day her marriage was arranged
into a family in Bombay who said that they were looking
for exactly that: a simple girl from a village. My parents
were flattered by their attention. They were high-caste
people like us, rich, living in a big city, and respected
within the community. My parents had no idea of the
people they were marrying their daughter to. They had no
idea because they had let themselves remain simple, they
had trusted in obsolete things like God and society and
morality. They barely knew what was going on in their
own world.

'I would have been like them if I hadn't realized that
this life of farming wasn't for me. I didn't want to grow up
like my uncle. I saw how people my age could go and rape
some low-caste woman in the fields and think nothing of
it. I don't know where the feeling came over me but suddenly I didn't want to be like them. I wanted to go to a city
and study there.

'As I say I don't know where I got these ambitions. My
father certainly didn't understand them. He wanted me to
do what he and his brother did. He wanted me to take
over the running of the estate. He was getting too old.
He wanted to retire and devote his life to religion. He
couldn't understand why I even wanted to finish my
schooling. One day he saw the schoolmaster and asked
him why he had put strange ideas in my head. The schoolmaster got so scared that he told my father that he would
have been ready to confine me to the same class for a few

years on his instructions and that would have killed my desires for further education. But when I insisted my father finally sent me to the nearest high school, which is in a kasba called Mehmoodganj. It wasn't much of a school. The teachers rarely turned up, and then often dismissed the class because so few students had come. On examination days they helped the students cheat.

'How can you learn anything in these conditions? I didn't and I began to try to persuade my father to send me to Allahabad. I had heard so much about it from one of my cousins, about the grand buildings the British had created. I remember how impressed I was by the university when I went to get admission there. I saw that they were indeed palaces, with domes and towers.

'But perhaps they were fit for only kings to live in; they weren't for students. And not such students as you found in Allahabad: boys from poor families whose fathers were breaking the bank to give them higher education so that they can get a degree and be eligible for a job somewhere with the government. I went with such high expectations but it was the same story at the university: teachers not showing up for classes, the exams being delayed for months, sometimes years.

'Criminals roamed the campus with guns and home-made bombs. Some of these were boys who came from my own district. I tried to do what I could. I read on my own. I took private classes from the same teachers who did not show up for classes at the university. I was very privileged. You have seen my house. How big it is. But these privileges didn't help. What can you do if you haven't got a decent basic education? I found myself working very hard, but I felt unmotivated. I asked myself: What was I working so

hard for? The British had created universities like Allahabad so that they could get educated Indians to help them
exploit this country. And now people went there so that
they could get a job with the government, become part
of the elite class, and plunder the country just as the
British used to. I didn't want to work for the government.
I wasn't interested in making money. I hoped I could do
something else.

'I had also started reading other books. These weren't
things I had ever found in Gorakhpur, where the bookshops had cloth editions of the *Mahabharata* and
Ramayana. Nothing I had read had told me about my own
world. In Allahabad, I discovered Osho Rajneesh, I read
Swami Vivekananda. These philosophers taught me to
think, to see things in a new way. I felt on my way to some
kind of personal liberation.

'I began to see how much of what I had grown up with
and come to accept as common sense was ignorant prejudice. For instance, our society had arranged things so that
you could not satisfy your sexual urge outside marriage.
The sexual repression in our society kills so many sensitive
and intelligent people; that is also why you have so much
rape and violence against women. I think from Osho I
gained at least the knowledge that sex is a natural thing
and nothing to be ashamed of.

'Swami Vivekananda taught me to see that our society
has grown corrupt and feeble, how it has lost its manhood.
Of course, this wasn't just something I got out of books.
You can see it in the world around you. The peasants
breed mindlessly, live in poverty and disease, and then die
as ignorant and trampled-upon as ever. The shopkeeper
adulterates the food and oil he sells. The policeman wants

a bribe before he can register your report, and will implicate you falsely for the sake of money. The student is not interested in education; he only wants a degree. The teacher will supply it to him at a price. And he will become a government official. What will he do then? Go to the civil hospital. Go to the district collector's office. The men working there collect their salaries, like the family planning man, and they extort money from the poor people who come to them for help. They have lost all idea of what they are supposed to do.

'It is people like Gautama Buddha and Gandhi who have misled us. They have taught us to be passive and resigned. They have told us of the virtuous life; they have told us to deny ourselves in order to be content. But they haven't told us how to live in the real world – the world that grows bigger and bigger and more complex all the time. This is why Vivekananda is important. He could see why the old habits of fatalism and resignation – the habits of village people – wouldn't work any more. He saw that they had made us the slaves of the Muslims and then the British, why these people coming from outside could rule over India for so long. He was totally unsentimental, and he was brutally frank. He told us that we were sunk in *tamas*, darkness. There was no point in trumpeting our spiritual success, our philosophical wisdom. All that was in the past. It was meant for primitive people. This was now the age of big nations. India was one such nation but it was way behind Europe and America. The West had technology, it had mastered nature, it had exploded nuclear bombs, it had sent people to the moon. When someone asked Gandhi what he thought of western civilization, he made a joke. He said that western civilization would be a good idea. But Vivekananda knew that the West had much to teach us. The first lesson was that we have to be materialists first. We have to learn to love wealth and comfort; we have to grow strong, know how to take pleasure in things, and recognize that there is no virtue in poverty and weakness. We have to know real manhood first. Spirituality comes later, or not at all. Perhaps we don't need it.

'I wish I had known this before. I could have avoided much confusion and pain. I could have seen the hollowness of the life and the values I had known. Perhaps, it is not too late to make something of myself. I fear sometimes that I will have to make my peace with what I had. But if I can't go forward then I can't go back either. I can't unlearn anything I have learnt. And now with these different ideas I have, the new vision of things, I find it very hard to come back home and find the same old complacency. The fields are still ours, the peasants still work on them, the servants haven't left, the house still stands. But people don't even know where they are in the larger scheme of things. They have no future. They need to change but don't know how. The world has moved on. People have gone to the moon, they are conquering space and time, they are living in the nuclear age. We are stuck in our old ways. You saw my father and mother. You must have wondered about my silence before my parents. But I find it too hard to say anything to them, and then I feel ashamed of the impatience and contempt they provoke inside me. They have spent the last five years mourning my sister, and will mourn her until the day they die. But she is not going to come back to life, and for me the worst thing is that they don't, they can't, even see what killed her. They have no idea of the world outside their little fiefdom here. In Allahabad, I took a course on western philosophy and the first thing I learned was about Plato's cave. I thought then that my parents were like the people in Plato's cave, who watch shadows and images on the walls and imagine that there is a clear sky and sun outside the cave and the shadows they see are reflections of the realm of eternally true laws and ideas. They think that there are rules out there, some kind of divine morality, governing life and society. But they are mistaken. And perhaps this is what I discovered for myself. There is no clear sky and sun out there, no great ideals or values to appeal to. You have to live in the dark cave and there are no rules there except those that strong men make for themselves and enforce upon others.'

It was in this mood Vinod spoke again about Gandhi and the Buddha: as luxuries India could not afford. It was why, he said, he had not been interested in visiting Lumbini. He said that he had been once to Kushinagara, the town where the Buddha is said to have died. He had seen a huge brick mound over the supposed site of his death. There were people worshipping there – people from South-east Asia and western countries, but not, as far as he could see, from India. He thought it fitting that the affluent countries should rediscover the men whose ideas of self-denial and passivity were no longer relevant in India and make them their own.

I listened, but didn't feel I had much to add. What I knew of Gandhi and the Buddha resonated as little with me as with Vinod. It was hard to see, while living in Allahabad, much virtue in poverty and weakness. Perhaps,

Vivekananda's ideas could better illuminate our peculiar circumstances and show a way out of them. But I didn't know enough about him to speak confidently.

We left the next morning for Allahabad. I had expected Vinod to stay a little longer. But he was in a hurry to leave. He was already dressed and packed and had ordered the tonga when he woke me up. I came out of my room to see him watching his mother praying before the tulsi plant in the sun-drenched courtyard. He said nothing to her, only touched her feet as she pulled the edge of her sari back from her head, and then before she could even ask where he was going, he turned his back upon her and walked out of the courtyard.

I followed him after a swift embarrassed *namaste* in his mother's direction. I passed his father sitting where I had first seen him the previous evening, in the room that was still dark and gloomy, although the light outside was dazzling. He came out, walking slowly with his stick, and then as the tonga lurched off he stood there for what seemed like a long time, a small diminishing figure against the white house.

The autumn sun was warm. The bare-bodied men in the stripped-down rice fields looked exposed; the pipal trees with their ample spread and shade stood even more self-assuredly in the vast flatness. It was the same landscape we had passed through before. But the twilight and the rain of the previous evening had given it a gentle aspect. In the bold exposing sunshine it was touched by what Vinod had told me. Poverty and disease and neglect seemed to mark the low huts with the bare front yards where low-caste peasant women in colourful saris sat slapping together cowdung patties, and children who had been playing with paper boats the previous day looked under-fed and malnourished with their rust-coloured hair and protruding, hard bellies.

Vinod sat next to me on the tonga and then the bus. But he didn't speak much during the rest of the journey back to Allahabad. We met again several times. I went to his flat and found myself staring at the photo of his sister. We talked about Vivekananda; he gave me pamphlets and booklets to read on the subject of India's regeneration. But we never talked about that evening.

At the end of three years, I left Allahabad and moved to Delhi. I heard intermittently about Vinod. He had become a lawyer; he had married; he had become a social worker; he had become very devout. It didn't surprise me much when I heard that he had become a politician and joined the Hindu nationalists who were then rising to power on a wave of anti-Muslim violence all across North India and would soon form the federal government in New Delhi.

It was many more years later that I began to see differently the thoughts he had expressed that evening, and I realized that the certainties he longed for could have been supplied to him only by a radical political ideology.

I realized, too, that no one had ever spoken more directly to me of my own situation than he had that evening on the roof of his house. There were the obvious similarities in our circumstances: I had no difficulty in recognizing the picture of the colonial-age university, the sense of futility and doom the students lived with. But I had also heard for the first time a description of my own young life – of growing up bewildered and ignorant and frightened.

My own ancestral past was much like Vinod's, if less constricted and exposed earlier to change. My father, who was born in the mid-1930s in a small village close to India's north-western border with Nepal, belonged to a family of Brahmins. They had worked as priests at some point in the past, but for at least a century they had been farmers, small landowners, relatively rich but unambitious. They had invested their money in property and jewellery, patronized a temple or two. They were otherwise fully absorbed by the peculiarly demanding routine of agricultural labour. At best, they probably had what Nietzsche once called the 'cheerfulness of the slave who has nothing of consequence to be responsible for, who does not value anything in the past and future higher than the present'.

India was then under colonial rule but it wasn't easy to see that in my father's village. The institutions of British colonialism – the courthouse, the tax collector's office and the police station – were in the nearest town, which was several hours away by bullock cart on an unpaved road. My father, who never saw a British person and rarely travelled outside his village in his early childhood, later had to work hard to imagine a big country called India, which had been enslaved by white people from the West, and which some great Indian nationalists had then liberated.

By the time he knew about India, it was free of colonial rule, but his family had grown poor. And the unsentimental western ways of organizing human society that Vinod admired had begun to shape his future.

After replacing their British masters, and declaring

themselves democratic, socialist and secular, some Indians in remote New Delhi had gone after large landowners. Like the French revolutionaries of the eighteenth century, whose example most postcolonials consciously followed, they proposed to sweep away all signs of what they called feudalism. As in much of Europe, changes in ownership of land were to begin the process of modernizing India. Land, individually and efficiently farmed, was to produce the capital for industrialization; some part of the rural population had to be weaned away to the cities to work in the factories and offices of the urban world.

And so one day an official from the nearby town came to my father's village with a ball of string and the fresh stationery of independent India, with which he measured and recorded my father's family fields, and then parcelled it out among several peasants.

My father was forced to leave his impoverished home and to begin his life on an altogether new basis in the city of Lucknow, where none of the advantages his family had enjoyed were of much value. He found that the bonds of caste and community could no longer be the source of identity and security; rather, they were the badges of backwardness.

Millions of human beings had known this experience: the displacement from their native habitats, the arrival in large anonymous places and the exposure to new kinds of uncertainty, freedom and suffering. It was what the Buddha had addressed, and what Vinod had also spoken of. But each person still had to bear in solitude the knowledge that the old props of caste and community were gone and that the awareness of being an individual brought both freedom and pain.

The simple fact of poverty probably blunted some of my father's more existential anxieties, and both limited and clarified his choices. He had to educate himself in western-style institutions – liberal arts universities, or medical and engineering colleges – where thousands of young men like himself acquired degrees and prepared themselves for the few jobs available in newly independent India. Failure meant a return to the fresh deprivations of village life. If he succeeded, then there would be things he could acquire and enjoy – electric fans, running water, even the bungalows, servants and motorcars the British had previously enjoyed.

The new world came as a shock to him. Everything was regulated: from the arrival of the street cleaners in the morning to the big noisy railway station from which steam-engined trains travelled over rivers, lakes and canyons, across vast empty lands, and many small cities and settlements, to the unimaginably large bureaucratic and financial capitals of Bombay and Delhi.

All this had happened over the previous century, while my father's ancestors were tilling their land and hoping for plentiful monsoon rains. And the change wasn't random. There seemed to have been a will and a purpose behind it.

Men from distant Europe, such as those I first read about in Mashobra, had long moved away from the passivity and fatalism our ancestors still lived with. They had, in Marx's words, 'been the first to show what man's activity can bring about'. They did not take the world as they found it. Rather, they studied it rationally, and proposed to change it, in accordance with the laws of science that they had developed through close observation and analysis of the empirical world.

Marx had seen these men – the European bourgeoisie – as temporary, soon to be overthrown by the working classes. But he couldn't stop himself from celebrating their achievement in almost lyrical prose:

> The bourgeoisie, during its rule of scarce one hundred years, has created more massive and more colossal productive forces than have all previous generations put together. Subjection of nature's forces to man, machinery, application of chemistry to industry and agriculture, steam navigation, railways, electric telegraphs, clearing of whole continents for cultivation, canalization of rivers, whole populations conjured out of the ground – what earlier century had even a presentiment that such productive forces slumbered in the lap of social labour?[7]

Marx thought that this class of Europeans had 'accomplished wonders that far surpass Egyptian pyramids, Roman aqueducts, Gothic cathedrals'; it had 'conducted expeditions that put all former migrations of nations and crusades in the shade'.

Young British men, who laid gigantic railway networks and dug canals across the world, had brought the same energy to India. They had brought, along with their high sense of self and economic calculation, the precise ways of science: the fixing of that elusive thing called 'reality' by the weighing and measuring of experience and the drawing of universally verifiable results. They had not only rediscovered India's past and catalogued it exhaustively, they had classified India's population by religion and ethnicity, created new political identities of Hindus and

Muslims, delineated India's most inaccessible borders and linked India's economy into the system of international trade and industrial production.

Confident that their conquests would make the world a better place, the busy men of Europe had also given their actions a high moral meaning. In the British books my father read, he was told that the British had brought the best of modernity – technology, secularism, the rule of law, civil society – to India, which had been a barbarous place ruled by tyrannical Muslims until the arrival of the Europeans. The Indian books he read denounced the British for exploiting India. But they conceded that, despite the oppression and violence, the British had inadvertently exposed many Indians to the benefits of the modern world, which the independent nation state of India was bound to enter much faster.

What was this modern world? How did one get into it? What were its benefits?

My father was too much under its spell to know how it worked. But both the British, and the Indians who replaced them, seemed to know what was needed. The guidelines had already been set by the political, economic and scientific revolutions of Europe in the eighteenth and nineteenth centuries: a country dependent upon agriculture was backward and feudal; it had to industrialize its economy, embrace science and technology, organize itself along rational lines, and reduce the power of religion and other superstitions.

But as the English and then the Americans and the French seemed to have proved, a country couldn't do any of this if it didn't reconstitute itself as a nation state with a cohesive national identity. It seemed clear from their example that only a relatively homogeneous nation state was capable of defending itself and reconstituting disparate human beings into citizens of a productive and efficient society.

Much of Europe tried to adopt what became a means of survival: an independent and strong national state, the desire for which led to the remaking of Europe along nationalist lines in the nineteenth century and, among other things, forced de Körös to go searching for the origins of the Hungarian people in the vast spaces of Central Asia.

Already in the seventeenth century, with the decline of religion and moral philosophy, politics had emerged as a major human preoccupation in Europe. Individuals, it had begun to seem, could not achieve happiness and virtue without reorganizing their societies – the secular vision that later inspired the western idea of revolution, which contained the promise of building society on entirely new foundations, after destroying the remnants of the past.

Writing in the mid-seventeenth century, in an England ravaged by civil war, Thomas Hobbes set out his alarming vision of individuals ruled by appetites and aversions, pursuing their own interests and locked in perpetual mutual enmity. Hobbes believed that only a ruthless centralized state, which subjugated all other forms of human association, could preserve the peace and save individuals from endless fear and insecurity.

Hobbes spoke on behalf of the then emerging bourgeoisie; his values were drawn from a market society, which was freeing Englishmen from the constraints of tradition and hierarchy, and upholding the ideals of equality and freedom. He couldn't have been much heard outside Europe, in places where the idea of the individual defined by a desire for free trade and profit was still alien.

In 1616, when Sir Thomas Roe, the first accredited English ambassador to the Mughal Empire, arrived in India, seeking a formal trade treaty, he had been treated with suspicion. The aesthete Mughal emperor Jahangir, who spent his days recording flora and fauna, commissioning miniature paintings, designing gardens in Kashmir and smoking opium, was sceptical about a supposedly great English king who concerned himself with such petty things as trade. But in less than two centuries, the petty traders turned into the conquerors and rulers of much of the known world. Hobbes's vision of amoral individuals pursuing their self-interest and bound together by the state received its apotheosis in the nineteenth century when the new bourgeoisie of Western Europe established rival empires across the world.

It seemed clear to many educated men in the conquered countries of Asia and Africa that the superior organization of the nation state had helped western nations in amassing their superior resources, inventions and firepower. Forced to consider how their inheritance of ancient tradition had failed to save them from subjection to the modern West, they concluded that it was now up to Asia and Africa to work hard and hope to emulate the success of the West.

Catching up with the West: this was the obsession of many people, even in Russia, which was an empire, not a European colony, and where there was hardly a writer or intellectual in the nineteenth century who did not either favour or oppose strongly westernization. If Alexander

Herzen and Ivan Turgenev spoke of the benefits of liberal democracy and the need for reason in human affairs, the Slavophiles – Fyodor Dostoevsky and, later, Leo Tolstoy among them – asserted the moral superiority and instinctual wisdom of the devout Russian soul. In 1868, the new Meiji rulers of Japan started on their own a programme of modernization designed to bring the country level with Western Europe – a programme that eventually led Japan in the early twentieth century into war against Russia and colonial conquests in Asia.

However, it was people in countries conquered by European nations who were most acutely preoccupied by the perceived challenge from the West. They included such Muslim intellectuals as Mohammed Iqbal, the poet advocate of Pakistan, the Egyptians Mohammed Abduh, the intellectual founder of modern radical Islam, and Sayyid Qutb, the fundamentalist activist who inspired Osama bin Laden. These were mostly middle-class men who were educated formally in western-style institutions; their most crucial encounter was with the West, whose history they learnt before they learnt anything else, and whose power they felt daily in their lives.

Travelling to the West in the late nineteenth and early twentieth centuries, they came up against the paradox that the western nations, which were mortal enemies of each other and ruthless exploiters of their colonies, had created admirably liberal civilizations at home. These thinkers remained opposed to the western presence in their countries and aspired for independence. But they were also dazzled by the power and prestige of the West, and they couldn't but grapple with the complex question of how much space to give to western values of science, reason, secularism and nationalism in the traditional societies they belonged to.[8]

This question began to haunt Vivekananda when in 1893 he travelled to the West for the first time in his life. Born to a middle-class family in Calcutta, he was studying law, in preparation for a western-style professional career, when he met the mystic Ramakrishna Paramahamsa and renounced the world. As a monk, he travelled all across India and first exposed himself to the misery and degradation most Indians then lived in. When he travelled to the World Parliament of Religions in Chicago in 1893 as a representative of the Hindu religion, he hoped partly to raise funds for a monastic mission in India and, more vaguely, to find the right technology for alleviating poverty in India.

The World Parliament of Religions was part of a larger celebration of Christopher Columbus's so-called discovery of America. The organizers planned to 'display the achievements of western civilization and to benefit American trade'. Vivekananda, who then had a low opinion of western civilization, addressed himself directly to such self-absorption. At Chicago, he spoke eloquently on Hinduism, drawing on his great knowledge of western philosophy. He claimed that it was an Indian achievement to see all religions as equally true, and to set spiritual liberation as the aim of life. Americans received his speech rapturously. He lectured on Hinduism to similarly enthusiastic audiences in other American cities.

The news of Vivekananda's success flattered insecure middle-class Indians in India who wished to make Hinduism intellectually respectable both to themselves and to westerners.[9] But Vivekananda himself, during the next few years spent travelling in America and Europe, was to move away from an uncritical celebration of Indian religion and his hostility towards the West. He came to have a new regard for the West, for the explosion of creative energy, the scientific spirit of curiosity and the ambition that in the nineteenth century had made a small minority the masters of the world. He could barely restrain his admiration in letters home: 'What strength, what practicality, what manhood!'[10] Vivekananda was among the first Indians to see clearly the fact of western dominance over the world, and to attest to the inevitability of the West's presence, even superiority, in almost all aspects of human life. His own conclusion was that India should regenerate itself with the help of such western techniques as reason, nationalism and science. And he wasn't alone in his admiration for western masculinity.

> Europe is progressive. Her religion is . . . used for one day in the week and for six days her people are following the dictates of modern science. Sanitation, aesthetic arts, electricity, etc are what made the Europeans and American people great. Asia is full of opium eaters, ganja smokers, degenerating sensualists, superstitious and religious fanatics.

This could be either Vivekananda or Iqbal. It is actually Anagarika Dharampala, one of the greatest figures of modern Buddhism. Born in Sri Lanka (then Ceylon) in 1864, Dharampala was just a year younger than Vivekananda. He also went to the World Parliament of Religions in Chicago, though as a representative of Buddhism, and was much less prominent than his Indian colleague. Like Vivekananda, Dharampala was influenced by the West, particularly by the Protestant missionaries, who came with British rule over Sri Lanka, and grew to denounce traditional religion in Sri Lanka as corrupt and unmanly. He wished both to modernize Buddhism and to give it a political role. Following these contradictory desires, he became an anti-colonial nationalist; he was the major icon of the Sinhalese nationalism that later brought Sri Lanka to civil war in the 1980s.

Compared to such Hindu and Buddhist modernists as Vivekananda and Dharampala, the Muslim intellectuals were more divided in their attitudes towards the West. Some of them, such as the young Turkish intellectuals of the early twentieth century, wished to totally remake their countries along western lines so as to achieve the power and affluence that the West possessed. There were many others who chose the way of suspicion or antipathy. Iqbal stressed the need of Indian Muslims to form their own state where they could follow Islam in its most spiritual form and resist the material ways of the West. Qutb advocated a return to the Koran and preached revolutionary violence against the West and its values, which he saw incarnated in Arab nation states.

But whether choosing nationalism or revolution, almost all of these intellectuals from colonized countries seemed inadvertently to admit that the West had become the best source of ideas about effecting large-scale change and organizing human society. They admitted the need for modernization, even in the sphere of religion, and for cultivating a rational and scientific outlook.

The issue had been settled in India long before independence in 1947. India was obsessed with catching up with the West. In the 1950s, as my father left his village for the city, everything – newspaper editorials about five-year plans, advertisements for family planning, the grand schemes for dams and steel plants coming out of New Delhi – underlined the same shared objective.

These efforts towards western modernity were driven by an almost religious belief in history – history not as something that happened in the past and which is worth remembering and commemorating, as Thucydides and Herodotus, the first great historians, had seen it; history not as a series of unrelated events, but as a rational process, through clearly defined stages, towards a higher state of progress and development, a process which was shown in the West's movement from the Medieval Age to the Reformation and the Renaissance and on to its many revolutions, the process that people in the rest of the world could duplicate with the right outlook and means.

The guarantee against failure seemed to be the West's own tremendous success, beginning in the nineteenth century – the time when history acquired its prestige as a guide to understanding the confused tangle of human motives and actions which the past presented to ordinary eyes; when, popularized by intellectuals such as Hegel and Marx, this new teleological interpretation of human life began to help predict, even plan, an otherwise unknowable future, in which things would be even better than they were now.

India was not considered part of this forward movement of reason and humanity, which had achieved its apotheosis in nineteenth-century Europe. For Hegel, Indians had long been sunk in 'magic somnambulic sleep'. For Marx, India was 'an unresisting and unchanging society', marked by an 'undignified, stagnatory and vegetative life'.

It had fallen to Europeans to bring places like India into the mainstream of human progress. In the course of their conquests of the so-called undeveloped world, they had propelled whole continents, isolated for centuries from the West and from each other, into history – or what Marx called 'universal history':

> The more the original isolation of the separate nationalities is destroyed by the developed mode of production and intercourse and the division of labour between various nations naturally brought forth by these, the more history becomes world history. Thus, for instance, if in England a machine is invented, which deprives countless workers of bread in India and China, and overturns the whole form of existence of these empires, this invention becomes a world-historical fact.[10]

Marx deplored the oppression and violence of colonialism. But he could also slot it into his dialectical schema, as a necessary stage in the process of raising India's consciousness and bringing it into history. This task, which the British colonialists had begun, was deemed no less essential by the rulers of postcolonial India. They sought legitimacy by claiming they were there to fulfil it – to set up, as Nehru had said in his speech on Independence Day, India's 'tryst with destiny'.

Growing up in the late 1970s and 80s, I still heard much about the national aspirations for India to achieve its rightful place, level with, if not above, the West. But these aspirations had lost some of their old force. One idea of that West still lay around us, in the schools and universities, the administrative and legal system, the cuisine and the clothes that the British had introduced to India during two hundred years of colonialism.

But these western-style institutions had deteriorated fast in independent India, and no one seemed to know what could renew or even replace them. By the time I got to my undergraduate university in Allahabad, once known as the 'Oxford of the East', it had long ceased to be a place for higher learning. It had become a battlefield for rival caste groups, a setting for the primordial struggles for food and shelter, of violence and terror. The grand buildings on the campus – what Vinod called its 'palaces' – swarmed with the bemused sons of peasants, but to no one's benefit.

The general mood was one of disappointment and cynicism. Rebellious ethnic minorities in Punjab, Kashmir and the north-eastern states were threatening India's nationhood, and were being brutally suppressed. India had joined the march of history, but still appeared to be lagging behind not just Europe and America, but also much of the rest of the world. It was still known as 'underdeveloped' despite its big industries, dams, scientific manpower and military strength. It had grown into a more violent place; and a vast majority of its population existed on the verge of destitution. Millions of Indians, lured out of their villages by the promise of jobs, swarmed in the gigantic slums of the main cities and towns, where riots between Hindus and Muslims were commonplace. Only a tiny fraction of India's population was anywhere near the living standards of the western middle class.

I found it much harder than my father to match the high-sounding words emanating from the politicians and bureaucrats of independent India with the realities of corruption and crime and anarchy I lived with. It was no longer possible to be moved by the nationalist passions of my school textbooks, where colonialism was presented as the last and sorry phase before the eventual victory of the idea of India, the India hallowed by great names and achievements: the discovery of zero, Sanskrit literature, the *Mahabharata*, the Buddha, Mughal art and architecture, Gandhi, Nehru, non-violence, spirituality, democracy, nuclear bombs and military victories against Pakistan.

These contradictory ideas formed this exalted idea of India – the India we were told we lived in but couldn't quite recognize because what we lived with was the chaos and conflict of a wretchedly poor country, and what we still sought shelter in were the institutions that an alien people from a dynamic civilization coming into India had created in the process of consolidating and expressing their power: the incomplete projects of colonial modernity – industrialization, education, transport and health systems – that appeared to have given an old country something of a future in the modern world.

We had to work with what we had. And so, in Mashobra, I often became impatient with Mr Sharma when he spoke glowingly of India's past. Like many Indians of his age, he was full of speculations and grand ideas about this past. Sanskrit for him was the oldest language in the world and the mother of all languages of Europe. The *Bhagavadgita* contained all that men needed to know to achieve salvation. Modern physics was now discovering what the *Upanishads* had said all along about the unity of the *atman*, self, with the *brahman*, universe. India had once been the fount of wisdom, where the rest of the world slaked its spiritual thirst. But it was now engaged in slavishly imitating Western countries and industrial civilization.

Mr Sharma spoke at length about what I thought couldn't be my concerns. There was, it seemed to me, no going back to the spiritually whole Indian past for people like me, even if that past existed somewhere, ready to be possessed. I had to look ahead, and, in some ways, my desire to be a writer had clarified my way.

That ambition was inseparable from the modern bourgeois civilization of the West; and from my earliest days as a reader I had sought, consciously or not, my guides and inspirations in its achievements – in the novels of Flaubert, Turgenev, Tolstoy and Proust; the music of Brahms and Schubert; the self-reckonings of Emerson, Thoreau and Nietzsche, and the polemics of Kierkegaard and Marx.

It was clear from the works of these men that to be a writer was to engage rationally with, rather than retreat from, the world; it was to concern oneself particularly with the fate of the individual in society.

There was relatively little of profit in arcane-seeming ideas in the *Upanishads* about the self and the universe. Reading about the Buddha I came across fewer such abstractions. But the long discourses with their many repetitions could be wearying. I couldn't hold my meditative states for long. And I admired rather than followed the Buddha's briskly practical advice to shun desire in order to avoid suffering.

So when Mr Sharma spoke about the spiritual and moral decline of India and the devastation caused by modern civilization, I didn't react. I listened, shook my head positively once or twice, and tried to divert the conversation to more mundane matters, thinking slightly resentfully sometimes that a less prejudiced awareness of modern science and hygiene might have helped Mr Sharma in resolving the longstanding problems with my leaking toilet.

It wasn't that I, waiting to leave Mashobra for the bigger world, failed to see dignity in the simple life Mr Sharma led, or looked down upon his lack of ambition and energy. A part of me envied him for the things that kept him rooted to Mashobra: the apple orchard, the cows, the Sanskrit magazine, his father who foretold the future and performed sacrifice rituals and his mother who sat knitting near the window all afternoon long – he appeared lucky to have preserved the life his ancestors might have lived for centuries, the life that myth and ritual shaped from birth to marriage to death.

By appearing to change little during my first three years, Mashobra itself made continuity appear attractive. Few cars ever disturbed the dust that lay in soft piles on the road through the village. The shelves in the grocery stores remained half empty. The hunchbacked man came every day and worked in the small field of corn beneath my balcony. The old press underneath my cottage rattled and clanged; and on the fifteenth day of each month, Daulatram walked up the hill to the post office with the printed copies under his arm.

I occasionally had visitors: my parents, sisters, friends from Benares, an American art historian I had known for some years, a British diplomat I had met in Mussoorie and his wife from Delhi. Briefly, the cottage filled up, and I was always surprised to rediscover my own voice, the sudden garrulousness that came over me after weeks of solitude.

The summer remained serene for the rest of the village. The afternoons were particularly still, for the inhabitants found the 30-degree heat excessive. The grocery stores remained closed; the men retired for siestas behind wooden multi-hinged shutters covered over with faded photos of Bombay film stars endorsing soaps and perfumes.

Montu, the dhaba owner, replaced his noisy kerosene stove with a gas stove. For some reason, this made his food taste slightly better. His son, Neeraj, grew taller; wispy hairs appeared around his mouth, making him look even shyer. At noon, I walked through the deserted road to Montu's dhaba, where a still unread copy of *Punjab Kesari* awaited me on the sunmica-topped table.

It was the only newspaper I read in Mashobra. It had gossip about film stars on the front page; its jaunty tone relieved some of the grim news of the outside world. Still, I couldn't help but feel relieved at my distance, both physical and emotional, from what seemed to go on endlessly in the heat-stunned plains – the religious riots, the massacres of low-caste Hindus, the deaths by starvation, the environmental catastrophes caused by big dam projects, the corruption scandals.

During its overcrowded summer season, Simla seemed a disturbing symbol of that world. I hardly went there, except to look for books, and returned strangely fatigued by the press of tourists on the Mall, and the constant blaring of car horns and diesel fumes on narrow winding roads.

It was to the regions of Kinnaur and Spiti that I went

travelling during the summer months. I stayed in monasteries and cheap roadhouses, went walking through gorges and across quiet glacier-strewn slopes, and I returned to Mashobra, the roadhouse smells of tobacco and burnt manure still sticking to my clothes, with memories of early morning mists, bright dry afternoons and brisk sunsets.

The Long Way to the Middle Way

THERE IS A FAMOUS legend about the Buddha's renunciation, which turns up everywhere. It reached Europe, modified into the legend of Barlaam and Josaphat, as early as the eleventh century, and inspired Hermann Hesse's cult novel *Siddhartha*. Like many Indians I first heard about it as a child. It describes how the sheltered and spoiled prince of the Shakya clan called Siddhartha makes four visits to a park outside the city of Kapilavastu and encounters, successively, an old man, a sick man, a corpse and a wandering ascetic, a *sramana*. He is much disturbed by these sights; they tell him of the decay, suffering and death that come everyone's way. He decides to renounce the world, and one night, when he is twenty-nine, he leaves his wife, Yashodhara, and young son, Rahula, and goes forth into the world as a seeker of wisdom.

The legend emphasizes the fact that suffering is universal and, like most other legends, appears too neat. But it may be right in its broad details. The Buddha was most likely not a prince, but a member of a republican oligarchy. Prince or not, he did claim, however, to have known a sheltered youth, and his naivety in worldly matters probably gave him his peculiar advantage: of noticing suffering as if no one had noticed it before him, which also helped him to discover in suffering a fundamental truth of the human condition and made him dwell at length upon its causes and cure.

The early canonical texts barely mention the Buddha's marriage, and it is also not clear from them whether the Buddha had a son. It is the biographies written early in the Christian era, many centuries after the early texts, which present Siddhartha as a householder.

They claim that his mother, Maya, died seven days after giving birth to him and that he was brought up by Maya's younger sister, Mahaprajapati, whom Suddhodhana married, and who was later the first female monk in the Buddha's *sangha*. According to them, the Buddha had a half brother called Nanda, as well as several cousins, including Devadutta, who later became his great detractor.

Though unreliable, the later biographies offer many more vivid details than the canonical texts. For instance, the *Nidanakatha*, the introduction to the *Jatakas*, describes a 'sowing festival', which is supposed to have occurred in Kapilavastu not long after the birth of the Buddha.[1] Such festivals were obviously important to a community like the Shakyas, which was then moving away from the mechanical rituals of sacrifice, unlearning its dependence on invisible gods, and discovering the fertility of the land and its own ingenuity and skill.

On the morning of the festival, the city was decorated. Everyone, including the slaves and servants, wore new clothes and perfumes and garlands. Some hundred and seven ploughs were yoked to oxen on Suddhodhana's rice field. They, along with the oxen, the reins and the whip, were ornamented with silver and gold. Suddhodhana left the city for the field in a procession of brightly dressed relatives, retainers and citizens. In the middle of his field there was a large jambu (rose-apple) tree. It was where the future Buddha sat, under a canopy patterned with golden stars, surrounded by his retainers, and watched his father and his servants ceremonially work the field.[1]

The scene still remains fresh two and a half millennia later: a bright morning, the southern slopes of the Himalayan foothills shimmering on the horizon, a young man lolling under a tree in the middle of a field while all around him sparkles the gold and the silver of the ploughs, and men reaffirm their link with the land.

What it doesn't reveal, of course, is what is going on inside the young man's mind. The Buddha talked wryly to his disciples of how slender and delicate and protected he was in Kapilavastu. He wore the finest clothes of Benares; walked day and night under a parasol; divided his year between three separate mansions, and was rich enough to give his servants not broken rice and sour gruel but white rice and meat.

But it also made him lonely, more vulnerable to the perceptions which the tasks of everyday living mercifully delay or obscure. The Buddha himself confessed the self-doubts that weighed upon the young man who sat under the canopy with the golden stars:

> And though I was blessed with prosperity . . . I thought,
> The ignorant ordinary person, subject to old age and
> unable to avoid old age, when seeing another who is old
> and weak is troubled and feels anxiety, shame and

disgust, overlooking the fact that oneself also is subject to old age. But I too am subject to old age and cannot avoid it, and seeing one who is old and weak, I will probably be troubled and feel anxiety, shame and disgust. This seemed to me not to be fitting. At this thought, all pride in my youth vanished.[2]

The Buddha went on to describe his arrogant assumptions about his youth, his good health and life in general – the assumptions he thought only 'ignorant ordinary people' had. He, too, believed that he would be eternally young, healthy and alive. And questioning those assumptions he, even as a young man in his father's palace, had begun to see how desire drove human life, how it made people seek permanence – of youth, health, life – in the midst of flux. He knew, he told Mahanama, also a Shakya and one of his great disciples, 'that there is little that is pleasurable in desires, that they bring suffering and anxiety and misfortune'.

The sequence of events leading to the Buddha's enlightenment may be hard to trace, but it does seem clear that at some point he grew weary of the life he was born into. And at the sowing festival, he couldn't help but see through the celebratory ritual, and observe the labouring oxen and men, the insects and worms, which their ploughs turned up and which the birds swooped upon. Meditating on them, he quickly entered a trance of sorts:

> I well remember how once, when I was sitting in the shade of a jambu tree on a path between the fields while my father was attending to the affairs of government, I became detached from desire and from that which is wrong and attained the pleasant state of that first stage

of meditation, born of detachment, the contemplation accompanied by reasoning, and the contemplation accompanied by investigation. I thought this was truly the path leading to enlightenment.[3]

He may well have thought so, but this was an isolated moment, and it seems not to have gone very far or deep. For, as the Buddha told Mahanama,

all the same I did not experience zest and pleasure outside the desires, outside wrong dispositions, and I did not reach anything that was of higher goodness. So I could not say that I was not ensnared by desire.[4]

It is likely that while in this state of mind the Buddha saw a *sramana* – one of the many who wandered across North India, and whom the Buddha often listened to in the park outside Kapilavastu. Their presence – no less ubiquitous than that of old, sick or dying men – may have suggested to the Buddha that escape from desire and suffering was possible, even desirable.

The legends diverge at this point. One of them asserts that the sight of the *sramana* helped the young prince decide that the homeless life was for him. He decided to leave Kapilavastu on the same night, and told his servant, Channa, to keep his horse ready.

According to another version, the Buddha's son Rahula was born seven days before he renounced the world. Apparently, the Buddha's parents lived in fear that he would one day emulate the *sramanas* who passed through Kapilavastu, and they managed to persuade the Buddha to wait until his son was born. This might explain his relatively late renunciation, thirteen years after his marriage.

As the *Nidanakatha* relates it, the Buddha wished to

see his son before his departure. He walked into his wife's
room.

> At that moment the lamp of scented oil lit up. Rahula's
> mother was sleeping on a bed strewn with . . . flowers,
> her hand resting on her son's head. The Bodhisattva
> stopped, standing at the threshold and gazed (at his wife
> and son).
>
> 'If I take my wife's hand off (his head) and hold my
> son, she will awaken, and will be an obstacle to my leav-
> ing. I will come back and see (my son) after I have
> become a Buddha.' So thinking he descended from the
> flat roof of the palace.[5]

It was midnight. Channa was waiting downstairs with
his horse. There were guards at each of the four gates of
the city, especially placed by Suddhodhana to prevent his
son from leaving. But as the Buddha rode towards the
north gate, it opened by itself. The tempter Mara, the
divinity of desire, now appeared before him and told him
to turn back since he was destined to be the ruler of a great
empire. This was the first of the many temptations Mara
would hold out to the Buddha.

He refused and rode through much of the night, across
three different republics. On the sandy beach of a river
called Anomiya, he dismounted. He told Channa he
wished to renounce the world. Channa said he would follow his master. The Buddha told him he was not allowed
to do so, and that he should return to Kapilavastu.

He then cut off his hair with his sword and took off his
princely clothes and ornaments and put on the robe of a
sramana – these acts later became part of the ordination
ceremony for Buddhist monks, *bhikshus*. He sent Channa

back to Kapilavastu with his horse and other things and then proceeded on foot to a mango grove where he spent the first week of his freedom.

The Buddha's own words, as recorded in the Pali texts, present a less dramatic account of his departure. While in Kapilavastu, struggling with his self-doubts, he had begun to wonder:

> The thought came to me: The household life, this place of impurity, is narrow – the *sramana* life is the free open air. It is not easy for a householder to lead the perfected, utterly pure and perfect holy life. What if I were now to cut off my hair and beard, don yellow robes, and go forth from the household into homelessness?[6]

The impulse to renounce all social responsibilities, to put an end to role-playing, and gain the freedom to remake oneself had come over countless people living in the increasingly regulated societies of post-Vedic civilization, and had led to the *sramana* movement. Its popularity explains partly why the Brahmins stipulated renunciation as the last phase of life. They acknowledged its appeal and hoped to incorporate it into their world view. But they didn't want to see the young set free from their obligations to society, and undermine its very basis, the family.

The Buddha's mind, however, was made up:

> And I, being young, a youth with black hair . . . cut off my hair and beard, although my father and foster mother opposed this . . . donned the yellow robes and went forth from the household life into homelessness.[7]

According to some texts, the Buddha returned to Kapilavastu about eight years later, some months after his enlightenment. He stayed outside the city, in a grove frequented by *sramanas*, under the shade of a vast banyan tree, and on his first morning he went around the city with an alms-bowl.

News of his presence reached his family, and the first meeting between father and son was tense. Suddhodhana accused the Buddha of degrading himself as a beggar in his hometown. The Buddha calmly responded that looking for alms was the custom of the *sramanas*.

They must have parted well, for a week later the Buddha visited his old house. His wife had been living there since he'd abandoned her, and it may have been with some bitterness that she sent their eight-year-old son, Rahula, to the Buddha, saying 'Rahula, that is your father. Go and ask him for your inheritance!'

Rahula was polite with his father, asking him only as he left the house for his inheritance. The Buddha reacted by asking his close disciple, Sariputra, to accept Rahula as a novice monk.

Rahula's grandfather was extremely unhappy when he came to know that another member of his family had become a *sramana*. There was not much he could do. But he did make the Buddha promise that he would never again accept a young man as a novice monk without the permission of his parents.

On the whole, the Buddha's first visit to Kapilavastu after his enlightenment was not wholly successful. He dismayed his father and wife by taking Rahula as a novice monk, and although a few of his kinsmen – notably Nanda, his half brother, and cousins Devadutta and Ananda (who later became his personal attendant) – were won over by his teaching, he did not gain a sizeable following. His links with Kapilavastu were to grow stronger only over the next few decades. He visited the city again after his father's death and he accepted his stepmother as a nun – she was the first woman to be so ordained. He is also said to have intervened successfully in a dispute over water the Shakyas had with their neighbours. And he lived long enough to hear about the destruction of Kapilavastu by a vindictive and powerful new king.

The Buddha knew great fame in his lifetime. But when he first left Kapilavastu, he was only twenty-nine years old and insecure and anxious. Like the countercultural wanderers of his own and later eras, he wished to attach himself to a guru-like figure in order to learn the secret of salvation. But Kapilavastu was at the edge of the urban civilization of the Indo-Gangetic plain, where the *sramana* movement had originated. The big cities where the *sramanas* found both their patrons and recruits, and which the young Buddha had dreamed of visiting, lay to the south and to the east of the Shakya city-state. Leaving Kapilavastu, the Buddha was faced immediately with a long journey.

According to the *Nidanakatha*, after a week at the mango grove, he travelled to the city of Rajagriha, the capital of the kingdom of Magadha, four hundred miles east of Kapilavastu. The ancient city, whose modern extension is now known as Rajgir, lies in a small valley surrounded by hills, sixty miles south-east of Patna, the present capital of the Indian state of Bihar. Close to a mineral-rich region, it was once the largest city in India and known as a centre of wealth and culture. Mahavira, the founder of Jainism and the Buddha's rival, is also supposed to have lived here.

In what may be the most crucial event in the history of Buddhism, five hundred monks met in Rajagriha in the first 'Buddhist council' held three months after the death of the Buddha and agreed to systematize his teachings.

The Buddha spent much time in the hills around the city. Eight miles north of Rajagriha lies Nalanda, where the Buddha found his closest disciples, Sariputra and Maudgalyayana, and where a famous monastic university set up in the fifth century AD attracted Buddhist scholars from China, Central Asia and Tibet.

On his first visit to Rajagriha, the Buddha had a crucial encounter with Bimbisara, who was then the young king of Magadha. While standing on the terrace of his palace, Bimbisara noticed and was greatly struck by a young *sramana* who looked as if he belonged to a noble family. He ordered his servants to find out about him. They came back with the information that the *sramana* was staying in a cave on one of the five hills. Bimbisara got into his chariot and drove to the hills; he then walked to the cave from the foot of the hill.

This moment would become a famous episode in the legend of the Buddha. In April 1963, Allen Ginsberg climbed the steps leading to the cave. Ginsberg was then spending a year in India, 'dreaming', as he later described it on the back cover of his published journals, 'about holy-men and visiting some few'. In his poem 'Howl', published in the same year that his mother died in a mental hospital, 1956, Ginsberg had spoken of the spiritual exhaustion and anomie that existed in the midst of the unprecedented prosperity of post-war America. In India, looking for salvation through eastern wisdom, he was one of the earliest and most famous of the disaffected members of the western middle class who wandered across Asia in the 1960s. Ginsberg later found his guru, a Tibetan, in Colorado. Walking on a hot April afternoon up the hills where the **Buddha first met Bimbisara**, he reflected, perhaps inevitably, on the insubstantiality of history and the transience of empires:

> I've got to get out of the sun
> Mouth dry and red towel wrapped
>   round my head
> walking up crying singing *ah sunflower*
> *Where the traveller's journey*
> Closed my eyes *is done* in the
>   Black hole there
>   Sweet rest far far away
> Up the stone climb past where
> Bimbisara left his armies
> Got down off his elephant
> And walked up to meet
> Napoleon Buddha pacing
>   Back and forth on the platform
>   Of red brick on the jut rock crag
> Staring out lidded-eyed beneath
> The burning white sunlight
> Down on Rajgir kingdom below
>   Ants wheels within wheels of empire
>   Houses carts streets messengers
>   Wells and water flowing
>   Into past and future simultaneous
>   Kingdoms here and gone on Jupiter
> Distant X-ray twinkle of an eye
> Myriad brick cities on earth and under
> New York Chicago Palenque Jerusalem
>   Delphos Macchu Picchu Acco

Herculaneum Rajagriha
Here below all windy with the tweetle
Of birds and the blue rocks
Leaning into the blue sky—
Vulture Peak desolate bricks
Flies on the knee hot shadows
Raven-screech and wind blast
Over the hills from desert plains
South toward Bodh Gaya—[8]

The 'platform of red brick on the jut rock crag' Ginsberg refers to is on the summit of the hill called Grihadrakuta; its oddly shaped rocks and boulders gave it the name 'Vulture Peak'. The Buddha is said to have stayed in the caves around the hill during his time in Rajagriha, and to have meditated sitting on Vulture Peak.

It was here that the Buddha received Bimbisara in one of the first momentous meetings between sage and king that often feature in Indian myths.[9] On being asked about his family, he said that he had belonged, before renouncing the world, to the Shakya clan and that he had travelled to Rajagriha from the kingdom of Kosala in the foothills of the Himalayas. Bimbisara apparently responded by offering him the 'generalship of a splendid army headed by a band of elephants'.

This may have been Bimbisara's attempt at realpolitik. The kingdom of Kosala was the most powerful rival of Magadha in North India. Although Bimbisara was married to the sister of king Prasenajit of Kosala, and had received the state of Benares as his dowry, he still looked for ways to contain Kosala, and probably thought that it was a good idea to have a Shakyan nobleman on his side.

The Buddha turned down his impulsive offer, saying

that there was no meaning for him in things and lustful desires and that he had left the world in order to seek enlightenment. Bimbisara persisted, but the Buddha was firm. According to the *Nidanakatha*, Bimbisara left after requesting that the Buddha visit his kingdom first after becoming enlightened, or a Buddha.

The exchange with Bimbisara hints at the determination of the Buddha. He wasn't going to be distracted, even though, at that early stage in his renunciation, he couldn't have known what he was looking for. His self-confidence probably helped him through the next few years as he wandered across the basin of the Ganges, still seeking, adopting and then rejecting the prevalent ways of wisdom.

After some time in Rajagriha, he travelled to the hermitage of a guru called Alara Kalama. The latter's name does not feature among the main *sramana* teachers mentioned by Buddhist texts, but his reputation must have been strong enough among the many gurus then flourishing in North India to attract the Buddha. One of Kalama's disciples, who later joined the Buddha, claimed that Kalama taught a special technique of meditation, which makes him seem a practitioner of *yoga* – a yogi.

The Buddha told Kalama that he wished 'to lead the religious life according to your discipline and teaching'. Kalama told him that his teaching was 'such that an intelligent man can, in a short time, attain to understanding equal to that of his teacher, and dwell in it'.

This was indeed the case, as the Buddha found out. But as he said later in the autobiographical *sutra* called *Discourse on the Noble Quest (Aryapariyasena Sutra)*, 'I was only paying lip service and reciting a doctrine I had picked up from the older (pupils), and as others did also I maintained I had known and understood the teaching.'

Soon, the Buddha began to have doubts. He began to think that 'Kalama only has faith in this teaching and does not proclaim: "I myself know, realize, and take upon myself this teaching, abiding in it".' He went up to Kalama and asked him: 'How far have you yourself realized this teaching by direct knowledge?'

In response, Kalama told him about the 'Sphere of Nothingness', which most likely was a kind of trance induced by meditation. The Buddha soon realized 'the teaching and abode in that state'. Impressed by his disciple's progress, Kalama invited him to join the hermitage as a co-teacher. But the Buddha was not satisfied. As he told his disciples later, 'This teaching does not lead to disenchantment, to dispassion, to cessation, to calm, to knowledge, to awakening, to *Nirvana*, but only to the Sphere of Nothingness.'

The Buddha turned down Kalama's offer; he obviously couldn't see himself spending his life as the manager of an ashram. Still seeking a guru, he went next to a teacher called Udraka Ramaputra. He later described his time with Ramaputra in terms similar to those he used to describe his months with Kalama.

He learnt whatever there was to learn, and then grew restless. He began to consider that Ramaputra only had faith in his teaching and hadn't realized it within himself. When he asked Ramaputra, Ramaputra told him about what he had learnt from his father: the 'Sphere of Neither Perception nor Non-perception'; about how people may see the blade of a well-sharpened razor but not be able to see its fine edge. The Buddha understood this truth quickly enough. He was once again offered the leadership of the ashram and once again he declined and left.[10]

When he left Ramaputra's ashram, he had been on the road for a few months. He was still as far from enlightenment as when he had first left Kapilavastu. But he hadn't entirely wasted his time. From both his gurus he picked up ideas and techniques he would later rework into his own teachings.

The most important of these seems to have been meditation, a spiritual exercise common enough at the time to be used by the yogis, the *sramanas*, the Brahmins and both of the Buddha's earliest gurus. It did not vary greatly at a basic level: it involved sitting cross-legged with a straight back in a quiet place, the posture ensuring a certain wakefulness, and concentrating on an object – image, sensation, sound, colour or the rhythm of breathing – which excluded all other objects, up to the point where the meditator felt comfort and pleasure, and detachment from his surroundings and preoccupations.

There are deeper stages that meditation leads to. The Buddha described after his enlightenment a series of four Absorptions (*dhyana*). In the first, the meditator grows oblivious to everything around him and though still capable of causal thinking he is free of desires or other strong emotions and feels a high degree of comfort. In the next two stages he stops thinking altogether and also transcends his feeling of comfort before reaching the fourth stage when he is aware only of the object of concentration and indeed has become one with that object.[11]

Meditation retains the central place in Indian religions it seems to have acquired even before the Buddha's time. The Indian ascetics who manage to suppress their breath or slow down their heart rate show thereby their mastery of meditative practices. The Buddha wasn't convinced, however, that meditation, as practised by the ascetics of his time, alone could lead to spiritual transcendence.

For one, the states achieved by meditation, no matter how deep, were temporary, 'comfortable abidings', as he put it, 'in the here and now'. One emerged from them, even after a long session, essentially unchanged. Concentration and endurance were important means, but without a corresponding moral and intellectual development, they by themselves did not end suffering.

The Buddha saw this more clearly later. At the time, he knew only that the techniques of both Kalama and Ramaputra had taken him thus far and no further – an important awareness in that it already set him apart from those *sramanas* who were merely seeking to justify their escape from social obligations, and easily fell prey to pseudo-wisdom. His experience had also taught him – a lesson he would later emphasize before his disciples – that mere faith in what the guru says isn't enough and that you have to realize and verify it through your own experience.

Perhaps, coming from the backwaters of Kapilavastu, the Buddha still lacked the confidence to break with existing pieties. For his next move was just about as conventional as seeking wisdom from gurus.

As he described it, he walked south from Rajagriha and arrived in the region of Uruvela, where he saw a 'delightful land with a beautiful grove, a flowing river, a well-constructed and attractive embankment . . .'[12]

Uruvela is now called Bodh Gaya, the most important

pilgrimage site for Buddhists. Some of the forests that the Buddha spent his time in have disappeared. But the land is otherwise unchanged. Gaya, the nearest town, has the sweet-smelling squalor of a Hindu pilgrimage site: a maze of tiny alleys, where men and women in clean starched dhotis and saris walk gingerly past mangy dogs nuzzling heaps of rubbish, thick incense smoke trails from the many barber shacks with the garish paintings of tonsured heads, and flowers fallen off marigold garlands lie pressed neatly upon the muddy ground.

Bodh Gaya lies in Bihar, the poorest and second most populous state in India; on cold winter nights, countless bodies huddle on the floor of the railway platform, often rising to reveal hollow dark eyes, while rats roam intrepidly across the first-class waiting room upstairs. But a few minutes away from the railway station the land is empty, and on late mornings, the white temples on top of the cactus-craggy hills stand against a clear sky, the river glitters through the dark shades of the palm and tamarind trees, and out in the mustard fields peasants in white dhotis move slowly with their water buffaloes.

The Buddha spent more than six years as an ascetic in Bodh Gaya. Self-mortification was then a feature of Jainism, and many other religious and philosophical sects. Ascetics were a common sight in forests or groves near villages. They enjoyed much prestige, which has survived to this day, and even their rivals, the Brahmins, spoke highly of *tapas*, the spiritual power the body amassed through self-denial.

In Bodh Gaya, the Buddha tried to follow this well-established trend. It wasn't an easy time for him in all sorts of ways. He had been away from home for just a few months. His failures with Kalama and Ramaputra were fresh in his mind. It may be that to the Buddha the torments involved in asceticism might have made it seem more challenging than learning wisdom by rote, as Kalama and Ramaputra had proposed. In his old age he spoke often of the hardships he voluntarily underwent for six years.

Once, when a Brahmin came up to him and confessed how hard it had been for him to live alone in a forest, the Buddha agreed and shared with him the loneliness he, someone used to the bustle of town life, had felt often during those six years in Bodh Gaya; how fear and terror were his constant companions, aroused by the approach of an animal, a peacock dropping a twig and the wind blowing among the fallen leaves.

As an ascetic, he had to seclude himself from human company:

> When I saw a cowherd or a goatherd or someone going to cut wood or to gather grass or to work in the forest, I would run from thicket to thicket, bush to bush, valley to valley, peak to peak. Why so? So that they wouldn't see me and so that I wouldn't see them.[13]

But these were small deprivations compared to the arduous practices he attempted. He first tried to concentrate his mind in the way prescribed by the yogis: as he described it, 'I clenched my teeth, pressed my tongue against my palate, and by my mind, controlled, subdued, and dominated my mind.'

But as he confessed, the effort made sweat pour from his armpits, and while calming his mind, convulsed his body. He next tried to meditate by stopping his breath. This time 'an exceedingly great noise of wind' escaped from his ears, and he was 'frustrated by the painful effort and work'.

He kept trying but with the same effects. Yogic meditation having failed to bring insight, the Buddha decided to further limit his diet to soup or an occasional fruit. He now became 'exceedingly emaciated'. As he told his disciple Sariputra,

> Because I ate so little, my buttocks became like a camel's hoof, my backbone protruded like a line of spindles, my ribs corroded and collapsed like the rafters of an old and rotten shed, the gleams of the pupils in my eye sockets appeared deeply sunken, my scalp became wrinkled and shrunken . . .
>
> When I tried to touch the skin of my belly, I took hold of my backbone, and when I tried to touch my backbone I took hold of the skin of my belly . . . when I stroked my limbs with the palm of my hands to soothe my body, the hairs, rotted at the roots, came away from my body . . .[14]

His penances became more severe – akin to those followed by the sect of Naga Sadhus who still show up defiantly naked and ash-smeared at every religious fair in India. He went around naked and ate only once in seven days. He refused to sit down, preferring to stand or squat on his heels. The dust and dirt of many years accumulated on his body, as a 'natural moss on my skin'. He went to sleep in a cemetery, lying on a skeleton. Such behaviour was sure to incite some local malevolence. 'Boy cowherds then came up and spat and urinated on me and showered me with dust and stuck twigs in my ears.'

He might have had more respectful visitors from the nearby village, people who came to marvel at the spiritual seeker in their midst. At some point, a group of five Brahmins joined him. They were Shakyas from Kapilavastu, and in fact had renounced the world and taken to the wandering life not long after the Buddha had. They were also seeking wisdom, and, impressed by the Buddha's example, decided to follow him into asceticism. They agreed among themselves that the Buddha, who had started early and seemed fanatically committed, would reach wisdom before any of them. They even asked him to 'announce the Law' whenever he attained it.

They were shocked then to see the Buddha eating porridge and gruel one day. As the Buddha himself recalled, 'They turned away in disgust, saying, "*sramana* Gautama is luxury-loving, he has forsaken his striving, he has become extravagant".' This seems an exaggeration. But then porridge and gruel were an extravagance compared to the cow dung that the Buddha and his companions had often eaten.

The Shakyas felt betrayed partly because they had no idea of the great changes that had occurred within the Buddha even while he was with them. It had taken him longer than when he was with Kalama and Ramaputra, but once again, he had begun to question what he was doing; what, if anything, was the value of torturing himself.

He knew he had experienced 'painful feelings' that were more 'acute and fierce' than anyone else had and could experience. But, as he said, 'Though I have undergone severe ascetic practices, I cannot reach the special and wonderful knowledge and insight transcending the affairs of human beings. Could there be another way to attain enlightenment?'[15]

The answer bubbled up from an old memory. One afternoon, years before, when he had been a spoilt prince in Kapilavastu, he had lain one afternoon in the shade of a tree in the middle of his father's fields. He had let his mind drift and then grow still. Unexpectedly, he had found himself experiencing a great serenity. He had even wondered if this perfect equanimity was the way to enlightenment.

As the Buddha, whom starvation had by now brought close to death, remembered that afternoon, a great joyful peace suddenly came over him, and he asked himself if he had been trying too hard as a seeker, and whether excessive desire, even for enlightenment, wasn't the problem. Certainly, no desire had prompted the meditative bliss he had reached under the rose-apple tree: 'Do I need to be afraid,' he thought, 'of that happiness which is apart from sensuous desires and evil?'

He felt he could regain that felicitous state of mind. But he also realized that 'it is not easy to reach that well-being with such an extremely emaciated body'. Breaking the vows he had kept for six years, he ate some porridge, massaged his body with oil and took a warm bath.

All this greatly disappointed his companions from Kapilavastu, who promptly abandoned him. It is now that according to one tradition a local woman called Sujata offered the Buddha a meal of milk-rice, which was nutritious enough to sustain him for the next forty-nine days. Alone now in the forest, but physically much stronger than before, the Buddha seated himself one night under a pipal tree, vowed not to move until he had attained enlightenment, and began to meditate.

A Science of the Mind

THE INDIAN FIG, OR pipal, is a big, elegant tree. Its leaves are heart-shaped and glossily dark green, with a tapering, curling tip. They tremble constantly, even without a breeze. Trembling and striking each other, they produce a soft, soothing chorus, until the whole tree with its vibrating and sparkling mass seems alive with a vitality all its own.

The Buddha is said to have been sitting at the foot of one such tree on a full moon night in April or May when he achieved enlightenment. He claimed to have learnt then the four noble truths of human experience: suffering, its cause, the possibility of curing it, and its remedy. Knowing this, he felt liberated from ordinary human condition.

In the Pali text called the *Vinaya of the Mulasarvasti-vadins*, he is quoted as saying, 'Destroyed is rebirth for me; consumed is my striving; done is what had to be done; I will not be born into another existence.' In the *Nidanakatha*, he celebrates his liberating insight into craving, or *trishna*, which he now knows is a 'house-builder', responsible for continual rebirth:

I have run through a course of many births looking for the maker of this dwelling and finding him not; painful is birth again and again. Now you are seen, O builder of the house, you will not build the house again. All your rafters are broken, your ridge-pole is destroyed, the mind, set on the attainment of nirvana, has come to the end of craving.[1]

There is a quality of mystical revelation about the Buddha's truth. Like the crucial experiences of Jesus or the Prophet Mohammed, who founded world religions, it may be beyond verification through logic or intellectual concepts, but it doesn't imply that his enlightenment consisted of a lightning flash of inspiration.

The Buddha did not claim a divine origin for his insights. One of the legends about his life says that his four noble truths came to him over nine hours or so of meditation that night. It is more probable that they arose out of his six-year-long experiences as a meditator, ascetic and thinker, and that it took the Buddha more than one night to realize the full implications of what he had found, which he then refined over the next forty-five years of discussion with his disciples.

The Buddha set himself off further from recipients of esoteric wisdom by claiming that the truth he reached in Bodh Gaya is available to anyone willing to follow his example. The key was meditation – not meditation as others had known it, not the kind of yogic practice the Buddha had encountered before, but one which he perfected, and which he offered as a means to both knowledge and salvation.

During his time with the gurus Kalama and Ramaputra, the Buddha had encountered what were then the conventional Upanishadic-Brahminical theories of self-knowledge – the theories that remain at the spiritual and philosophical core of Hinduism. According to these, the microcosm (man) reflects the macrocosm (the universe). The essence or self of the individual is the same as the essence or self of the world; both partake of the same unchanging substance, the *brahman*. Meditation, in so far as it achieves a consciousness without an object, is the means to reach a profound knowledge that the self of the knower is identical with the self of the known; it helps one realize the truth of the Upanishadic formula 'Thou art that'; and to realize this is to be liberated.

The deeper states of yogic meditation that the Buddha came across promised human beings a grand vision of transcendence: that there was a Self, an eternal, seamless, and unborn whole which lay behind apparent multiplicity and change in the world, the unity that lay behind the obvious dualism of subject and object, individual and the world.

However, the Buddha claimed originally that such knowledge of the eternal self was fixed in advance. The meditator had actually trained himself to locate it in the attainment of a deep meditative state; he began with a particular frame of mind or intention, which then predictably led him to a particular form of knowledge.

As the Buddha saw it, the teachers preaching the so-called eternal, independent and unanalysable Self had not realized it from within; it was an abstraction, a product of speculation. He may have been thinking of his own experience with Kalama and Ramaputra. Both teachers, upon questioning by the Buddha, had admitted to having no direct knowledge of their doctrine. Rather, they assumed that it must be true.

This was not unusual. Spiritual teachers before the Buddha had been content with positing an eternal essence and claiming that it could be experienced in certain meditative states. The Buddha thought that such experience was *samskrta* (conditioned) – a word he made his own through frequent use. It sprang from certain clear causes – frame of mind, will and intention, and so it could not be identical with an eternal and unborn self.

In any case, the deep states created by such meditation did not last long. They arose out of certain causes and then disappeared. They could be analysed; they couldn't but be different from an eternal, unanalysable self.

The Buddha did not use such practical reasoning to discredit meditation. Rather, he showed that the yogic experience of meditation was limited to certain states achieved through concentration, and did not seek to go beyond them. His own meditative technique tried to combine concentration with mindfulness and self-possession. It led, he claimed, to a direct knowledge of the unstable and conditioned nature of the mind and the body.

This may sound odd to most of us, who live with the triumphs and triumphalism of science, and are used to seeing knowledge as something arrived at objectively, through a process of verification by physical means. Meditation may not seem a convincing way to attain it. It doesn't rely on logic, not even on the evidence of the senses. It is a purely subjective experience.

But the Buddha's own discoveries could not have been made in any other way. For they describe first and foremost the workings of the mind – the mind that determines the way we experience the world, the way in which we make it *our* world. The Buddha worked with the insight that the mind was the window onto reality for human beings, without which they could access nothing, nor even assume the existence of a world independent of their perception, consciousness and concepts:

> It is within this fathom-long carcass, with its mind and its notions, that I declare there is the world, the origin of the world, the cessation of the world, and the path leading to the cessation of the world.[2]

This was not the absolute idealism of the kind found in western philosophy. The Buddha did not assert that everything was a projection of the mind, or that there was a thing-in-itself out there. He spoke rather of the phenomenal world arising out of interdependent causes and conditions.

The world and its objects had no intrinsic characteristics or true nature – or at least none that could be perceived outside human mental processes. Their colours, sounds, smell and textures weren't independent of the perceiving mind. They came into being through the process of sense organs perceiving and interpreting data through instants of consciousness.

This is illustrated by a story in Buddhist scriptures about two blind men who wished to know what colours were. One of them, who was told that white was the colour of snow, assumed that white was 'cold'; the other man, who was told that white was the colour of swans, thought that white went 'swish-swish'.

Happiness and suffering, fulfilment and frustration –

the mind was indispensable in all of these processes, even when they emerged out of conditions seemingly external to us. To control the mind, then, was to change radically one's relations with the world. As the eighth-century Indian monk Santideva wrote:

> By the mind the world is led . . . The mind swings like a firebrand, the mind rears up like a wave, the mind burns like a forest fire, like a great flood the mind bears all away. The bodhisattva, thoroughly examining the nature of things, dwells in ever-present mindfulness of the activity of the mind, and so he does not fall into the mind's power, but the mind comes under his control. And with the mind under his control all phenomena are under his control.[3]

The enquiry into the nature of the mind which the Buddha tried to conduct is a task not easily performed even today by modern science, which charts the central nervous system, reducing consciousness to chemical and electrical reactions within the network of neurones. Psychologists still tend to focus on outward behaviour to study the workings of the mind.[4]

The Buddha, however, began with the assumption, now often shared by neuroscientists, that the mind alone can know and analyse the mind, and alone can observe the movement and nature of thoughts passing through it. Accordingly, the first tool, or prerequisite, in his contemplative science was a still mind.

This is not achieved easily for the mind is more or less identical with ceaseless activity. Thoughts and feelings flow in and out of one another – so fast that they can barely be separated from each other and the actions they give rise to. The Buddha used an unflatteringly Darwinian simile to describe this process:

> What is called 'mentality' and 'mind' and 'consciousness' arises and ceases, in one way and another, through day and night; just as a monkey ranging through a forest seizes a branch and, letting go, seizes another.[5]

William James, the father of modern psychology, asserted that it was impossible to stop the flow of thoughts. His failure, as well as that of many early psychologists attempting to study the mind through introspection, may have kept psychology from its inevitable encounter with Buddhism. Modern-day psychotherapists who recommend meditation to their clients are more aware that thoughts can be identified and isolated in a calm mind.

At the same time, it takes patient and sustained effort to sit still and grow aware of thoughts passing through. The first effort usually produces greater agitation. Thoughts seem more oppressively numerous than usual, bubbling up one after another, although their quantity may not be more than usual. The tormented narrator of Fyodor Dostoevsky's insightful psychological fiction *Notes from the Underground* describes the slippery quality of such self-consciousness:

> How am I to set my mind at rest? Where are the primary causes on which I am to build? Where are my foundations? Where am I to get them from? I exercise myself in reflection, and consequently with me every primary cause at once draws after itself another still more primary, and so on to infinity. That is just the essence of every sort of consciousness and reflection.[6]

As in the narrator's case, negative thoughts – resentment, envy and malice – tend to multiply faster, making the world seem dark and unyielding. But to be aware of these thoughts is also to feel one's ability to control them. This is what frustrates Dostoevsky's underground man, who can't even get himself into a state of anger because of what he calls 'those accursed laws of consciousness':

> You look into it, the object flies off into air, your reasons evaporate, the criminal is not to be found, the wrong becomes not a wrong but a phantom, something like the toothache, for which no one is to blame, and consequently there is only the same outlet left again – that is to beat the wall as hard as you can.[7]

Devoted to activity, however mindless, Dostoevsky's narrator is determined to repel consciousness, to 'hate or love', do anything, 'if only not to sit with your hands folded'. But those who make it a habit to sit with their hands folded discover that when discouraged, thoughts simply cross the mind and fade. Gradually, with increasing concentration, you see your mind slowing down. A slight pain in the knees during meditation, which ordinarily makes you change your position without thinking, or a pleasurable daydream which spins out scenarios without stopping, can be examined in isolation and resisted before they result in action: a change of position, more daydreams.

With regular practice of meditation, you become aware of, and learn to ignore, the random impulses and sensations which previously would have resulted in some sort of reaction, physically or mentally, but which now arise and fade without leaving a trace.

The thoughts then cease altogether until you are aware of being perfectly still in the present moment. This state is reached relatively quickly by disciplined meditation – the state where Buddhists begin to examine the nature of discursive thoughts and their influence over the human body.

This kind of energetic meditation, which the Buddha called Vipasyana, went beyond the regular states of concentration and equanimity achieved by the yogis with consistent focus. It called for a detailed objective observation of one's mind, which could strip thoughts of their usual solidity, the power with which they held sway over human beings, the power they transmitted to the world, making it seem something fixed and unyielding, desirable or undesirable, when it had no innate quality or essence, and was only a continuous process of transformation.

This kind of meditation did not concern itself with finding essences outside or inside the human body. It analysed how we experience reality, rather than describe what reality is. It undermined the misperception of things and situations as unchangeable. It offered a different way of perceiving the phenomenal world, by seeing through to its true nature as something impermanent, unsatisfactory and essenceless. In his exposition of Buddhist teaching, *Vishuddhimagga* (*Path of Purification*), the fifth-century Indian philosopher Buddhaghosa came up with several images to describe the transience and elusiveness of the world as experienced by the meditator: dew drops at sunrise, a bubble on water, a line drawn on water, a flash of lightning, etc.

In a discourse called The Setting Up of Mindfulness, the Buddha described the various forms of meditation he preferred. The word 'meditation' brings to mind a stereotypical image of a person seated cross-legged with eyes closed. But the original Buddhist word for meditation, *bhavana*, which means culture or development, conveys better what the Buddha wished to accomplish: the creation of a wholesome mental climate through constant awareness. Accordingly, he prescribed a posture for only one meditative exercise, which requires attentiveness to the rhythms of breathing. The rest of the exercises – which involved partly the study of desire, anger, hatred, torpor, anxiety, as they rose in one's mind – were designed to accompany the meditator's daily routine.

For the Buddha, to observe the processes that occur inside the mind, to be aware of the tiniest perception or thought, was to move towards a radical truth: that consciousness was not an independent or self-contained entity, that it was a perpetual flow of interdependent thoughts.

The contemplative who analyses the nature of the mind in this way also understands the nature of the self. For although both mind and body change over time, human beings nevertheless have the sense of something constant within them – what characterizes them as persons until their death, what gives them their sense of individuality, which is strong or weak depending on the culture or society they live in. From this feeling of an innate 'I' arises the sense of an autonomous ego, and the tendency to gratify and protect it – the tendency that dictates virtually all human activity.

Perceiving itself as separate, the ego turns the world and other people into means for its gratification, giving rise to desire, pride, revulsions, anger and other emotions. The ego seeks to gratify and protect itself through desires.

But the desires create friction when they collide with the ever-changing larger environment. They lead only to more desires, and more dissatisfaction; and so the effort to protect and gratify the self is constantly destabilized and perpetuated.

Meditation thus revealed to the Buddha the conditioned and unsatisfactory nature of the self. It produced the theory that supported his view of phenomena as processes rather than fixed essences. But theory meant little to the Buddha if it couldn't be verified and turned into a way to overcoming suffering. Meditation was, most importantly, a practice indispensable to attaining *nirvana*, which was none other than a full realization within one's own being of the insubstantiality of self, and liberation from its primary emotions, greed, hatred and delusion.

Buddhist philosophers, such as Asanga and Vasubhandhu, who belonged to the Yogachara school that flourished in north-west India in the fourth and fifth centuries AD, were to take the Buddha's view further.[8] They saw consciousness as a stream without beginning or end, which could be born only from a preceding instant of consciousness and result in the following instant of consciousness, and which continued after death. Just as modern physicists see mass energy, so they saw consciousness: something that can neither be created nor destroyed, but only transformed. It was able to interact with the human body, but, as modern Buddhists have asserted, it could not be reduced to chemical reactions in the brain, and did not disappear along with the material body itself, but went on to manifest itself in another body. The proof of this lay in reincarnation – people who remembered their past lives, such as the present Dalai Lama, who as a child identified the rosary and walking stick he had used in his incarnation as the previous Dalai Lama.

Later philosophers also refined the Buddha's view of phenomena as things that appear but have no fixed or autonomous entity. Unlike the mainstream of western philosophers, they did not attempt to find or assume a stable and permanent entity behind phenomena – something that could be the basis of knowledge about the natural world. They accepted that the laws of cause and effect worked in the everyday conventional world, but rejected the notion that there could be an independently existing reality behind appearances. The chariot on which the Greek king Menander had travelled to see the Buddhist monk Nagasena was real enough. It belonged to what the Buddhists called the realm of relative or conventional truth (*samvrti*). But the chariot was only the sum of its constituent parts which when separated, reduced to grains of sawdust and eventually into molecules and atoms, revealed their ultimate reality – what the Buddhists call *parmartha*.

For Buddhist philosophers, the particles that make up matter are not more real than their constituent parts; they are not solid and indivisible entities with intrinsic existence. Nagarjuna, the second-century philosopher, went on to assert that the ultimate nature of phenomena was emptiness, which explained their ability to manifest themselves infinitely. This is close to what the physicist Werner Heisenberg believed: that atoms or the sub-atomic particles 'form a world of potentialities or possibilities rather than one of things or facts'.[9]

But Buddhist philosophical analyses of the phenomenal

world never broadened into a scientific explanation. This was because Buddhist philosophers had different, more pragmatic, goals. They aimed not so much to transform the external world through science and politics, or to build nuclear bombs, as to help human beings understand the nature of mind and rid themselves of the negative emotions – anger, hatred, malice, jealousy – caused by their attachment to such solid-seeming entities as self and world.

Turning the Wheel

THE BUDDHA SPENT A few days after his enlightenment in Uruvela. At first he doubted that he could share with others his ideas – which he thought were 'against the current', 'difficult to see, difficult to understand', and which he claimed 'men who are overpowered by passions and surrounded by a mass of darkness cannot see'.[1]

According to legend, Lord Brahma himself appeared to persuade the Buddha to become a teacher. The Buddha said that 'the world delights in the pleasures of the senses, but my teaching aims at the renunciation of all attachments and the destruction of craving'. He worried that people would not understand him. To this, Brahma apparently responded that there existed people with 'only a little dust in their eyes' who were likely to respond well to him.

When he finally overcame his doubts, the Buddha wondered with whom he should share his insights. He thought of his two gurus, Kalama and Ramaputra, but both of them had died in the previous six years. He then remembered the five Brahmins from Kapilavastu who had joined him briefly in his ascetic practices; he knew that they were staying in a deer park near Benares, and although they had denounced him for abandoning asceticism, the Buddha hoped that they would be receptive to what he had to say.

When, soon after his enlightenment, he set off for Benares, which lay several arduous days on foot away, the Buddha was only thirty-five years old. He had been a householder, a *sramana* and an ascetic. He had known sexual love, political power, the homelessness of a *sramana,* the trances of a yogi and the self-mortifications of an ascetic. And now after this range of human experience he had known what he thought was true wisdom.

A naked *sramana,* one of the Ajivikas who were extreme determinists, met him on his way to Benares, and was clearly struck by his confident mood. He asked the Buddha who his teacher was. The Buddha declared that he was the enlightened one, had no teacher and was a teacher himself. Instead of falling at his feet, the *sramana* merely said, 'It may be so, brother,' and walked away.[2]

If this wasn't deflating for the Buddha, the initial response from his erstwhile companions at the deer park near Benares must have been discouraging. For, when they saw him approach, they decided neither to greet him nor to rise in his presence. But as he came nearer they sensed the state of grace that had come over him, and their resolve weakened.

They received the Buddha courteously. They took his alms-bowl and his robe and washed his feet. But when they addressed their former companion as a 'friend', the Buddha told them that he was now a *tathagata arhat*, an enlightened sage, and should be addressed as such.

The ascetics may have been sceptical, if not dismissive, of their fellow Shakya. They had last seen him breaking his vows and eating porridge; it had seemed clear to them then that his search for enlightenment had ended.

Wishing probably to persuade them, the Buddha went on to preach his first sermon, what came to be known later as Setting in Motion of the Wheel of the *Dharma*. He first sought to establish that he had already experimented with the extreme ways – the life of the householder with its sensual fulfilments and the asceticism of the *sramanas* – and what he taught was the Middle Way:

> There are these two extremes, monks, which one who has left the world should not pursue. Which two? (On the one hand) giving oneself up to indulgence in sensual pleasure; this is base, common, vulgar, unholy, unprofitable. (On the other hand) giving oneself up to self-torment; this is painful, unholy (and also) unprofitable.[3]

He then explained the four noble truths:

1. *Duhkha*.
2. *Samudaya*, the arising or origin of *duhkha*.
3. *Nirodha*, the cessation of *duhkha*.
4. *Marga*, the way leading to the cessation of *duhkha*.

The first noble truth, from which the other three flow, is often taken to mean that life is *duhkha*, which in Sanskrit literally means pain or suffering. The second noble truth is that suffering is caused by *trishna* (craving), which binds us to the phenomenal impermanent world, and gives rise to rebirth. The third noble truth is that the suffering can be cured. The fourth noble truth lays down the eightfold path, which describes a journey from high moral behaviour to meditation to wisdom, and culminates in the cessation of suffering. They were:

1. Right View.
2. Right Intention.
3. Right Speech.
4. Right Action.
5. Right Livelihood.
6. Right Effort.
7. Right Mindfulness.
8. Right Concentration.

It is no coincidence that the four noble truths take the form of a medical diagnosis and cure. From his very first sermon, the Buddha tried to identify and then propose solutions to what he saw as the fundamental problem of life – suffering. His aims were therapeutic and ethical rather than metaphysical or theological. Pursuing them, he either ignored or denied just about every piety – God, soul, eternity – that was current in his time and was to form the basis of many subsequent religions and metaphysics in India and elsewhere.

He also refrained from proposing a new theology or dogma. It may seem that the four noble truths form part of Buddhist dogma, or creed, but the Buddha meant them to be a description of things as they actually are, self-evident things that we nevertheless do not see. It is why he didn't seek to persuade. He spoke as if the fact of suffering was universal, felt by almost everyone alive; he also assumed that it was individual misperception or ignorance of the true nature of the self which caused this suffering.

Life in its normal course produced several forms of

suffering: old age, sickness, death, and the mental and physical pain – depression, melancholy, grief – that couldn't but be *duhkha*. This was the suffering that the Buddha had first witnessed when as a young sheltered rich man he saw old age, decay and death. As he put it, 'birth is suffering, ageing is suffering, sickness is suffering, dying is suffering, sorrow, grief, pain, unhappiness, and unease are suffering'.

In nineteenth-century Europe, Schopenhauer chose such words to advance his view of Buddhism as an especially pessimistic religion. But the Buddha held out ultimately a promise of bliss; and he had much more in mind while speaking of this suffering. He meant also the discontent and unease that was caused by the impermanent nature of things. 'Being united with what is not liked is suffering, separation from what is liked is suffering, not to get what one wants is suffering.'

This was the suffering that lies in wait while we know happiness, when something or someone we like changes, or an unpleasant event breaks into our life; the suffering that is greater because it replaces happiness, and seems to rest on the unshakable reality that, as the Buddha put it, 'the world is in continuous flux and is impermanent' and 'human life is just like a mountain river, flowing far and swift, taking everything along with it; there is no moment, no instant, no second when it stops flowing, but it goes on flowing and continuing'. Here, *duhkha* acquires more meanings: it refers to the impermanent, uncontrollable and imperfect nature of the phenomenal world.

The suffering that is all-pervasive and everyday – part of a world of change and decay – was what the eighteenth-

century Scottish thinker David Hume had in mind when
he wrote:

> Were a stranger to drop in a sudden into this world, I
> would show him as specimen of its ills, a hospital full of
> diseases, a prison crowded with malefactors and debtors,
> a field of battle strewed with carcasses, a fleet foundering
> in the ocean, a nation languishing under tyranny, famine
> or pestilence. To turn the gay side of life to him and give
> him a notion of its pleasures – whither should I conduct
> him? To a ball, to an opera, to court? He might justly
> think that I was only showing him a diversity of distress
> and sorrow.[4]

For the Buddha, as much as for Hume, happiness was
too closely bound together with suffering. Even the happiness caused by meditation was fleeting and so part of
duhkha. Happiness could never be fully and permanently
possessed as long as it arose from conditions external to
us, conditions that changed all the time.

Part of the problem was that the so-called self that
experienced the world was innately unstable, changing
from moment to moment, and therefore insubstantial. 'Me
at this moment and me this afternoon are indeed two,'
wrote Montaigne, a close examiner of self.[5] Man, the
sixteenth-century French humanist said, was 'a marvel-
lous, vain, diverse and undulating object', who 'in all
things and throughout is but patchwork and motley'. In
the hands of this changeable man, even reason revealed
itself as 'an instrument of lead and wax, extendable,
pliable and accommodating to any bias or measure'.[6]

His vision of the self and the world as marked by

diversity and perennial movement led Montaigne to declare that in his essays,

> I do not portray being. I portray the passing. Not the passing from one age to another, or, as the people say, from seven years to seven years, but from day to day, from minute to minute.[7]

A similar view of changeable man prompted the Buddha on several occasions to provide close analytic descriptions of the series of events which, according to him, constitute the process of experience:

> In dependence upon the eye and upon visible objects visual consciousness arises. The union of these three (the eye, objects and visual consciousness) constitutes contact. Dependent upon this contact feeling is constituted. One perceives what is thus felt; what one perceives one considers; and what one considers one develops all sorts of notions about.[8]

In the Buddha's view, none of the stages in this process can be isolated from the others. Perception, feeling and consciousness form part of a dynamic complex, which individuals can call their self for the sake of convenience, but there is nothing stable or enduring about it. It was why *duhkha*, suffering, or impermanence and discontent, resides in the very nature of human existence.

This austere vision is not far from the one found among the greatest of modern novelists, Flaubert and Proust, who wrote about how human beings desiring happiness and stability were undermined slowly, over the course of their lives, by the inconstancy of their hearts and the intermittence of their emotions.

Personal experience and a habit of close analysis seem common to both the meditator and the artist in their discovery: they see that the human being is a process, a shifting web of relations among such changing aspects of his person as perceptions, desires and ideas, and that by presuming to possess a stable self he sinks deeper into ignorance and delusion.

For the Buddha, however, such discoveries were important only in so far as they led to the possibility of salvation. From his vision of the individual with the elusive self who is discontented and restless, who desires some kind of permanent happiness, security and stability and is constantly, pointlessly active, the Buddha drew a conclusion: that there is, as the second noble truth put it, a discernible cause of suffering.

He didn't blame the individual for his suffering, using concepts like 'sin' and 'evil'. It would have been easy, if banal, to do so. But it would have contradicted his own experience – reached through meditation – of the individual self as a process without essence. He knew about the thoughts and feelings, good or bad, which caused suffering by being uncontrollable and ever-changing. There had to be another cause, not personal, of suffering, and the Buddha found it in *trishna*, craving:

> And this, O *bhikshus*, is the Truth of the Arising of Suffering. It is just thirst or craving (*trishna*) which gives rise to repeated existence, which is bound up with impassioned appetite, and which seeks fresh pleasure now here and now there, namely thirst for sensual pleasures, thirst for existence, thirst for non-existence.[9]

Trishna literally drives human beings. It was different

from desire – the Buddha does not seem to have disapproved of wanting per se, or felt he was contradicting himself when he set off each morning to look for alms. To want something out of one's free will, and with the right intention, was not craving. Craving came into being 'wherever that is which seems lovable and gratifying, there it comes into being and settles'. It made individuals seek 'fresh pleasure now here and now there', in this life as well as the next. There was a craving to escape pain as well as a craving for wealth, power and status; a craving for sensual pleasures as well as for right opinions.

Each instance of craving involved an escape from the here and now, a desire for becoming or being something or someplace other than what the present moment offered. But to seek ceaselessly some new state of being while at the same time striving for permanence was to expose oneself to frustration:

> The world, whose nature is to become other, is committed to becoming, has exposed itself to becoming; it relishes only becoming, yet what it relishes brings fear, and what it fears is pain.[10]

Rebirth, whether in another moment of experience, or in another life, was caused by precisely this craving for new forms of existence, by the desire to be something or somewhere.

As a grand principle purporting to explain all of human life, *trishna* doesn't seem much unlike Hegel's Spirit of History, Schopenhauer's Will, or Nietzsche's Will to Power: something we can't actually observe or verify, something vaguely metaphysical. The closest western parallel to *trishna* is Schopenhauer's will to live, the blind force that lies behind life on earth, which the German philosopher held responsible for all suffering in the world and which he thought was best denied, either through asceticism or through aesthetic contemplation.

But the Buddha insisted on tracing *trishna*, like his other discoveries, to actual human experience; it wasn't for him, as the will was for Schopenhauer, the 'Thing-in-itself', something separate from the conditioned and phenomenal world. Meditation had revealed the human mind to him as a receptacle of random and short-lived impulses, one that made you change your posture, another that plunged you into a daydream, yet another that made you want to take a break.

As the Buddha saw them, these impulses, ceaselessly coming and going, and constituting what human beings think of as their experience, worked in a mechanical fashion. They were not the result of an active decision by the individual, which is why the individual can't be the cause of his own suffering.

These unbidden impulses seemed to amount to a basic tendency within human life, one which replicates itself endlessly. The Buddha called this tendency 'clinging' (*upadana*), which flourishes because of man's profound ignorance (*avidya*) of the nature of self and things as they actually are: impermanent, unsatisfactory, essence-less.

Clinging produces our typical and renewable desire for status, power, wealth and sexual love. But, as the Buddha never tired of repeating, to desire complete and secure happiness with an elusive self and in an impermanent world is to court frustration and discontentment. Even the fulfilment of all of one's desires could bring only short-lived happiness. For as Oscar Wilde had put it, 'In this world there are only two tragedies, one of not getting what one wants, and the other of getting it.'

The Buddha was categorical about the effects of uncontrolled *trishna*. 'All aspects of experience,' he declared, 'in the mind and body, in which clinging inheres, are suffering.'[11] This reduces the individual to a collection of impulses, doomed to repeat a pattern of craving, ignorance and clinging. But the Buddha was doing little if not creating through his seemingly bleak diagnosis the way to a cure.

As he saw it, impulses that arise in the mind, however automatic or habitual, also present the individual with choices. The individual can choose to act on them or not. Whatever decision he takes defines him for better or worse. Thus, for the Buddha, choice and intention shape the human being. They create his emotional and psychological world; and they add up to what the Brahmins called *karma* – the *karma* that for the Buddha resided in intention, expressed or not, as much as in action.

Previously, *karma* had been the act or deed the individual performed as part of a Brahmin-ordained social order, which then determined his social position in his next life. The Buddha rejected this definition, which enjoined the individual to see his salvation in serving the social order. 'It is,' he said, 'choice or intention that I call *karma* – mental work – for having chosen, a man acts by body, speech and mind.'[12]

With these apparently innocuous words the Buddha introduced an idea in India no less radical than the one the thinkers of the European Renaissance came up with when they stated that the good was defined by human will and not by God or nature. 'What good is man,' Erasmus had asked, 'if God acts on him as the potter acts on the clay?'[13] He was intervening in the centuries-old western debate between free will and determinism, the terms of which were set by Saint Paul when he declared that human beings were like inert clay in the hands of God. Erasmus and humanists like him wished to assert the dignity of human beings, their capacity to exercise their will and opt for goodness.

The Buddha reacted to a similarly reductive view of salvation – of grace through ritual, through socially pre-scribed deeds – when he defined *karma* as intention, and offered the possibility that individuals could break out of the over-determined universe of suffering.

Although their capacities are formed partly by the *karma* of their previous lives, human individuals are still able to exercise their free will within their present life. *Karma* was partly fate, but fate of which individuals could become, as it were, the authors. They can dispel the veil of ignorance, see things as they are, and control their desires. This is what the third noble truth asserted: that suffering can be overcome; that liberation is possible. It leads to the fourth noble truth, which prescribed the exact means – the eightfold path – by which greed, hatred and delusion could be overcome, and nonattachment, loving kindness and wisdom cultivated.

The first of these, Right View, means that action, speech and thought should flow out of an awareness of things as they really are, impermanent and unsatisfac-tory. Right Intention involves freeing oneself from selfish-ness and sensual pleasures, and acting with compassion and benevolence. Right Speech implies a rigorous dis-tance from false, hurtful and idle chatter. Right Action proscribes violence, stealing and sexual misconduct. Right Livelihood means not working anywhere that forces one into violating the rules of Right Speech and Right Action. Right Effort involves a constant vigilance against unwholesome mental states (anger, greed, malice). Right Mindfulness is perpetual awareness of the body, feelings and thoughts. Right Concentration involves focusing the mind on a single object, and is the first stage of the meditation that leads to profound and lasting equanimity.

'It seems to me,' Nietzsche once wrote, 'that most people simply do not believe in elevated moods, unless these last for moments only or at most a quarter of an hour – except for those few who know at first hand the longer duration of elevated feelings. But to be a human being with one elevated feeling – to be a single great mood incarnate – that has hitherto been a mere dream and a delightful possibility; as yet history does not offer us any certain examples.'[14]

The Buddha could be said to have described a path to a single great mood incarnate. Modern science may support his method – a recent article in *New Scientist* claims that the left prefrontal lobe of the brain, which is 'associated with positive emotions, good moods, foresight, planning and self-control' is remarkably active among Buddhist meditators.[15] In wishing to concentrate rather than dissipate the will, the Buddha stands opposed to the mystics and romantics who attempted to create this exalted mood through emotional reverie and dissipated attention. His emphasis was on self-control, best summed up by these lines from Milton: 'He who reigns within himself and rules passions, desires, and fears, is more than a king.'

In his distrust of desire and preoccupation with suffering, the Buddha resembles more the Hellenistic philosophers, the Epicureans, the Stoics and the Skeptics, who flourished in the wake of Socrates, Plato and Aristotle. In the fourth century BC the skeptic Pyrrho is supposed to have accompanied Alexander the Great to India. But the resemblance is striking even if Pyrrho didn't bring back with him some aspects of the Buddha's teachings.

> Empty are the words of that philosopher who offers no therapy for human suffering. For just as there is no use in medical expertise if it does not give therapy for bodily diseases, so too there is no use in philosophy if it does not expel the suffering of the soul.[16]

The words are those of Epicurus. But they could be the Buddha's. The Hellenistic philosophers also sought to avoid suffering and achieve a state of tranquillity by controlling desire. Their primary means was virtue, which they often equated with reason. But for the Buddha, the life of virtue, though essential, was a preparation for the tasks of meditation – an experience unknown to Hellenistic or any other form of western philosophy.

A virtuous life was for the Buddha the first of three stages on the path to *nirvana*: moral self-discipline, meditation and wisdom (*sila, samadhi, prajna*). As he saw it, a life lived truthfully and pacifically, in voluntary poverty but without self-mortification, a life lived, in short, with *sila*, created a suitably wholesome frame of mind. It set up the bare minimum required to achieve concentration and equanimity, which then made possible the special kind of meditation to follow: one in which the meditator remains in clear awareness of his inner and outer states of mind, his surroundings, his experiences, his actions, his thoughts and their consequences as they unfold moment by moment.

As with any kind of mental training, the discipline of meditation steadily equips the individual with a new sensibility. It shows him how the craving for things that are transient, essence-less and flawed leads to suffering. Regular meditation turns this new way of looking into a habit. It detaches the individual from the temptations of the world and fixes him in a state of profound calm: a 'single great mood incarnate':

> [The monk] neither constructs in his mind, nor wills in order to produce, any state of mind or body, or the destruction of any such state. By not so willing anything in the world, he grasps after nothing; by not grasping, he is not anxious; he is therefore fully calmed within.[17]

It was this unconditioned state of freedom that the Buddha reached one night sitting under the pipal tree in Bodh Gaya, the state that he called *nirvana* and described as the true goal of all sentient beings: a *nirvana* which did not consist of a mystical union with God or, as often supposed, the annihilation of the individual, but the end of craving and ignorance that causes the cycle of rebirth and suffering.

The deer park where the Buddha preached his first sermon is now called Sarnath. It lay forgotten for several centuries until a British amateur archaeologist excavated the site in the nineteenth century. He found *stupas* and a pillar originally erected by Emperor Ashoka in the third century BC.

The biggest *stupa*, called Dhamekh, was on the site where the Buddha supposedly gave his first sermon, sitting with the Brahmins from Kapilavastu. Later archaeologists discovered the shrine where the Buddha apparently had sheltered from the rains; they also found monasteries, which seemed to have been destroyed by a great fire. A temple built by the Sri Lankan Buddhist Anagarika Dharampala now stands in place of the shrine. The ruins of the monasteries lie amid vast green lawns. The grounds also include a deer park and a zoo.

Soon after completing his sermon to the five Brahmins from Kapilavastu, the Buddha won his first disciples. The Brahmin from Kapilavastu called Kondanna declared his wish to be ordained as a monk by the Buddha. The Buddha obliged, thereby inaugurating the *sangha*, the order of monks – probably the first such monastic sect in the world.

The other four ascetics from Kapilavastu soon joined Kondanna, after receiving separate instruction from the Buddha. But the Buddha's more important disciples were still to come. Not long after he preached his first sermon a young man from Benares called Yasa appeared one morning at the deer park.

According to the legends about him, Yasa was a rich young man much given to introspection.[18] Like many rich people of the time, including the Buddha himself in his youth, Yasa had three mansions, in one of which he spent four uninterrupted months during the monsoons, carousing with female musicians. His disillusionment apparently began when he woke up one night, and, in the light from an oil lamp, he saw the women sleeping in various postures of indignity.

Suddenly full of disgust for his life, Yasa left the

mansion and went to the deer park where the Buddha and other *sramanas* used to gather. The Buddha sensed that he was unhappy. He invited Yasa to sit beside him and gave him his first 'graduated discourse'; this was a pedagogic method he used, in which he began first with ethical rules for a good life, and moved onto the more complex part of his teaching only when he felt sure that he would be understood.

He told Yasa first about the importance of charity, ethical rules, and the futility of chasing after sensual desires and the benefits of abandoning them. When Yasa proved receptive and eager to hear more, the Buddha revealed to him the deeper truth of suffering, its cause, its extinction and the way to *nirvana*.

While Yasa was at the deer park, eagerly absorbing the Buddha's teachings, his anxious father was looking for him. He eventually reached Sarnath and asked the Buddha about his son. In response, the Buddha asked him to sit down and gave him the same graduated discourse he had given his son. Yasa's father was quickly converted.

But as he sat there he saw his son in the crowd surrounding the Buddha. He told Yasa about his distraught mother and begged him to return home. Yasa kept looking helplessly at the Buddha, who finally said that Yasa despised worldly life too much to be able to return to it. Yasa's father could not argue with this. He invited the Buddha and Yasa to a meal at his house, and then returned home.

As soon as his father left, Yasa asked the Buddha to ordain him as a monk. The Buddha obliged, making Yasa the seventh *bhikshu*. He went the next day to Yasa's father's house, where he delivered a graduated discourse to

Yasa's mother and his wife. The two women, instead of being angered by Yasa's rejection of them, became the Buddha's lay followers.

News of Yasa's conversion spread fast and puzzled many people, who wondered why a privileged young man would give up everything to become a *sramana*. Soon, four of Yasa's friends, also sons of merchants in Benares, came to the Buddha and were accepted by him as *bhikshus*. They were followed by fifty more of Yasa's friends from neighbouring parts of Benares.

Such dramatic conversions have a fairy-tale quality to them, as if they were invented by later biographers, eager to credit the Buddha with miraculous powers of charisma and persuasion. What, one wonders, did the Buddha say that was so compelling to these affluent citizens of Benares?

But then it is easy to miss the originality of what the Buddha said and how he said it, because we see him across packed centuries of history and not through the fresh eyes of someone in North India two and a half millennia ago, who wants, more than an abstract explanation of his world, advice about how to live.

Socrates was responding to the same spiritual need. Around the sixth century BC, the pre-Socratic philosophers, rough contemporaries of the Buddha, had begun to move away from traditional mythology and seek physical explanations for such observable phenomena as the motion of the stars and eclipses. They turned to cosmology, trying to find a unifying principle for the bewildering multiplicity of phenomena in the world. Thales suggested that everything was composed of water. Heraclitus posited flux as the universal law observed by the senses. Parmenides and his disciple Zeno denied the reality of appearances altogether. Anaxagoras proposed the mind as the cause of all physical processes.

Until Socrates appeared, philosophy had meant anything from metaphysics to ethics to medicine, mathematics, geometry and astronomy. It was the sum of what the Greeks had learned about *phusis* – the phenomenon of the growth of living beings and of man, but also of the universe. The Sophists gave it a practical component by making it part of the cultivation of young Greeks with political ambitions; the Sophists were itinerant professional teachers imparting a general sense of what we now call 'culture' through the art of oratory.

Socrates was the first among Greek philosophers to assert that acquiring know-how from external sources wasn't the same as acquiring knowledge itself, which involved continuous self-examination. Plato has him remark at the beginning of *Symposium*, 'How nice it would be if wisdom were the kind of thing that could flow from what is more full into what is more empty.'

Socrates wasn't much interested in utilitarian knowledge: 'I have no concern at all for what most people are concerned about: financial affairs, administration of property, appointments to generalships, oratorical triumphs in public, magistracies, coalitions, political factions. I did not take this path . . . but rather the one where I could do the most good to each one of you in particular, by persuading you to be less concerned with what you have than with what you are; so that you may make yourselves as excellent and as rational as possible.'[19]

For Socrates, to be rational and excellent was to know

about moral choice, about choosing the good, and about knowing how to live. Knowledge lay not in concepts, but in virtue; and it was available to everyone since the capacity and desire for the good existed within all human beings. The philosopher merely alerted individuals to these inner possibilities, which they had to excavate on their own. For, as Socrates famously put it, 'an unexamined life is not worth living for man'.

Socrates represented the achievement of the Greeks at a high stage in their culture: the individual philosopher who exhorted his audience to move beyond conventional forms of knowledge and towards rational self-awareness and moral choice. Even Nietzsche, who blamed Socrates for a host of evils, admitted that 'in ancient Greece Socrates was defending himself with all his might against . . . (the) arrogant neglect of the human for the benefit of the human race', and loved to indicate the true compass and content of all reflection and concern with an expression of Homer's: it comprises, he said, only "that which I encounter of good and ill in my own house".'

One could say almost the same about the Buddha. There had been dissenters before him: the *sramanas* who felt that life as lived by custom and convention left many questions unanswered. They rejected the authority of the *Vedas* and of the Brahmins; it did not seem to them to lead to wisdom. They thought that ordinary life itself was incompatible with the higher truths one gained through solitary thinking or asceticism; it had to be spurned before it could be examined.

But, although the *sramanas* carried on much dialogue among themselves and before large audiences, they dealt primarily in assertion. Reality consisted of this and that;

and there was no basis for morality. They lived in what the Buddha, commenting on the intellectual ferment of his time, later called the 'jungle of opinions'.

Unlike them, he was concerned to examine the nature of human experience rather than speculate about its supposed object – the world, its many components, their essence, etc. To this end, he proposed a description of the experiencing mind and body – the primary human means of grasping reality.

Sitting under an asoka tree, he took a few fallen leaves in his hand, and asked the *bhikshus*, or monks, whether the leaves in his hand or the leaves on the tree were more numerous. When the *bhikshus* stated the obvious, he told them that in the same way he knew more than he had revealed to them, because they were of no use in the pursuit of wisdom.

Thus he ignored the question, which obsesses Christian theologians, of how suffering arose in a world created and supervised by an eternally loving God. He denied that there could be a powerful divine creator God of a world where everything was causally connected and nothing came from nowhere. For him, neither God nor anything else had created the world; rather, the world was continually created by the actions, good or bad, of human beings. He didn't dwell on large abstract questions, preferring to goad the individual into facing up to his immediate situation.

As he told a disciple who had asked him whether the world was eternal and infinite, or the soul and body one and the same thing,

It is as if there were a man struck by an arrow that was

smeared thickly with poison; his friends and companions, his family and relatives would summon a doctor to see to the arrow. And the man might say, 'I will not draw out this arrow as long as I do not know whether the man by whom I was struck was a brahmin, a kshatriya, a vaishya, or a shudra . . . as long as I do not know his name and family . . . whether he was tall, short or of medium height . . .' That man would not discover these things, but that man would die.[20]

He concerned himself instead with suffering, its causes and its cessation. Preoccupations with eternity and the soul were either irrelevant or shot through with faulty assumptions that led to suffering. The individual had to take responsibility for his condition:

> It is not the case that one would live eternally by holding the view that the world is eternal. Nor is it the case that one would live the spiritual life by holding the view that the world is not eternal. Whether one holds that the world is eternal, or whether one holds that the world is not eternal, there is still birth, ageing, death, grief, despair, pain, and unhappiness.[21]

It was the Buddha's achievement, as it was that of Socrates, to detach wisdom from its basis in fixed and often esoteric forms of knowledge and opinion and offer it as a moral and spiritual project for individuals. As a teacher, he offered no dogma – he asked his disciples not to trust him until they had realized within themselves the truth of what he had taught. The unexamined life was no more worth living for him than for Socrates. He worked to enhance the feeling, latent in everyone, that we are not what we ought to be. He assumed that the good exists in all human beings, if veiled by ignorance, and that evil, not wisdom, was an aberration.

Self-discipline was the way to realizing the essential moral nature of man. At Sarnath, the Buddha spoke of the stages by which gold was refined: how coarse dust and sand, gravel and grit had to be removed before the gold dust could be placed in a crucible and melted, and its impurities strained off. The way to higher consciousness required this gradual purging of impure deed, work and thought, through gross impurities to coarser ones, until the time when the dross disappeared and there remained only the pure state of awareness.

With sixty *bhikshus* as attentive listeners, the Buddha would have become a confident man in Sarnath and might even have begun to long for a bigger audience. One day, as the monsoon ended, he decided to give up his by then exclusive claim to teaching and exhorted his sixty *bhikshus* to become preachers and missionaries themselves:

> Go forth, *bhikshus*, on your own way for the profit and happiness of the many, out of compassion for the world, for the profit, gain and happiness of gods and men. Let no two go together . . . There are beings whose eyes have little dust on them, who will perish if they do not hear the teaching. But if they hear the teaching, they will gain liberation.[22]

The *bhikshus* left Sarnath, travelled to various places, and came back with several people who wished to be ordained by the Buddha himself. The Buddha realized that he had to delegate even further and give his monks the responsibility to ordain new people into the *sangha*. It was now that he first set out the rules of the ordination:

> Now, *bhikshus*, you yourselves may grant ordination and the precepts in various places and various countries. However, you should grant ordination and the precepts in this way. First cut off the hair and the beard (of the aspirant), robe him with a yellow robe so it covers one shoulder (leaving the right shoulder bare), and have him bow down at the feet of the *bhikshus* (with his head on the ground), sit down squatting, place the palms of his hands together, and say: 'I take refuge in the Buddha. I take refuge in the *dharma*. I take refuge in the *sangha*.'[23]

The Buddha conceived of the *sangha* as a group of self-reliant *bhikshus* undergoing the spiritual training necessary to escape suffering and attain enlightenment. The individual *bhikshu* worked through the three-fold process of enlightenment – morality, meditation, wisdom – and also created the atmosphere for other *bhikshus* to do likewise. Over time, the Buddha codified the arrangements of the *sangha*. Later Buddhists developed elaborate procedures to deal with issues arising out of the *sangha's* internal complexity and relationship with the larger world. There were some basic rules. The monks had to live a life of voluntary chastity and poverty. They could not possess anything more than three robes, a begging bowl, a razor, needle, belt, water strainer and medicine. They had to observe decorum, which meant walking with slow measured steps. They could eat only what they had been given as alms, except for fruit; eating meat was permissible as long as the animal had not been killed specially for them.

The daily routine was simple. In the morning they went looking for alms, and took their only meal of the day in the shade of a tree. They then wandered until midday when they rested from the heat. For the rest of the day, they wandered, had conversations about the *dharma*, and meditated. For the three months of the monsoons, when it rained incessantly and the rivers burst their banks, making the roads impassable, they had to confine themselves to the so-called 'rains retreat' during which they stayed under a roof, either of a temporary hut or a monastery. In the autumn, they were free to wander again.

The appearance and routine of the *bhikshus* changed little over centuries. In the fourteenth century, almost two millennia after the Buddha first formulated their rules, an emissary of the then Pope, Benedict XII, described what he had seen of *bhikshus* in Ceylon, Siam and China:

> These monks only eat once a day and never more and drink nothing but milk and water. They never keep food with them overnight. They sleep on the bare ground. They walk barefoot, with a stick, and are satisfied with a robe rather like that of our Friars Minor (Franciscans), but without a hood and with a cloak over their shoulder in the manner of the apostles. Every morning, they go in a procession to ask, with the greatest possible reverence, that rice be given to them in an appropriate quantity for their number . . . These people lead a very saintly life – albeit without Faith.[24]

With the *sangha*, the Buddha was partly following a tradition of renouncers in India. It included the thinkers of the *Upanishads*, who had retreated to forests, and the wandering *sramanas*, of whom the Buddha himself was one, along with Mahavira, the founder of Jainism. Their rejection of the sensual life and voluntarily chosen hardship inspired respect among the ordinary people they approached for food, clothing and shelter. The renouncer continues to be revered in India today, sometimes for no more than his act of renunciation. They had become the rivals of Brahmin priests, who were dependent on the same ordinary people for their own livelihood.

As always, the Buddha looked for the middle way between extreme rejection of the world, which some of the more ascetic *sramanas*, such as Mahavira, espoused, and the deeper and corrupting involvement with it that the Brahmins largely embodied. According to the Oxford English Dictionary the word 'monk', which is often used as a substitute for *bhikshu*, originally meant 'religious hermit or solitary', and then later, 'member of a community or brotherhood living apart from the world'. But the Buddha didn't wish his *bhikshus* to live apart from the world; he had already rejected the way of private salvation in Bodh Gaya, soon after his enlightenment.

In setting up the *sangha*, he hoped to achieve something more than the secluded community in which individuals could find the right conditions to achieve personal spiritual satisfaction. This is implicit in the word *bhikshu*, which means one who receives a share of something. This 'something' is nothing other than the common wealth of society that he is dependent upon. The *bhikshu* had renounced private property, but by this act he had earned an exalted place in society, and the promise that he would be fed and clothed by the general population. In exchange, he offered himself to society as a model of virtuous behaviour and self-awareness.

As the Buddha saw it, the *bhikshus*, who had reduced their personal desires and lived interdependently with like-minded human beings, had much to teach a society that was involved increasingly and fractiously in the pursuit of wealth and pleasure. This is why the *bhikshus*, unlike Christian or Jain monks, usually stayed close to urban centres of trade and business, and did so even during the Buddha's time.

In any case, to be enlightened was to understand the sources of suffering not only within oneself but also within all beings. The wisdom this brought could not remain a personal achievement; it was inseparable from the feeling of universal compassion, or *karuna*.

A Little Dust in the Eyes

THE *SANGHA* MIGHT HAVE expanded quickly had the Buddha gone into Benares. The city was already a centre of commerce and manufacturing, famous for its cotton and brocades, and the place where people went to wash away their sins in the Ganges and hope for a better rebirth.

However, the Buddha rarely ventured into Benares, though he passed very near to it several times in his long life. He was probably deterred by the dominance of the Brahmins, who claimed many rich clients in the city. He knew that the Brahmins despised *sramanas*, whom they saw as likely competition. He in turn was scathing about the Brahmin insistence on ritual bathing, sacrifices and Vedic cults; he claimed that they brought no merit to anyone.

As elsewhere in India, the Brahmins seem to have won their argument with the Buddha. There is little trace of the Buddha in Benares today, where India's pre-Buddhist Vedic religions still flourish. Temples to every conceivable deity (snake, monkey, river) crowd the old city's alleys, along with countless sacred cows and old widows.

Millions of Indians still crowd the riverside ghats (bathing steps), hoping to wash away their sins in the waters of the Ganges, first considered holy by the Aryan settlers of North India. Brahmin priests with little top-knots on their shaven heads form a mafia of sorts; they supervise the post-funeral ceremonies and other Hindu rites, routinely ripping off hapless pilgrims from villages and small towns across India.

Five miles away, on a flat land dotted with mango groves and rice fields, lies Sarnath, where the Buddha spent a few months after his enlightenment in Bodh Gaya. It is the most picturesque of Buddhist sites in India, its wide open spaces always bracing after the chaos – the heat, noise, dirt – of Benares. But its great peace is easily shattered, and there are days when the gaggle of shops and dhabas outside the lawn of Sarnath blare Hindi pop songs from morning till evening, middle-class Indian picnickers gather on the lawns, leaving small mounds of plastic bags and cups on the grass, and teenage boys in imitation Levi jeans and Nike sneakers go around asking white female tourists to have sex with them.

It was partly in connection with this new Indian middle class that I went to Benares in 1994, and then found myself one afternoon revisiting Sarnath. One afternoon in Mashobra, when I hadn't gone out to Montu's dhaba for lunch, the postman brought a letter from a publisher in Delhi. He had seen my reviews in Indian newspapers and wanted to know if I was interested in writing a travel book.

By then, I had been working on a book about the Buddha for more than two years. I had acquired many books, read quite a few of them, and made notes, but somehow the book refused to grow beyond a point. I was also bored by the Buddha's dialogues, which were long-winded and repetitious. I found little of the artistry so evident in Plato. And so although I had no particular wish to write a travel book, when I heard from the publisher in Delhi it struck me as an opportunity to redeem, at least partially, the promise I had long ago made to myself: the promise that I would be a writer, and would do nothing else.

Besides, the idea of the travel writer was not unattractive: I imagined myself as Jacquemont, moving serenely through a picturesque landscape and recording everything in a cool, jaunty tone.

I wrote back to the publisher, proposing a book on Indian small towns – somewhat thoughtlessly, since I disliked even the trip I had to make to Simla once a month in order to stock up on provisions, magazines and books. The publisher offered a tiny advance, and it became clear that I would have to finance my travels out of my own resources. But it was too late to withdraw.

For the next five months, I travelled across small-town India. During this journey, I continually missed Mashobra, never stopped wishing that I was in my cottage instead of the grim hotel with the overused bed sheets and television echoes where I usually found myself at the end of a day's journey.

The towns I saw were no better than extended slums: crammed with economic migrants from villages, congested and unsanitary. The wealthier towns were no better than the poorer ones. In fact, the more prosperous a town was, the greater seemed its moral and physical squalor. From Kanyakumari, the town at the southernmost tip of the

Indian subcontinent, where Vivekananda had meditated before leaving on his historic trip to Chicago, to Simla, there seemed to have come into being an urban landscape of glass-and-concrete mansions, stunted shacks, naked-brick box-shaped houses, broken roads and stagnant malarial ponds.

Much of this came as a shock to me. In Mashobra, the cruel, garish world of middle-class India felt remote, and I was happy to think that I had managed to escape it. In fact, I had grown used to living in the simpler India of my own small-town past. It never seemed closer to me than in the fair the village held each summer, where on sheets spread on the ground, or on ramshackle wooden stalls, lay all the things that I as a child, sitting on my father's shoulders, had once thought amazing and longed to possess: pyramids of powdered orange and yellow spices; knives with lacquered and carved wooden handles, towers of bangles and bracelets, garishly coloured photos of Indian film stars, pink cotton candy, painted wooden toys and countless booklets about Hindu gods or litanies.

Mr Sharma stayed away, but almost everyone else in the village – shopkeepers, farmers, government employees, the servants in the big houses, the lone taxi driver heading fast towards prosperity – came to the fair with their families, dressed in unfamiliarly bright clothes, and mingled in what seemed an egalitarian spirit of bonhomie. Among the assorted crowd – of visitors, basket makers, knife sharpeners with their grinding wheels, aphrodisiac sellers with what looked like pieces of dry intestines in vials, and screaming children on the mini Ferris wheel – the local legislator, though still radiating power through his starched white kurta, always looked a bit lost.

*

A moderate climate and long years of communal living seemed to have given even the poorest people in Mashobra an air of calm and dignity. In contrast, most of the people I met on the plains during my travels seemed to be living on the edge.

One of the most volatile places was Bihar, once part of the kingdom of Magadha, the first great Indian empire. In this poor and densely populated Indian state, where rich landowners travelled in private planes while a caste of rat eaters starved to death due to a shortage of field mice, brutality seemed a casual everyday affair. The stories came in from every direction. Private armies of upper-caste landlords massacred low-caste landless peasants. Communist activists retaliated with massacres of upper-caste families. Doctors going on strike pulled out transfusion tubes from the veins of their patients.

This was especially unsettling given Bihar's history. The Aryan settlers of North India had created their first urban civilization in this exceptionally fertile and mineral-rich part of the Indo-Gangetic plain. The first post-Vedic religious and spiritual movements of India had occurred in the same parts. The Buddha had spent much of his life visiting the cities of Magadha and preaching to their wealthy classes. Ashoka had made the region the centre of his Indian empire. Teachers and missionaries trained at the famous fifth-century AD university in Nalanda, whose ruins still spoke of splendour, had taken the Buddha's ideas to remote parts of Asia.

There were days in Bihar when the disappearance of Buddhism from the land of its origins, and a politically driven and ethically empty Hinduism, appeared part of a catastrophe that was still working itself out. In the town of Gaya, where the Buddha gave a famous sermon, I met some middle-class Brahmin students who boasted to me of how their grandfathers had resolved a dispute with low-caste Hindus in their village by burning them alive. A few miles away at Bodh Gaya, the Mecca and Jerusalem of Buddhists, Hindu nationalists had started a violent agitation to claim for the Hindu community the temple standing on the site of the Buddha's enlightenment. Heavily armed policemen stood everywhere in the dusty town, even inside the temple complex, frisking the South-east Asian monks who had walked for miles to reach the spot, and who prostrated themselves full length, hurling themselves on the muddy ground, after every two steps.

Such ancient gestures, performed by foreigners, expressed what remained alive of Bihar's long past. From the summits of intellectual and spiritual achievement, Bihar had fallen to become the most derelict place in India. How had it happened? It was an obvious question, to which the disappearance of Buddhism and its replacement by Hinduism were only partial answers. But having taken Jacquemont as a model, and hoping to imitate his easy wit, I hadn't prepared myself for such questions before setting off on my travels.

The history books quickly made it clear that Jacquemont had moved through a simple world, in which the British colonial elite together with their native feudal collaborators had presided over an invisibly wretched peasantry. The books told me about the ignorant and rapacious officials of the British East India Company, who had destroyed the system of collective ownership of land; they described the role of the all-powerful Indian zamindars, who on behalf of the British had taxed the peasantry into debt and destitution.

I learnt about the devastating industrialization that had destroyed small-scale manufacturing not only in England but also in distant Bihar, which was transformed from an exporter of raw cotton into an importer, and then reduced to farming opium, which British traders – those whom Jacquemont met in Calcutta's elegant riverside mansions – then cynically smuggled into China.

The deprivations of medieval Europe, the exploitation of the early capitalist period, and the political chaos of modern times: the worst experiences of the West seemed to have been duplicated and speeded up in Bihar. History showed a cruel, unforgiving face in this place; and for many people who felt oppressed by it there was no release from it, except through more violence.

In a small, windowless room in a shanty town not far from Bodh Gaya, I met young low-caste activists from a Communist group who read Marx, Lenin and Mao in Hindi translations, organized landless peasants against exploitative landlords and the police, and spoke, quite seriously, of pulling off a revolution in New Delhi.

I had known activists from their group at the university in Allahabad. Mostly very poor, they weren't among the students who went to Nepal to buy baseball caps. They organized demonstrations and Communist study groups. Gaunt and virtuous in their cheap synthetic shirts and rubber slippers, they were described, mockingly, by upper-caste students as followers of 'Chou-Mao'.

A generation ago, they would have been in their villages and towns, not thinking or reflecting much, but simply living the life of deprivation they had been born into. Education and exposure to the wider world, and the accompanying bewilderment and pain – all the things that had led Vinod to Vivekananda – had led them to Marx, Lenin and Mao. They now possessed the words to describe the causes of their suffering and the means to end it. And they could also lay claim to the promises – democracy, socialism, secularism – made them by the western-educated idealistic men who had framed the Indian constitution.

The young men I met in Bihar had witnessed rape, killing, torture in their own families. They were outwardly gentle, but full, as I discovered, of a disquieting intensity. In the room we sat in one afternoon, as clouds of dust kicked up by passing trucks and buses on the broken road outside kept bursting in through the open door, faintly powdering the hair and stubble of the thin young men, they told me about what they called their 'struggle': the agitation to raise the minimum daily wage; their ongoing battles with a pro-landlord police; the recent attack on the home of a local Brahmin landowner who turned out to have several mistresses. They told me about the rise of self-respect they sensed among landless peasants who no longer let their sisters and daughters be kidnapped and raped by local landlords; the things that had to be achieved when the revolution comes.

'When the revolution comes': many of their sentences began with these unsettling words, which seemed to promise them freedom and happiness. They weren't worried about the terror and the violence it involved, the demonizing of entire sections of the population as 'class enemies'. Like other high-minded revolutionaries –

Jacobins, Bolsheviks, Khmer Rouge – they too spoke casually of the necessary elimination of 'decadent' Brahmins, 'kulak' landlords, 'reactionary' government officials and the 'comprador' class of shopkeepers.

In Allahabad, I had also been stirred by the thought of revolution: nothing seemed more necessary in the degraded conditions of India than the brutal and swift cancelling of the past, and a fresh beginning in a new world of justice and equality. And even now, when I knew more about the fate of revolutions, I didn't feel unsympathetic to these young men. But I knew that the revolution they hoped for was not going to come. Worse, there was going to be no place for these men in the new India that was beginning to emerge.

I was then at the end of my travels for the commissioned book. In the past, I had visited many places in India, but never with a view to writing about them. It was easier to make an itinerary than to know what to look for, and where to find material. These uncertainties disappeared fast as I began to travel and found my subject: the middle class was becoming visible in small towns and cities after the Indian economy was liberalized in the early 1990s and opened to foreign investment.

When Jacquemont visited India and for decades afterwards, the middle class in India had consisted mainly of clerks, educated at the European-style institutions that Macaulay and others had promoted in order to help the British administer India. From this small class had emerged modern India's great men. Just as the first urban class in India had produced the Buddha, so the nineteenth-century middle class had brought forth men like Gandhi, Nehru, Tagore and Vivekananda.

It was this class of politicians, doctors, lawyers, industrialists, engineers and teachers that Vivekananda had exhorted to embrace materialism and science and to weld India into a manly nation. This class had taken over the reins of government from the British in 1947, and had grown rich partly by plundering the immense resources available to the centralized Indian state. But it had had to wait for fifty years after independence, and an economic boom, to expand and begin fulfilling Vivekananda's vision of a strong materialist India. Though still a minority – less than 20 per cent of the population – the Indian bourgeoisie appeared, by the mid-1990s, as big and important as the middle class that emerged in Europe in the nineteenth century and began to reshape the continent's history, politics, religion, art and architecture.

On my travels I saw the particular sensibility this class had brought into being, one reflected in the opulent small-town mansions with Palladian facades, the raunchy songs, the violent films, and a vivaciously ignorant and biased media. This new wealth amid the restive slums and villages knew it was vulnerable, a minority of mostly upper-caste men among low-caste Hindus and Muslims. And so, like the European bourgeoisie, it had a defensive ideology, nationalism, through which it sought to represent, and legitimize its rule over, the majority of the country's population.

This nationalism derived its energy from a special kind of history: one that spoke of Islam destroying Hinduism and Buddhism in India, of lost Hindu glory, and of the national strength and international eminence that could be regained through nuclear bombs. The message spread quickly, embraced by people newly empowered and seeking to define themselves in the big world in which they suddenly found themselves.

The aggressiveness it had provoked did not need to conceal itself in euphemism. In a famous temple complex in Rajasthan, a teenage boy from Gujarat, where Gandhi was born, declared to me that the only way to deal with the 'Muslim problem' was to kill them all. I found soft-spoken, well-educated men revealing suddenly an inexplicable murderous rage they harboured towards Muslims, Pakistanis and low-caste Hindus.

What I saw was at least partly the effect of the Hindu nationalist movement which had developed fast in the 1990s. Middle-class people from small towns had been among the crowds that in 1992 demolished a sixteenth-century mosque in an ancient North Indian city which the Buddha had once known. They had turned into solid supporters of the Hindu nationalists who promised to guarantee their political and economic dominance, and keep all their rivals, real as well as imagined, poor Hindus as well as poor Muslims, at bay.

Vivekananda, of whom Vinod had spoken to me so admiringly, had become the patron saint of the BJP (Bharatiya Janata Party), a political party of mostly upper-caste, middle-class Hindus who strove to boost India's capabilities in the fields of nuclear bombs and information technology and also revered the cow as holy. Even Vinod couldn't have expected that the BJP would come close to realizing his project of fully westernizing Hinduism and turning it into a full-fledged nationalist ideology: one which had pretensions to being all-inclusive, but which demonized Muslims and sought to pre-empt the long over-due political empowerment of India's lower-caste groups with its rhetoric of egalitarianism.

That empowerment seemed inevitable, and destined to incite more violent struggles between classes and castes over India's limited resources. In the meantime, power still lay with the upper castes, and those who clamoured too stridently for justice and equality, such as the young men I met in Bihar, could only appear doomed.

The promise of violent change, of security and dignity in a new political order, was all that kept them from sinking into utter hopelessness and despair. Yet while sitting in their dark and shabby one-room office, where the world appeared infinite and threatening, I could not help feeling how absurd and futile was the task to which these young men had devoted their lives.

In many ways, this task had barely begun, but the Communist young men already seemed to wear an aura of heroism and tragedy. I saw them destined to be the usual victims, like many thousands of 'troublemakers' before them, of the periodic middle-class outcry for 'law and order', for 'ruthless crack-downs'. Easily trampled upon, they were likely to become a statistic: among the thousands of men who were tortured and executed each year while in police custody.

These emotions of dread and pity were still with me when I went to Bodh Gaya one drowsy winter afternoon and saw again the place where one night the Buddha had his great awakening.

In the sunken courtyard of the tall Mahabodhi temple, peasant Hindu women waved *diyas* before the small statues and *stupas*, making egg-shaped circles of fire. The shrine was very dark, and heavy with incense. Behind the temple was the Bodhi tree, allegedly a descendant of the one the Buddha knew, with its trunk tattooed all over with gold leaf and ochre, and strings of coloured prayer flags running wild across its branches.

Policemen played cards on a lawn not far from the Mahabodhi temple, where a famous Tibetan monk was giving a lecture. I went and stood at the back of a bright yellow tent, where an audience made up exclusively of foreigners, some of them in ochre robes and with tonsured heads, sat on the grass, their clear solemn faces turned towards the monk on a platform draped with marigolds.

The monk – surprisingly young for someone so famous, slightly plump, but serious in his glasses – spoke of how rebirth was the most difficult thing to understand for people born outside the eastern traditions. He said that most people asked him: how could a person be reborn if he had no enduring self? What was it that was reborn?

He spoke of how the Buddha had altered the Brahminical notion of *karma*, exalting intention above action. This was because he knew that every deed couldn't possibly contribute to rebirth in all circumstances since action is unavoidable and there would be no release from painful existence.

The Buddha didn't think it necessary to be reborn in order to gain the benefits of good actions. What he stressed was self-control. The more successfully one disciplined the mind, the less likely rebirth became. The speaker quoted the Buddha:

If, *bhikshus*, an ignorant man produces a good intention,

then his consciousness will incline to the good. If he produces a bad or neutral intention, then his consciousness
will incline to the bad or the neutral.

I couldn't hear all the words, which boomed across to the
back from an antiquated sound system. I lingered for a
while, and then, growing tired of the indistinct earnest-
ness, decided to visit a Communist activist called
Dharmendra. I had heard about him from one of his colleagues in Allahabad. He worked as a servant in a Tibetan
monastery in Bodh Gaya. Unusually for a Communist
activist, he was also a Buddhist, or a 'neo-Buddhist', as the
followers of B. R. Ambedkar, the leader of the untouch-
ables (Dalits) and the framer of India's constitution, were
called.

Ambedkar, a disciple of the American philosopher John
Dewey, had grown disillusioned with the egalitarian promise of independent India soon after 1947. He had wished
to lead the Dalits out of Hinduism and give them a new
religious and political identity as they fought against
upper-caste prejudice and violence. He chose Buddhism
over Islam and Sikhism – the other options he considered
– since he saw the Buddha as a radical thinker, the Karl
Marx of his time, for rejecting the caste system, positing
the equality of man and advocating the end of misery and
sorrow. In 1956, a few weeks before his death, Ambedkar
ceremonially converted to Buddhism along with more
than three hundred thousand other Dalits.

But the Dalit converts had not revived Buddhism,
which had vanished from India centuries before. As a
political movement, too, neo-Buddhism seemed to have
stalled. And at the monastery, where white men and

women in kurta and lungis sat meditating in the front garden, and where a small, stocky Tibetan suddenly appeared
and in a low, sibilant voice demanded to know what I
wanted, I began to wonder about the kind of status the
Indian neo-Buddhists had among the richer Buddhists of
other countries.

Dharmendra was not among the boys in the backyard,
squatting over the dusty ground, raking it with a short
broom. It turned out that he had gone for the day. On the
way to my guest house, I passed a chai shack. The stall
with its grimy kerosene stove and blackened and dented
kettles stood next to a stagnant open gutter. The stench
was overpowering and had kept away, it seemed, most
customers, except one Buddhist monk.

He sat on a tiny bench, drinking sticky-sweet tea from
a glass tumbler. He was either from Europe or North
America: tall, in his late thirties or early forties. His head
looked freshly shaven and gleamed in the afternoon sun.
He was watching two boys in rags fish what looked like a
newspaper boat out of the slimy water of the gutter. He
appeared amused by them.

He was a common enough sight in Bodh Gaya, which
received Europeans, Americans, Tibetans and South-east
Asians in large numbers. They came more often as seekers
than as monks, sometimes as curious tourists. They usually stayed half hidden in the monasteries and guest houses
around Bodh Gaya, meditating in the gardens or listening
to discourses by Buddhist teachers. But when out in full
strength at the temple they seemed to easily outnumber the
natives.

The monk looked new to Bodh Gaya and to India,
easily distracted by unfamiliar things, still to learn the self-

absorption of experienced travellers. There was nothing more remarkable about his appearance or manner. But abruptly, on that alley with its reminders of the wretchedness of Bihar that no revolution could ameliorate, walking back to the gloom of my mosquito-infested room, I found myself full of resentment.

It occurred to me – words bubbling up to match thought – that the monk was play-acting, like the people meditating in Indian clothes at the Tibetan monastery, that the privileges of wealth and travel had allowed him to become a Buddhist monk just as they would allow him to return to what he had been before.

I don't remember thinking more about him. But some of the resentment he abruptly incited must have clung to me when I travelled to Benares and learned that Helen had become a Buddhist nun.

I had first met Helen while I was in Benares for a few months in the late 1980s, just after finishing my undergraduate degree in Allahabad. My admission to a university in Delhi had been delayed for a year, and instead of going home to my parents, I had decided to spend the year in Benares. Helen was a student of literature, from San Francisco, spending a year in Benares as an exchange student at the Hindu University. She lived in the alley next to mine in the southernmost part of the old city, where, among the cows and small shrines to Hanuman, she was an intriguingly exuberant presence in a salwar kurta, her long blonde hair tied in an Indian-style pony-tail, one hand holding a poetry paperback, as she walked with quick purposeful strides, smiling and nodding at the boys playing cricket on the cobblestone path.

One evening, the son of my landlord introduced us as I walked with him back to the house. I knew few people in Benares. Much of my day was spent at the library at the university, randomly reading books and magazines that I thought might help me become a writer. In the evenings, when I came back from the university, I walked to the ghats and sat on the stone steps there watching the light fade over the placid river. I returned home through half-lit alleys to a dinner served by my landlady in her smoky kitchen. I rarely spoke to anyone, and when I first met Helen, standing in a dark alley, I struggled at first to make polite conversation.

There was her obvious foreignness: the open white face, frank stare and quick smile. I didn't know at first how to deal with her curiosity about my life of reading; wasn't it unusual, she wondered, that I wasn't pursuing a professional career, like most Indian men? I didn't want to tell her about my literary ambitions, which I cherished privately, reluctant to expose them to the cold light of reality. So I gave her an involved explanation. She listened attentively. And then her face was sparkling again. She had a suggestion. She had many books in her room, which I could borrow any time I felt too tired to walk to the university library. In fact, she said, I could come tomorrow.

Shyly, I went up to her room the next evening. It was small, like mine, but colourful with printed bedcovers, pillows, small rugs, Tibetan wall hanging, and cluttered with many things – an electric kettle, a jar of peanut butter, a bottle of olive oil – that appeared new and exotic to me. She invited me to sit on the floor on a cushion and made me peppermint tea – another attractive novelty – with a teabag. We spoke of literature. It quickly became apparent that she and I had few books in common. She hadn't read much European fiction. She said she loved the American Beat poets: Allen Ginsberg, Gregory Corso, Lawrence Ferlinghetti. I had heard only of Ginsberg, and hadn't read anything by him. It came as news to me that he was also a Buddhist, and had spent many months in Benares, and had travelled to the sites connected with the Buddha's life.

She told me of the City Lights bookstore in San Francisco and the row of bookstores in Berkeley. I then looked at her books. There was little there along the row of American small-town fiction and Beat poetry that I wanted to read. But the books were new and beautifully printed, compared to the dust-laden, termite-ravaged volumes I handled every day at the library, and I was very pleased to be able to borrow, and overwhelmed when she insisted on giving me, one of the volumes of Ginsberg's poetry.

I came away that evening elated. I had never been so close to a woman outside my family, or talked to one with as little awkwardness as I felt with Helen. I wasn't unaware of her attractiveness. But there seemed something so particularly zestful and sympathetic about her, so without guile, that fantasy couldn't but come tainted with guilt.

Still, I was slightly disappointed to know that she had a boyfriend, back in what Helen called the Bay Area, marking it off, as it were, from the rest of America. He came visiting one day, a pleasant-faced, wiry young man, radiating the same effusive friendliness as Helen, and as eager to savour the alienness of Benares. I went walking with them on the ghats, where he challenged the kite-flying boys to a match and accepted a drag of cannabis from an ash-smeared Naga sadhu.

He spoke of Ronald Reagan, his conservative administration, of the hard decade it had been for many people in America, and I was struck by how people could define themselves and whole periods through reference to such remote things as presidents and administrations. It came out that he and Helen had gone coffee picking in Nicaragua in order to express their solidarity with the Nicaraguan Sandinistas who were then fighting guerrillas trained and armed by the Reagan administration; they had also worked for Mother Teresa's home in Haiti. All this they had done while still in their early twenties.

I told them about the violent student politics I had experienced at my university in Allahabad. They seemed shocked; they hadn't associated places of learning with homemade guns and bombs and daylight murders. I told them about my marginal involvement with a revolutionary student outfit. I gave them many more details than they probably needed. I may have been trying to impress. I had so little to speak of, so little to claim for myself. I couldn't stop being awed by what seemed to be their confident sense of who they were and what they could do. The privilege of having settled opinions and a steady view of the world: this was what people like Vinod and myself, all of us who had yet to know even ourselves, longed for in different ways.

I wrote to Helen after I left Benares, and she wrote back. She went back to California the next year. Her letters now came to me from San Francisco, bearing on their stamps the stern faces of Harry Truman and Abraham Lincoln. She wrote of going to protests, meetings, lectures; the Bay Area grew in my mind as the intellectual and spiritual capital of America. My life of reading and writing appeared complacent and futile in comparison; I tried to present myself as being aware, if not active, politically. The correspondence continued for some time. A few letters even came to Mashobra; then, they ceased. I heard nothing from her for some years, and when I thought of Helen I had the disquieting sense of her lost somewhere in the seemingly endless expanse of America.

Now, six years later, I had returned to Benares to write about it for my travel book. On my first morning, I went to a bookshop near the river in the old city. The amiable young man there seemed to know much of the expatriate population of Benares. I overheard him talking to a white-haired American woman in a sari who was complaining to him about sexual harassment in Sarnath, which had apparently grown worse in recent years. When the American woman had gone, he came over to me and began to mock her. Then, suddenly, he said, 'Do you know? Helen is here.'

It was one of those beautifully clear winter mornings I had come to love during my months in Benares, kites hanging high in the blue sky, and the river full of sparkle. The name 'Helen' rekindled the nostalgia I'd felt earlier as I walked through an alley where a radio in a paan shop played an old film song, and I remembered my months in the city, which, though shadowed by anxiety about my future, appeared, in retrospect, and especially when touched by the memory of her perennial confidence and optimism, a time when everything had gone well.

I thought how nice it would be to see her. I asked the young man if he knew where she was staying. He didn't know, but said he could easily find out. Looking at, but not seeing, the row of books before me, I began to imag-

ine the conversation I would have with her. There seemed
so much to tell. I was full of what I had seen in Bihar, but
had not found anyone to talk to about it.

I was standing there, daydreaming slightly, when the
young man added, 'You know, she is a Buddhist nun now,
hard to recognize. She shaved off her hair.'

I was jolted out of my daydreams. Strange, unsettling
images arose in my mind. I had known a few foreigners in
Benares who claimed to be Buddhists; it did not seem to
require more than an acceptance of the Buddha's teachings, regular meditation and a few wall hangings with
mandalas. I hadn't known any nuns, except the stern
Catholic ones who ran the small-town schools I had
attended. Helen suddenly appeared remote, more distant
than when I used to think of her as lost somewhere in
America.

I had read enough about Buddhism by then to realize
that it was not easily practised in the modern world where
almost everything was predicated on the growth and multiplication of desire, exactly the thing that the Buddha had
warned against. What the Buddha identified as the source
of suffering – greed, hatred and delusion – and wished to
extirpate, was also the source of life, and its pleasures,
however temporary.

I was full of wonder at the immensity and complexity
of Buddhist literature, the work of thinkers and scholars
now almost lost to memory. But I couldn't understand
much of what these philosophers had written. The most
fascinating among them was Nagarjuna, who had challenged even the Buddha by asserting that there could be no
such thing as a Right View since all intellectual constructs
had no essence. But how did one understand the concept

of Emptiness, not to mention the assertion that Emptiness itself was empty? Or, see that compassion flowed out of a realization of Emptiness?

Meditation might have helped me, but I couldn't sit still for too long. And although I couldn't admit it to myself, I was far from ready to embrace as rigorous a practice as Buddhism. I didn't know what had led Helen towards it. But she seemed not to have been daunted by its immense philosophical and practical difficulties. Or, perhaps she had gone only one step further than the people who meditated regularly and hung *thangkas* in their homes. In any case, her conversion appeared to me too easy, and my desire to see her vanished.

I spent the next day walking around the city. The changes I had seen elsewhere had not bypassed Benares. There were phone booths with gaudy acronym-rich signboards (STD-ISD-PCO) in the obscurest of side alleys. A pizzeria had opened at one of the ghats. There were indoor shopping malls in the newer parts of the city, their white facades already succumbing to the grime of the streets, and they were mostly empty inside, with more curious visitors than shoppers – peasant pilgrims from nearby villages reverent before the marble floors and the glass windows.

I was deep in my work and had almost forgotten about Helen when one morning I caught an auto-rickshaw to Sarnath. During my days as a student in Benares, I had often visited Sarnath, seeking a break from the Hindu city. I would walk through the museum that had the famous lion stone capital from Ashoka's iron pillar and then lie in the dappled shade of one of the big trees that fringed the vast lawns and read the book I had brought with me. I ate at one of the cheap dhabas to the east of the complex.

Back on the lawns, I would take a long nap, wake up refreshed to the sound of parakeets darting about in the branches overhead, and then read for a bit before returning to Benares.

I never paid much attention to the big *stupa*, the temple where the Buddha had spent a few monsoon months, or the remains of the monasteries. I regretted this while reading about the Buddha in Mashobra, when I often thought about Sarnath, and told myself that I would return to see the place with my newly educated eyes.

I had intermittently looked forward to it during the previous months of travel. But as the auto-rickshaw slowly negotiated the cluttered outskirts of Benares, often coming to a halt among the rickshaws, donkey carts, mopeds and trucks spewing black diesel fumes, and as the small-town scenes that had grown depressingly familiar passed again before my eyes – the mounds of rusty machinery, the pools of fetid water, the mess of illegal power cables, the young men idle and morose at chai stalls, the corpulent confectioner ensconced before a vat sizzling white with samosas – I began to feel numb.

The traffic cleared at last; the auto-rickshaw came on to a straight long road through mango and tamarind trees. A few miles away, there was Sarnath, with its deer park, *stupas*, temples, and its promise of serenity. But, for no clear reason, I didn't wish to be there.

When the auto-rickshaw stopped, I went first, trailed by a throng of beggars and mineral-water vendors, to the local museum. An old guard with a white moustache and an antiquated rifle stood at the door. There was no one inside the under-lit building, where, at the end of a long room, past the Ashoka pillar there was an image in sandstone of the Buddha seated in meditation. I stood before the statue, trying to summon up what I had read about it.

I left the museum and walked to the lawns. Although it was early and dew still lay on the grass, there were a few picnickers, unpacking plastic bags and spreading sheets on the ground. Not far from them, a lone monk moved slowly, apparently in walking meditation, around the big Dhamekh *stupa*.

I thought of visiting the *stupa* built by Ashoka on the spot where the Buddha had preached his first sermon to the five ascetics from his hometown, Kapilavastu. But there was only a circular platform where according to my map the *stupa* should have stood, littered with decayed flowers and incense and candle offerings. I stood before it for a while, wondering what to do next. I thought I would walk to the Dhamekh *stupa* and then catch an auto-rickshaw back to Benares.

I had walked a few metres when I saw the nun coming towards me. White, and of medium height, she was wearing an ochre robe and walked with quick springy steps. There seemed something both strange and familiar about her.

She came closer and then I saw her face. It was Helen, her head hairless and round but her mouth shaped as always into a smile.

My first panicked thought was: *Has she seen me?*

I wanted to hide. But the nearest tree was some metres away and in desperation I turned my back abruptly, shaded my eyes with my hand, hoping to appear to be looking at something in the distance.

I half expected her to say my name, and I wondered, my mind racing, how I would respond.

Tensely, I heard her walk past me, her robes gently rustling. I remained standing there for what seemed a long time, first wondering whether it was safe to move and then almost paralysed by self-reproach.

The shame and guilt receded as I returned to Benares and became preoccupied with writing. I spent a few more days in the city doing research for it and meeting middle-class people, and though I went again to the bookshop I did not ask about Helen.

I wrote my book over the spring and the summer in Mashobra. Much of my life had been sheltered, spent in reading and daydreaming. It seemed to me that my travels had exposed my naivety. I had seen a complex world which demanded an experienced mind to understand it. My travels had shown my notions about writing and the writer in general as a private and sterile indulgence. And so, defensively, what I wrote now had a harsh, satirical edge, half showy, half truthful.

In my over-earnest mood, I thought more about Helen's decision to become a nun. It now appeared to me to have cancelled out everything she had previously represented: an awareness of and engagement with the larger world, which I had once admired in her, and had even clumsily tried to imitate. I saw her efforts in Nicaragua and Haiti as another instance of the diverse advantages she enjoyed as an American – the same privileges that now permitted her to make herself into a Buddhist nun. I felt that we had moved in quite opposite directions, and that the meeting that I had avoided in Sarnath would only have been painfully awkward.

I was to see Helen again, in another place and time. But

now I was settling into my new self – the self that had travelled and imagined that it had learnt much. I didn't know
then that I would use up many more such selves, that they
would arise and disappear, making all experience hard to
fix and difficult to learn from.

The monsoons dragged on into late September while I
wrote my travel book in Mashobra. The drumming on the
tin roof rarely ceased; the bedclothes never lost their
slightly mouldy smell, and the road running through the
village more or less disappeared under intricate delta-like
formations of mud and rivulets of rain water.

Late in the evenings, I counted a few more lights on the
distant hillsides. Daulatram worked as always in the long
printing room, the tips of his fingers black, the printing
press steady in its rhythms during the long afternoons.
After days of absence, when I feared that he was either ill
or dead, the hunchbacked peasant would appear in the
orchard.

When the monsoons ended, I went walking again. The
shopkeepers looked older; the more prosperous of them
had small black and white television sets nestling amid the
jars of pickles and packets of Surf detergent. Montu
seemed to have more difficulty moving his enormous
weight around the dhaba and had to be helped by his
son, Neeraj. One afternoon, when his school had closed
early, Neeraj asked me shyly if I knew about computers,
what they did and whether he should learn to use them.
His mother, who was listening in the adjacent room
screened off by a torn sari, spoke up. She said that it was
my responsibility to find a vocation for Neeraj after he
finished his schooling.

A telephone line was laid through the village, involving

much digging beside the main road, and there suddenly appeared in the bazaar short dark men with flat noses and thick lips. They were dressed in rags and spoke a strange form of Hindi, and in the afternoons they stood knee-deep in the ditches, the sun blazing on their sweaty faces. They turned out to be labourers from the tribal regions of Bihar who moved across India, looking for work. They lived in tarpaulin tents by the road, next to the mounds of excavated earth, and their wives cooked on open fires in the way they would have done in the forests they had lived in on the plains.

The cows mooed forlornly in their shed, but Daulatram hardly ever took them out. I began to long for clean days, and when I finished my book I found myself eager to leave Mashobra, although it was still early in the autumn, with the most glorious days of the year ahead of me.

I had come to see the village as complete and, though I was waiting to move on, had considered myself content within it. But now I was restless, hungry for new sights and experiences. Confident that I would soon have more money from my book, I went travelling that autumn. I went to South India, Goa and Bombay. I returned north and went to Benares, then travelled, still thinking of the book about the Buddha, to Shravasti, Vaishali, Ayodhya and Kushinagara, the places the Buddha had travelled during the obscure middle years of his life.

At Shravasti, where a rich merchant had donated a grove to the Buddha, which had been the Buddha's preferred monsoon retreat for twenty-four years, there was a park with the bare remnants of what were probably the first Buddhist monasteries. Langur monkeys chattered in the bel trees, and even jumped on to the old pipal tree that stood behind railings in one corner. Out in the dry countryside of sheep and scrub, there were *stupas*, many of them plundered for brick. There was another park at Vaishali, with a dusty museum full of broken relics. At Kushinagara, abruptly in the middle of sugarcane fields, there was the brick mound where the Buddha had been cremated; a giant Buddha, gilded from head to toe, reclined in one of the nearby temples.

A wayside shrine to Hanuman appeared to contain more life than some of these sacred Buddhist sites. They were peculiarly dead places, long sunk into drabness, from which, it seemed, the elaborate piety, the orange, ochre, crimson, white robes and the new gold-plated monasteries of the Asian Buddhists had arrived too late to rescue them.

I didn't return to Mashobra that year. I lingered on in Benares. I was tense, waiting for nothing I could specify, but unwilling to re-enter the eventless life of reading and writing that I had known for some years.

When journalistic commissions took me to Europe and America the following year, I was happy to leave Mashobra. When I had taken that long bus journey to Nepal with Vinod, I had not expected to visit other foreign countries. But now I sat through the long monsoon months in Mashobra, hoping for the rain to stop, and fearing that it might cause landslides on the road to the plains from Simla and prevent me from reaching the airport in Delhi.

The weather was clear in London. People everywhere said that they were having the warmest autumn in many years. This talk of the weather was oddly exciting to me, in the way the sight of a cow on a street probably might be to a first-time visitor to India. The familiar cliché was something to hold onto amid the estranging newness of my surroundings. The weather also helped: the secretive autumn air, the sombre colours, the cold blue sky, the shortening days, things I had only read about, and which in my first few hours in England helped to suppress my great anxiety.

This anxiety had built up over the long hours on the plane. It surged up again in the queue at immigration, where the blank, uncomprehending Sikhs were being interrogated in sharp, severe voices. I took a black cab from the airport: an extravagance given my small budget, but I didn't feel confident about dealing with public transport.

The windows in the back were half down and, although I had already read many descriptions of the drive from Heathrow to south-west London as 'grim', on my first morning it was the unexpected delight of breathing large lungfuls of fresh air – bracingly sharp, like the air found in the Himalayas – and the ever-present greenness – glimpsed from the plane, but felt much more intimately on ground level – that kept at bay not only my nervousness, but also the passing shabbiness of warehouses and housing estates that I myself, in time, was to see as grim.

I was staying at the house of a British friend I had known in Delhi. When I arrived, it was empty, my hosts away at work, part of the busyness of London that here in East Sheen's quiet leafy lanes was hard to imagine. It was my first English house, semi-detached with pink wallpaper and thick carpets and a piano in the dining room. I heaved my bags up to the room on the first floor the letter on the carpet said was to be mine: a narrow bed, a radiator, a bookshelf, a picture of – what?

I didn't wait to look. I was impatient to see the view from the room's only window and, though tired and ready to fall asleep, I stood for a while with my nose pressed to the glass panes, enchanted by the vision of a miniature arcadia, the fenced back garden with its tiny greenhouse, tool shed and a patch of lawn bordered by hydrangeas and petunias on both sides. Towards the back of the yard, forming a natural screen, were the sycamore trees, serenely brown and red. I felt I could spend days there, lying on the grass watching soft white clouds glide across the patch of sky overhead.

Unwilling to sleep, I went walking around later that empty afternoon and stumbled, quite literally, into Richmond Park. I had seen the large spread of green on my map, but, accustomed only to the shanty-town sprawl of Indian cities, I hadn't been prepared for the proximity of city and country, the tree-lined avenues past drowsy front gardens that suddenly opened out into vast undulating immensities of green turf. Around the tiny still pond sat elderly men with dogs and walking sticks; the planes slowly circling above in the big pale-blue sky seemed almost to be keeping guard over this tableau of quiet contentment.

I walked through the wooded depths of the park and then stopped in the middle of a congregation of oaks – so sturdy, these trees, in such contrast to the nervous leanness of the common Indian type – to unpeel from my shoes the leaves they had collected on the damp paths. Later, light steadily diminishing, I lost my way while walking home and wandered around a couple of side streets, where the light falling out of curtained bay windows was to my weary traveller's senses the glow of domestic comfort and self-sufficiency.

I wanted to talk to someone. Standing in the kitchen from where I could see the back garden, I rang Sophiya. I knew her from Simla, where she had spent two years researching a thesis on imperial urban planning.

She seemed a bit subdued. She said she had just broken up with her boyfriend. It had been a stressful time for her, but she was coming out of it.

I didn't know what to say. She had never spoken to me about her private life before. In Simla, she seemed to work very hard, with a determination I put down to intellectual curiosity rather than professional ambition; she was always full of interesting details she had uncovered about the making of the city.

I began to ramble on about what I had seen: the lonely men with dogs in the empty park, the private houses with their living rooms facing deserted streets, and the vast city I had yet to visit, where I imagined the stupendous effort needed to make possible these quiet middle-class lives taking place.

She said, interrupting me, 'But where you are is actually a suburb. You should wait until you see the centre of the city.'

I went there the next day, partly to see Sophiya, who lived in Shoreditch. I went by train, and the men and women in dark suits who joined it at every stop, so preoccupied, so serious, as they unfolded and read *The Times* and the *Guardian*, were like a premonition of the city ahead. Outside, the moss-overgrown backs of houses, creepers on sooty walls, clothes lines, back lawns with a tricycle or playpen, a brief glimpse of the grey river and an island, and then warehouses, factories, squat office blocks.

Like much else, I knew the London light from books. But to see the accumulated mass and solidity of the cluster of buildings on the embankment, to walk through Westminster, past Whitehall and into Trafalgar Square – places bringing back memories of certain streets in Calcutta and Madras – was to know that light's extraordinary power to confer form and colour.

I had seen this part of London in old prints and photographs, greatly resembling Madras, Bombay and Calcutta, colonial outposts not untouched by the architectural movements of late eighteenth- and nineteenth-century Britain. In my mind London existed in an endless languid colonial afternoon, the loin-clothed natives resting in the shadows of the high walls, a rickshaw disgorging an overdressed official on the exposed empty street in front.

I hadn't been prepared for the crowds that worked there, for the certainty of purpose with which they strode across Waterloo Bridge, the resolute tick-tock of high-heels hitting the pavement. Few people ever looked so energetic in India, and if they did they were usually regarded as eccentrics. Wordlessly again, looking neither left nor right, as if impelled by a great inner panic, they flowed out of the underground station at Tottenham Court Road, a gaggle of pale autumnal faces over black or grey overcoats, among which, with a small twinge of disappointment, I recognized Sophiya.

In Simla, among the promenading men and women on

the Mall, Sophiya in her salwar kameez and with her British accent had seemed glamorous. She also had what appeared to me a highly unusual family history. Her grandfather, born in a remote village in the Punjab, had worked as a coolie in Simla before joining the British army and serving in the First World War. He had fought in Mesopotamia and returned with a wound to his village. His son, Sophiya's father, had also joined the British Indian Army. He had distinguished himself in the Second World War, during fighting in Italy, before settling down in London, where Sophiya was born.

Sophiya didn't talk much about her father and grand-father. She once described the wars they had fought in as 'white man's wars'. I was impressed by what seemed then both a considered view of the world and her ability to express it in casual conversation.

In Simla, the place where her grandfather had made a living by lifting heavy sacks of coal on his back, she had seemed consumed by her curiosity. But in London that morning, although as primly pretty as before, she was barely distinguishable from the crowd in her short skirt, sheer stockings and neatly cut hair. The lone item of Indian clothing she had on was a shawl, not spread around her shoulders Indian fashion, but wrapped around her neck – a sign of her personal style. In her own world – the streets and crowds of London, the vegetarian restaurant near London University where we presently went to have lunch – she appeared diminished.

And it was of this diminishment that she spoke to me, her voice low with complaint, when she told me that after-noon – assuming a personal intimacy we had never had before – of her frustrations at her as yet temporary job, the competitive spitefulness of her colleagues, the excessive formality and sterility of social life among academics – all this in the cramped restaurant, the pavement outside bright with the banter of students bathing in unaccustomed autumn sun.

We travelled together to the suburb of Southall. One of my briefs in England was to write about a gathering of Indian soldiers who had served in the Second World War. The soldiers had spent close to half a century in Britain; they felt that the British government had treated them shabbily during the fiftieth-anniversary celebrations of the end of the war, and had not even considered them for honours they had bestowed on former soldiers from Australia, Canada and other British Commonwealth countries.

Sophiya was restless in the room full of men with thick white moustaches and sticks and shiny medals, who sat on white plastic chairs, staring into space, animated only when lunch was served, when they queued up obediently before the table heaped with Indian food. Her own father wasn't there. He had done well out of Britain, she said bitterly, with a house in London and another house in the country, and his children in good jobs. He didn't much care about how other immigrants lived.

She carried her discontent back to the pub in central London where we had a drink. She was, she said, fed up with the Indians in London: they were self-seeking, aggressively ambitious, unscrupulous people. It turned out that her boyfriend was one of these Indians: a journalist who had used his ethnic identity strategically in the mostly white professional world that strove self-consciously for diversity and multiculturalism. He had risen fast at his moderately left-wing newspaper, from the sub-editor's desk to the newsroom. In the process, he had become conservative in his politics and insincere in his private life. He had bought a Saab convertible and started an affair with the female boss in his office.

I listened to her, slightly embarrassed and awkward, not always understanding the import of particular events, such as the buying of the Saab convertible, but also deeply fascinated. It was like being given another view of the hectic office workers of that morning, of the peculiar motives and tensions that swarmed at their workplaces and appeared to form the material of the arch young columnists and the writers of risqué novels about office life whose excepts I had seen in the newspapers – things which that morning had added to my nervousness and made me think that I had arrived in the middle of a long and complicated film.

It was a little later that evening – the pub full and often erupting into raucous laughter – when she told me she had a new lover, a French journalist she had met at a party in Islington. The story came out briskly. I couldn't make myself heard in the noise of the pub and was content to listen and nod. I must have seemed curious. She was slightly drunk.

As she described it, he had pursued her relentlessly, and she had finally given in, 'fed up', she said, with her loneliness. It had worked out for a while. She saw the French lover several times every week. They went out to a film or play, or simply came straight to his flat in Islington and made love; the vacant evenings ceased to be a threat.

But she was now fed up with him. The Frenchman was no reader, had no interest in art. He was also stingy.

Sophiya said, 'He never brings me flowers, never brings me presents, there is never any food in his kitchen.'

On the train back to East Sheen that evening, standing among the weary pale faces of people in dark suits, sinking deeper into my solitude and strangeness, I had a sudden vision of Sophiya: of her rummaging through the fridge and empty cupboards in a dark kitchen, loud TV voices echoing out of the bedroom, the light dead outside on rows and rows of identical houses of the kind I saw from the train.

From England I went to France and then to America. I passed through famous airports – Heathrow, De Gaulle, JFK, LAX – always gazing in wonder at the Mexicans, Russians, Indians, Nigerians, Iranians, Indonesians, Filipinos, Koreans who swarmed in those vast, shiny bazaars. It seemed that while I was growing up in India, many people like myself had longed for the richness of the world. Whether businesspeople, students, tourists or immigrants, they wanted to be accommodated beyond the life they had so far known, where they could shed the narrow racial or national identity they had been born into and devote themselves to the making of money, the pursuit of learning and the search for love and freedom.

I was relieved when, returning to Mashobra later that year, Mr Sharma did not ask me any questions about my travels: what I had seen, whom I had met. I never brought up the subject myself. I didn't want to encourage him. I was far from being able to articulate my experience even to myself.

I was surprised by this failure. I had had some experience of travel before I left the country. I had admittedly travelled late to London, after many of my opinions had already been fixed. I thought myself different from the Indians who had left India early in their lives. These were usually the sons and daughters of upper-class Indians, who after three or four years as students in England or America returned to inherit their privileges, with little more than a brittle sense of superiority and a sour-sweet memory of interrupted romances and friendships to mark their time in the West. I was not a tourist, looking for cathedrals, museums and monuments. I wanted to see myself as separate from the shamefully large number of Indian tourists shopping for bargains in electronics and kitchen gadgets. Nor was I an immigrant, predisposed to embrace, whatever its quality, his new life.

My motives were much more romantic. Walking across the island in the Bois de Boulogne in Paris, where Proust had set his own and his characters' longings for fame and love, visiting the New England town of Concord where Emerson had preached self-reliance, or nearby Walden Pond, where Thoreau had translated Buddhist texts and read the *Vedas*, I was hoping to bathe in the aura of men whom I had revered since the time when, in places scarcely unimaginable to them, I had first read their works and began to build a usable self and life.

Just outside the well-preserved haunts of famous writers and sages, there were shops selling souvenirs: wine bottles and parasols imprinted with the dark-eyed melancholy of Proust, coffee cups showing Emerson's gravely bearded profile. I let myself go at these shops, which with their imaginative merchandise seemed to me like the stalls that lined the path to famous temples in India, selling flowers, incense, sandalwood paste and other items of ritual worship.

It took me time to realize that my love of western writers and philosophers had been a form of idolatry, and that it had not prepared me to see them as people shaped by, and responding to, specific events – the break-up of the old moral and religious order, the economic and political revolutions, the making and unmaking of empires, and the rise of the bourgeois individual with his particular desires and pleasures. I still assumed then that people could be considered apart from the forces that had conditioned them.

On that first visit to the West, I had travelled mostly to a place in my mind. I was more surprised than I could have imagined by the sex-obsessed advertisements, magazines and newspapers, which I had already seen in India; by the graffiti-ravaged outskirts of Paris, which I had seen in a film about North African immigrants but never thought real; and by the stark wilderness of the malls and parking lots of suburban America, not far from Concord and Walden Pond, that I had read about in the fictions of John Updike. The platitudes of sociology – the mechanization of life, the culture built around the gratification of individual needs – that I had encountered many times before came back to me; they clarified nothing and only led to more platitudes.

This was why I couldn't have explained to Mr Sharma the everyday sight in London of black-clad commuters with expressionless faces pouring out from the trains in railway and underground stations and striding wordlessly towards their offices; or about the boisterous crowds of office-goers spilling out from street-corner pubs, the restless queues outside nightclubs on Friday evenings, the men and women staggering back late at night to the rows upon rows of houses with hard unyielding fronts; about the impulse to divide life into manageable parts, about the city as a collection of solitary individuals brought together briefly by a few shared interests.

It was also why I couldn't have told him about the dissatisfactions of a single girl in London; or even about something he, who had contentedly spent all his life in a village, might have recognized: the oppressive solitude that one could know in the large city, the lives of private longing and frustration which many of the people in the crowds seemed to lead, on whom the glittering past of the large metropolis that attracted a visitor like myself no longer cast its spell.

Looking for the Self

THE BUDDHA SPENT SEVERAL weeks in Sarnath. He made no attempt to conquer the orthodox centre of Benares, which lay disdainfully aloof a few miles away. Perhaps he was satisfied with what he had: there were the first loyal disciples, the five Brahmins from Kapilavastu, then Yasa had sparked a veritable rush to convert among his contemporaries.

The monsoons came after the long weeks of heat. The continuous rains swelled the rivers, flooded the roads and made travel impossible. There were then hardly any buildings in Sarnath, and the force of rain and gale must have threatened to bring down the leaf or bamboo huts of the monks. But amid what to the Buddha might have seemed minor inconveniences, he continued to develop variations on the themes he had sounded in his first discourse. He spoke of the need for systematic thought that had taken him towards enlightenment; he spoke of the need for *bhikshus* to rigorously examine themselves for flaws and faults.

The most important sermon he gave during this time developed his sceptical view of what individuals took to be their identity. This is probably the most difficult part of Buddhist doctrine, along with the related notion that all things in the world have a 'dependent origination'. Even the Buddha's personal attendant, Ananda, could not understand it, despite having listened to his master explain it several times. I couldn't cease to feel that no matter what the Buddha said about the insubstantiality of the self, there was an 'I' which performed the daily tasks of life, and ate, slept, read and thought in a consistent way over a long period. I couldn't deny this continuity, or accept that the person who went to sleep was different from the one who woke up the next morning.

Perhaps the problem lay with my early perception of the Buddha as a thinker, somewhat in the mould of Descartes, Kant and Hegel, or like the academic philosophers of today, presenting their own and debating each other's ideas. I looked for a coherent and systematic metaphysics and epistemology in the words attributed to the Buddha, when his aim had been clearly therapeutic rather than to dismantle or build a philosophical system.

In fact, the Buddha had made clear his distrust of abstract speculation. There were problems, he claimed, that eluded all linguistic and conceptual nets and whose solutions were inexpressible. It is why he famously remained silent when a wandering ascetic called Vacchagotta asked him if he thought there was an *atman*, or soul.[1] Faced with the Buddha's silence, the seeker asked, 'Then, there is no *atman*?' Again, the Buddha was silent.

After Vacchagotta had left, the Buddha was asked by Ananda why he had remained silent. He explained that if, when asked if there is a self, he had said, 'There is a self,' he would have sided with those who held the theory of the eternal soul, and if when asked if there is no self he had said, 'There is no self,' he would have sided with those who hold the theory of those who denied the self.

As always, the Buddha sought a middle way between these theories. Before the Buddha, the *Upanishads* had sought to console men with the promise of an everlasting *atman*. Residing in each human being, this soul or self was the thinker of thoughts, the feeler of sensations and the performer of actions, good or bad, for which it received the appropriate rewards and punishments after the death of the body it lived in. This self was furthermore an absolute entity; it was the same as the unchanging substance, *brahman*, that lay behind the changing world, and liberation, or *moksha*, consisted in realizing the unity of *atman* and *brahman*.

But the Buddha seems to have rejected more than the Upanishadic idea of an eternal self or soul. He rejected too the self residing in the mind that Descartes assumed when he declared that he was 'a thing that thinks' – a thing that doubts, understands, affirms, denies, is willing, is unwilling, and imagines and has sensory perceptions.[2] According to the Cartesian view, the self is a single unified substance with the capacity to experience, desire, think, imagine, decide and act. It does not change through time, and is ontologically distinct from other selves.

The Buddha seemed to reject this notion of the individual self as a distinct substance with identity. He said that it didn't correspond to any reality observable within the mind and the body, and, furthermore, its awareness of itself as separate from the world and other selves was false and the source of craving, pride, selfishness and delusion.

The Buddha's view sounds counter-intuitive, mostly

because the linguistic term 'I' that we use to describe a whole range of simple or complex experiences – for instance, 'I am sad' and 'I am happy' – presupposes the existence of an unchanging self that experiences these varying states. In fact, we lay claim to those experiences precisely through that 'I' or what we imagine to be a separate autonomous self within us, and they then go on to shore up our selfhood and identity.

The Buddha and Buddhists didn't forgo the word 'I' or individuals; they remain practical words, belonging to the realm of conventional or relative truth. But the Buddha denied them any stable reality. In many of his discourses and dialogues, he came back to the subject of the stable self, or the false views of it that an individual was prone to develop, leading him into habits of craving what he thinks is 'mine'. Unlike Descartes, he presented the self as a process rather than as a substance, by claiming that what we call a 'being' or an 'individual' is only a physio-psychological machine in which mental and physical energies constantly combine and change.[3]

In a sermon at Sarnath, he went on to list and analyse painstakingly the physical and mental events that he said constituted the human individual. He organized these events into five groups or aggregates called *skandhas*.[4] The first of these refers to material form: the body and its aspects – solidity, fluidity, heat and motion – which make possible the five material sense-organs, the faculties of eye, ear, nose, tongue, and body. The second group refers to sensations produced through the contact of the five senses and the mind with the external world and their quality. Then, there is the group of perceptions, which involves labelling and judgement of the feelings of pleasure, gloom, or indifference – experiences triggered off by the senses in contact with the physical world. We are constantly classifying these experiences, so that there is instant recognition of physical stimuli, such as a glass of wine, or a sharp blow.

These experiences in turn provoke desires, longings, traits, a whole set of circumstances in which we act. Seeing a glass of wine may lead to an irresistible desire to drink wine, or it may trigger associations that lead to different desires and actions. Desires, wishes, indeed anything that brings about action belongs to the fourth group. The last group consists of a basic self-consciousness, a sense of ourselves as sentient beings who think and perceive.

The Buddha claimed that there was nothing more to an individual than these five groups of causally connected and interdependent phenomena: bodily phenomena, feelings, labelling or recognizing, volitional activities and conscious awareness. He denied that the self could exist in any or all of these because they changed constantly, were impermanent and had no independent existence. He went on to assert that the human personality was unstable; a complex flow of phenomena; a set of processes rather than a substance; a becoming rather than a being. It was part of his larger claim that everything in the world is ontologically connected and in a state of change.

In the Buddhist view, not even consciousness amounts to a self or soul. For consciousness is primarily a reaction or response to stimuli. Consciousness is, as the Buddha put it, 'whatever condition through which it arises': because of the eye and visible forms there is a visual consciousness;

because of the ears and sounds there arises an auditory consciousness, and so on. Consciousness, which is always born out of contact with an object, does not exist on its own; it is not innate in objects. As a Zen poem puts it, 'To her lover a beautiful woman is a delight; to an ascetic, a distraction; to a wolf, a good meal'.

There may be an apparent continuity, but perception and discursive thought arise and fall constantly. Consciousness is a flow of tiny instants that have no separate existence or essence; they are constantly being triggered by each of the tiny changes in the world outside – the process creating the impression of what we call reality. When broken up into its aggregate parts, consciousness reveals itself as profoundly conditioned, ever changing and relative, and far from the substantial entity we believe the individual self to be.

David Hume among western philosophers had a view of the self closest to that of the Buddha:

> When I enter most intimately into what I call *myself*, I always stumble on some particular perception or other, of heat or cold, light or shade, love or hatred, pain or pleasure. I never can catch myself at any time without a perception, and never can observe any thing but the perception.[5]

From this Hume concluded that

> we are nothing but a bundle or collection of different perceptions, which succeed each other with an inconceivable rapidity ... The mind is a kind of theatre, where several perceptions successively make their appearance;

pass, repass, glide away, and mingle in an infinite variety of postures and situations . . .⁶

It was this theatre of the mind that the Buddha exhorted his son, Rahula, to observe during meditation. For to do so, he said, was to abandon the conceit 'I am'. Hume himself drew no such practical implications from his analysis of the data of consciousness, although he helped establish for later philosophers the roots of the intellect in feeling. The idea of reality as a process, first proposed by Heraclitus, entered the mainstream of western philosophy only with Nietzsche, Henri Bergson, William James and the discoveries of modern physics. It was the literary artists of the modern era, Flaubert, Baudelaire, Dostoevsky and Proust, who spoke in their work of the unstable nature of the experiencing self.

Proust in his evocations of memory seemed to hint that the self was nothing more than a convenient name for causally connected experiences. The narrator of his novel *In Search of Lost Time* wishes to be a writer but despairs of ever finding coherence in his life; of making sense of his many selves that have had love affairs, conducted friendships and travelled widely. In a famous passage, he describes how one day late in his life, when he has given up on his literary ambitions, he eats a pastry cake dipped in tea:

> No sooner had the warm liquid and the crumbs with it touched my palate than a shudder ran through my whole body, and I stopped, intent upon the extraordinary changes that were taking place. An exquisite pleasure had invaded my senses, but individual, detached, with no suggestion of its origin. And at once the vicissitudes of life

had become indifferent to me, its disasters innocuous, its brevity illusory . . .[7]

The taste brings back to the narrator his childhood in a country town where on Sunday mornings he had the same kind of cake dipped in tea. The town and its buildings and people suddenly arise into brilliant clarity in the narrator's consciousness:

> I feel something start within me, something that leaves its resting place and attempts to rise, something that has been embedded like an anchor at great depth; I do not know yet what it is, but I can feel it mounting slowly; I can measure the resistance, I can hear the echo of great spaces traversed . . .[8]

It is the epiphany brought on by the cake dipped in tea that suggests to Proust's narrator a self held together by involuntary memory, the self that reveals itself in particular experiences and can be recreated briefly only when certain causal conditions – smell, taste, sound – are present:

> But when from a long-distant past nothing subsists, after the people are dead, after the things are broken and scattered, still, alone, more fragile, but with more vitality, more unsubstantial, more persistent, more faithful, the smell and taste of things remain poised a long time, like souls, ready to remind us, waiting and hoping for their moment, amid the ruins of all the rest; and bear unfalteringly, in the tiny and almost impalpable drop of their essence, the vast structure of recollection.[9]

The series of mental and physical events that are the individual arise dependently at any given moment and over time. They form certain patterns, which tend to reproduce themselves and are relatively stable. You are not the same person at thirty that you were at five, but neither are you completely different. 'You cannot step into the same river twice,' Heraclitus claimed, implying that both the river and the person stepping into it change. But they don't become entirely different entities.

As Proust discovered, there is a continuous causal relationship between the patterns of mental and physical events that occurred then and are occurring now. It is why he is able to remember. According to Vasubhandhu, the fifth-century Indian philosopher, 'Remembrance is a new state of consciousness directed to the same object, conditioned as it is by the previous states.'

The Buddha often spoke of how without milk there can be no yoghurt, and without yoghurt there can be no buttermilk, etc; and how within this process nothing remains unchanged or is totally altered. This continuity also made it impossible for individuals to escape moral responsibility for their acts. As Nagasena explained to Menander, someone who stole mangoes from another man's trees couldn't plausibly claim that the mangoes he stole were not the mangoes their owner planted since the mangoes he stole arose dependently upon the mangoes that were previously planted.

The Buddha extended the principle of causality to human life. There is a short formula that explains how everything is connected and in a state of change and how this change is not random or chaotic but a stable process of causation:

When this is, that is
This arising, that arises
When this is not, that is not
This ceasing, that ceases.[10]

As the Buddha put it:

From wisps of grass the rope is spun
By dint of exertion
By turns of wheel the buckets are raised from the well
Yet each turn of itself is futile.

So the turning of all the components of becoming
Arises from the interaction of one with another
In the unit the turning cannot be traced
Either at the beginning or end.

Where the seed is, there is the young plant,
But the seed has not the nature of the plant,
Nor is it something other than the plant, nor is it the
plant –
So is the nature of the law of Righteousness, neither tran-
sient nor eternal.[11]

The more ambitious twelve-point chain of what Buddhists call dependent origination describes how life exists,
arises and continues:

1. Through ignorance, volitional actions or *karma-*
   formations are conditioned.
2. Through volitional actions, consciousness is
   conditioned.
3. Through consciousness, mental and physical
   phenomena are conditioned.
4. Through mental and physical phenomena, the six
   faculties (five senses and the mind) are conditioned.

5. Through the six faculties (sensory and mental), contact is conditioned.
6. Through (sensory and mental) contact, sensation is conditioned.
7. Through sensation, desire is conditioned.
8. Through desire, clinging is conditioned.
9. Through clinging, the process of becoming is conditioned.
10. Through the process of becoming, birth is conditioned.
11. Through birth, decay, death, pain etc are conditioned.

The general idea here, rendered obscure by the technical language, is no different from the one the Buddha proposed elsewhere: that ignorance as to the impermanent nature of reality and grasping make for continuous rebirth and suffering. As the Buddha told Ananda,

> Were there no grasping of any sort of kind whatever of anyone at anything – that is to say, no grasping at things of sense, no grasping through speculative opinions, no grasping after mere rule and ritual, no grasping through theories of the soul – then, there being no grasping whatever, would there, owing to this cessation, be any appearance of becoming?[12]

Since nothing could arise out of nothing, the Buddha denied the notion of an omnipotent creator God. Instead, he posited a world which with its diversity, its structures and capacities had come into being as the result of prior actions of living beings motivated by greed, arrogance, passion and envy – by what he called *klesha*, afflictions, and their latent counterparts: ignorance, desire for sensual pleasure, thirst for existence, grasping onto identity, etc.

{ 263 }

*

For Proust, sensual memory lay dormant within human beings and managed to outlast all changes of personality in our entire lifetime. For the Buddhists thinkers of the Yogachara school, the traces of previous actions outlast even death. Using terms close to the Freudian notion of the unconscious, they asserted that every thought, utterance and action deposits a karmic trace upon the consciousness, which already contains the residue of past lives and so is a bridge across not one lifetime but several.

The Buddha once spoke of the infant who lies prone and does not even have the notion of 'personality', of sensual pleasures, or of aggressiveness towards others. But these dispositions lie latent within him, waiting to mature and influence his actions. As the Yogachara philosopher Vasubhandhu put it:

> The world in its variety arises from action (*karma*). Actions accumulate by the power of the latent afflictions; because without the latent afflictions (they) are not capable of giving rise to a new existence. Consequently, the latent afflictions are the root of existence.[13]

The 'subject as multiplicity', man as nothing other than 'the totality of his drives' – this was how Nietzsche saw human personality. For him, too, the body was a dynamic process, in which a number of thinking, willing and feeling subjects constantly ebb and flow. The person was a constellation of fluctuating forces, where such impulses as love, malice, sexual desire, pride, cunning and jealousy dominated, and in which even 'conscious thinking is secretly directed and compelled into definite channels by instincts':

The course of logical thoughts and inferences in our brains today corresponds to a process and battle of drives that taken separately are all over illogical and unjust; we usually experience only the outcome of the battle: that is how quickly and covertly this ancient mechanism runs its course in us.[14]

As Nietzsche saw it, all human beings came into the world with the same animal-like impulses. What distinguished them from each other was the particular pattern created by the past struggle among these impulses – the pattern that the higher type of man, the self-aware superman, has the ability to override. This was Nietzsche's own version of *karma*: man as a psychological complex, who is a consequence of his past dispositions, of how and what he thought and said and did.

For the Buddha, it was the variously configured psychological complex of human beings that determined their next form of existence – what he called *nama-rupa* (name and form, denoting the incorporeal and physical aspects of the new person). Consciousness carried over from previous lives could alone explain the presence of consciousness in living creatures:

Consciousness conditions name and form (i.e. the new empirical person). That should be understood thus: If the consciousness (of one who has died) were not to descend into the mother's womb, would name and form (the new person) develop there?[15]

There were other, more mundane causes attending birth, apart from a conditioned consciousness: a woman and a man. When they come together, new life sprang into being. The conditioned consciousness of a dead man kindles new life, and a new flame burned in the womb, conditioned by, but not identical with or different from, the spark of the dead man's consciousness. Consciousness thus was conserved in the same way that energy was conserved in the world of matter: something that was never destroyed but only transformed.

Rebirth will seem impossible only if you think of the self as a stable, enduring substantial entity instead of, as Nietzsche partly understood it, a series of mental and physical events – a conditioned stream of consciousness. According to the Buddha, death doesn't break the causal connectedness of these events. It breaks up only a particular pattern in which they occur. And such is the nature of causal connectedness that these events start forming another pattern as soon as rebirth takes place. The Buddha thus made rebirth somewhat plausible, even though this remains the one part of his teachings that requires a leap into faith.

This was not as deterministic for individuals as it may appear. It is true that there is no such thing as an absolutely free will in this Buddhist view of the world. For will and freedom are conditioned by cause and effect, like all other phenomena; the idea of free will is itself conditioned. But as the 'self-overcoming' man in Nietzsche's optimistic vision can rise above the reality of his basic drives and change the pattern formed by them, so the individual in the Buddha's vision is free to act within this conditioned realm, and strive for liberation from the cycle of rebirths.

Salvation exists in the purest kind of awareness, which consists of knowing the conditioned nature of phenomena:

of knowing how past karmic activities become present predispositions and determine the quality of the current of consciousness that survives the death of the physical body. This awareness was reached through meditation, which weakened preconceptions and psychological constructs formed during these previous karmic activities.

The acts with the least karmic consequences are those that flow from this awareness: that we lack a fixed or unchanging essence but are assemblages of dynamic yet wholly conditioned mental and physical processes; and that suffering results when we seek to assert our autonomy in a radically interdependent world, when a groundless self seeks endlessly and futilely to ground itself through actions driven by ignorance, greed and delusion, which when frustrated lead to even further attempts at self-affirmation, making suffering appear inevitable and delusion indestructible.

In the second century AD, Nagarjuna took further the Buddha's notion of dependent origination.[16] He systematized the Buddha's rejection of theory and concepts; he asserted that all known realities are constructed realities used to order the world and make it intellectually comprehensible. He asserted that nothing can be known except in terms of something else. In itself, each entity is empty of essence.

We move in our quest for knowledge from concept to concept, but no concept exists on its own: it depends for its existence on other concepts. Analytic and rational thinking produces ideas and opinions, but these are only conventionally true, trapped as they are in the dualistic distinctions imposed by language. Reason throws up its own concepts and dualisms, and tangles us in an undergrowth of notions and views, whereas true insight lay in dismantling intellectual structures and in seeing through to their essential emptiness (*shunyata*).

For Nagarjuna, the only right view is no view at all. His suspicion of metaphysics and his view of language as embodying cultural presuppositions make him appear an early precursor of the structuralists and deconstructionists of today. Claude Lévi-Strauss may have been thinking of Nagarjuna's attempt to deconceptualize the mind when he spoke of the 'decisive wisdom' of the Buddha, 'to which my civilization could contribute only by confirming it':

> Every effort to understand destroys the object studied in favour of another object of a different nature; this second object requires from us a new effort which destroys it in favour of a third, and so on and so forth until we reach the one lasting presence, the point at which a distinction between meaning and the absence of meaning disappears: the same point from which we began.[17]

The Fire Sermon

THE WORLD AS A network of causal relationships, the emptiness of the self, the thirst for stability, the impermanence of phenomena, the cause of suffering, its cessation through awareness – all these ideas formed the systematic view of human existence that the Buddha offered in Sarnath during the first weeks after his enlightenment.

When the monsoons ended, he decided to return to Bodh Gaya, where he had spent six years as an ascetic before reaching enlightenment. In a forest on the way, he ran into a group of thirty friends, sons of rich people, much like Yasa and his companions. They had come to the forest on a picnic of sorts. One of the men had brought a courtesan, who had stolen some of their belongings and escaped while they were distracted. The men were looking for her when they came across the Buddha and asked him if he had seen a woman.

According to some texts, the Buddha asked them if it was better to seek a woman than the self. When they conceded that it was better to seek the self, the Buddha asked them to sit down. He then taught them the four noble truths. The men were promptly converted.

What this episode further highlights is how almost all the Buddha's first lay followers were people from the commercial class – the class that had begun to emerge in the new urban centres of North India just a few decades before the Buddha's birth. These were people who, in the new conditions of urban living, had slipped out of the Aryan four-fold caste system that held sway in the villages. The old rules didn't apply to them; they were still outsiders in their new society.

Like mercantile classes everywhere later, they were insecure, yet to find their intellectual and spiritual culture and construct the grand monuments to reflect it. They chafed at the continuing dominance of the Brahmins, who denied them the status they now felt they had earned through the creation of wealth, and who reserved the right to bestow religious merit. The Buddha's lesson – that it was up to the individual to examine himself and strive towards goodness – couldn't but be gratefully received and promoted by the new business class.

In Bodh Gaya, however, the Buddha faced tougher resistance to his teachings than he had met so far in the callow merchants or the decadent young men of Benares. It is likely that he was tempted to return to the site of his enlightenment by the prospect of converting an old ascetic called Uruvela Kashyapa, who lived on the banks of the river in Bodh Gaya and was respected and revered all across the kingdom of Magadha. He, his brothers, who lived downstream from him, and his hundreds of followers followed the sacrifice-based religion of the *Vedas*. The Buddha may have seen their conversion as a propaganda coup for himself.

Apparently, the Buddha didn't think that a simple presentation of his ideas, which had worked upon the Brahmins
from Kapilavastu, Yasa and his friends, and the young men
in the forest, was going to impress Kashyapa. At any rate,
the legend records that he performed three and a half thousand miracles, which include flying through the air and
ensuring that the ascetics could not kindle their sacrificial
fires. Finally, the Buddha bluntly informed Kashyapa that
he hadn't attained enlightenment and never would if he continued with the same means of sacrifice and asceticism.

Convinced of the Buddha's superior ways, Kashyapa and
his followers cut off their matted locks and threw them into
the river. His brothers and their followers saw the locks as
they floated past. Wondering what was going on, they
walked up the river to where the Buddha was. The Buddha
led them to a hill, where he preached them the famous fire
sermon.

There is a hypnotic quality to this sermon, which was
one of T. S. Eliot's multicultural borrowings in his poem
The Waste Land. The effect is more dramatic when you
imagine the scene, about a thousand matt-locked ascetics
sitting on top of a hill near Gaya, being told that the fire
they worshipped could be looked at differently, that there
was no better metaphor than fire for the volatile nature of
the senses and the desires they perpetually engender. 'Everything is ablaze,' the Buddha said:

> What is ablaze? The eyes are ablaze. The form (objects
> seen by the eyes) is ablaze. The mental functions (based
> on eyes) are ablaze. The contact of the eye (with visible
> objects and mental functions) is ablaze. The sensations

produced by the contact of the eye, whether pleasant, unpleasant, or neither one nor the other, are ablaze.

The ears are ablaze. Sounds are ablaze . . . the nose is ablaze. Smells are ablaze. The tongue is ablaze. Tastes are ablaze . . . The body is ablaze. The objects (felt by the body) are ablaze . . . The mind is ablaze. Objects of thought are ablaze. The mental functions based on the mind are ablaze. The contact of the mind (with audible objects and mental functions) is ablaze. The sensations produced by the contact of the mind, whether pleasant, unpleasant, or neither one nor the other, are ablaze.

By what are they ablaze? I tell you they are ablaze with the fire of greed, with the fire of hatred, with the fire of delusion, ablaze with birth, old age, death, grief, lamentation, suffering, sorrow, and despair . . . A disciple who is well-learned, *Bhikshus*, when he considers things in this way, grows . . . weary of the eye . . . He grows weary of the ear, grows weary of objects seen by the eye, grows weary of the mental functions (based on) the eyes, grows weary of the contact of the eye . . . Growing weary of them, he rids himself of greed. Being rid of greed, he is liberated. Being liberated, he becomes aware of his liberation and realizes that birth is exhausted, that the pure practice is fulfilled, that what is necessary has been done, and that he will not return to this world again.[1]

From Bodh Gaya, the Buddha moved with his new followers to Rajagriha, the capital of Magadha, where six years previously he had met Bimbisara and turned down the opportunity to command his army. This time he went at the invitation of Bimbisara, whom he had promised to visit soon after his enlightenment.

Bimbisara had heard vaguely about the encounter between the Buddha and the Kashyapa brothers in Bodh

Gaya, but it was not clear to him who had converted whom. He went out to meet the Buddha accompanied by the Brahmins and wealthy people of Magadha. When they met, the Buddha encouraged Uruvela Kashyapa to speak. Kashyapa told the court of Bimbisara why he had abandoned his ascetic practices and taken refuge in the Buddha's *dharma*. The Buddha then preached a sermon to Bimbisara, who expressed his desire to be a lay disciple and donated a dwelling to the Buddha in his own pleasure park, a bamboo grove not far from Rajagriha.

While at the bamboo grove, the Buddha met the two men who became his closest disciples, Sariputra and Maudgalyayana. His fame was obviously growing at the time for one day Sariputra, who was a *sramana* affiliated with a Brahmin teacher called Sanjaya, met one of the Buddha's disciples in Rajagriha and asked him about his teacher. The disciple told him that the *sramana* Gautama of the Shakya clan taught a doctrine which, though difficult, could be put in verse:

> All things arise from a cause
> He who has realized the truth has explained the cause
> And also how they cease to be
> This is what the great *sramana* has taught

Much taken by this description, Sariputra returned to his companion Maudgalyayana and repeated the verse before him. They then went together to the bamboo grove and asked the Buddha to accept them as *bhikshus*. Other followers of Sanjaya followed them in joining the Buddha, inciting rumours around Rajagriha that the Buddha, who had already poached the followers of Sanjaya, had come to take away the sons of the city's citizens. The Buddha told his disciples to ignore the accusations, which he said would last for all of seven days and disappear. He now had more than a thousand *bhikshus* in the *sangha*.

The Buddhist texts are not very forthcoming with biographical or physical detail. They describe the Buddha as very tall and handsome; his voice as cultivated and his language as elegant and clear and full of imagery and metaphor. The texts are more or less silent about the Buddha after his enlightenment and his early successes with converts. One has to infer from the stories and discourses how the Buddha passed more than forty years of his life.

A broad picture emerges from them: of the famous and charismatic figure in yellow-brown robes walking barefoot across the Indo-Gangetic plains with a small entourage of *bhikshus*, the man who is courted by kings and frequently approached for instruction and clarification, who is requested to provide relief from famines and personal distress, and even coerced into opening an order for Buddhist nuns.

He acquired three of his most important lay followers during these years: Jivaka, a physician, Anathapindika, a banker and gold-dealer, and Ananda. Jivaka became a doctor on call for the *sangha*. Anathapindika bought and donated to the *sangha* a park near Shravasti, the capital of Kosala, where the Buddha spent many of the monsoons of his mid-life. Ananda became his personal assistant, bringing him water, washing his alms-bowl, screening visitors and keeping him in touch with the *sangha*.

There are stories of the miracles he performed during these years. Most famously, he converted a highway robber called Angulimala (literally, Finger-Necklace), who operated in the Kosala region and wore a necklace made of the knuckles of the people he had robbed and murdered.[2] Prasenajit, the king of Kosala, whose police had been hunting Angulimala, came to see the reformed criminal in his new robes. But the citizens of Kosala were less tolerant. They stoned Angulimala as he walked around Shravasti looking for alms. When, bleeding, he appeared before the Buddha, he was told to endure his pain for he was experiencing here and now the ripening of his evil deeds for which he otherwise would have had to endure hellish pains for a long time.

Once, when the Buddha was in Rajagriha, a messenger came from Vaishali, the capital of a people called the Licchavis, who formed one of the self-governing republics in the Vrijji confederation. He brought news of cholera and death from his town, where drought had led to famine, and he asked Bimbisara to persuade the Buddha to help the Licchavis. The Buddha had praise for the Vrijjis' democratic and consensual style of politics. He travelled to Vaishali, where he was received heartily at a great hall in the city. According to the texts, the rains followed in due course, and the cholera retreated.

On his later visit to Kapilavastu, after the death of his father, the Buddha had been accosted by his stepmother, Mahaprajapati. She said that she wished to join her stepson and step-grandson in renouncing the world. The Buddha had replied evasively and discouraged her. Mahaprajapati went away in tears, but persisted nevertheless. She cut off her hair and wore the yellow robes of a monk. Accompanied by a few women from the Shakya clan, she followed the Buddha on his tours. She arrived in Vaishali while the Buddha was there, being feted by its grateful citizens. Outside the hall where the Buddha was staying, his assistant, Ananda, noticed her, covered in dust and with swollen feet.

Tearfully, she told Ananda of her wish to persuade the Buddha to let women join a *sangha*. Ananda took her case to the Buddha. But the Buddha was adamant. Ananda began to argue with him. He asked the Buddha if women who went into homelessness and followed his teachings would be able to attain enlightenment. When the Buddha said yes, Ananda wondered why in that case he wouldn't ordain a woman who had been his guardian and nurse after his own mother died very early in his childhood.

The Buddha relented, but only after suggesting eight severe conditions to Mahaprajapati. She accepted them. They effectively subordinated the nuns, or *bhikshunis*, to the *bhikshus*. He was still full of regret when he told Ananda that his teachings, which he expected to last a thousand years, were now, after the admission of women into the *sangha*, going to last for only five hundred years.

The Buddha was understandably anxious about admitting women into a celibate order of men. But his decision was a radical step for its time, for there was no comparable place for women in the religious and spiritual traditions of the Brahmins, or other *sramanas*.[3] The Buddha did not consider gender a factor in attaining enlightenment. In a collection of poems by early Buddhist nuns, a *bhikshuni* is quoted as saying, 'What does womanhood matter at all when the mind is concentrated, when knowledge flows on steadily as one sees correctly the *dharma*? One to whom it might occur, "I am a woman" or "I am a man" or "I am anything at all" – is fit for Mara to address.'[4] In other texts, the Buddha is quoted as criticizing the prejudices that con-

sider a woman to be successful if she performs her household duties well.

Nevertheless, women remained subordinate to men in
Buddhist monastic institutions. It was the movement of
Tantric Buddhism, emerging in India around the seventh
century, which overturned many of the old patriarchal rules
of monastic orders. Respect for women became one of
the prerequisites of enlightenment. All dualism had to be
rejected in this later tradition of Mahayana Buddhism. This
meant giving up attachment to gender distinctions. The
most important goddess, Prajnaparamita, was the embodiment of wisdom. Tantrics revered *yoginis*, goddesses
uniquely equipped to cut through attachments and take
practitioners to *prajna* (wisdom). Sujata, the woman who
had given the Buddha his last meal before enlightenment,
came to be honoured in the Mahayana tradition.

His scepticism about *bhikshunis* did not stop the Buddha
from befriending women. One of his closest personal relationships seems to have been with a rich laywoman called
Vishakhā, who lived in Shravasti with her husband and
many children. She was a prominent benefactor of the
sangha, to which she gave clothes, food and medicines. She
also established a monastery outside Shravasti.

On one occasion, the Buddha was denounced as an idler
by a rich Brahmin farmer he had approached for alms. He
replied that far from being an idler he was working harder
and more profitably than the farmer. He said, 'Faith is the
seed, penance the rain, understanding my yoke and plough,
modesty the pole of the plough, mind the tie, thoughtful-
ness my ploughshare and goad . . . exertion my beast of

burden.'⁵ It was through such strenuousness that one achieved the 'fruit of salvation'.

The texts are full of such exchanges. They speak of a self-confidence bordering on arrogance. But then the Buddha did not ever seem to have ever pretended to humility. He had the brusqueness of a busy doctor. He seems to have been convinced that he not only spoke the truth but also that what he said could be objectively verified. It may be why he avoided contact with other *sramanas* and teachers, and avoided getting into metaphysical speculation. He spoke more than once of the 'jungle of opinions'; he plainly thought himself well above it.

His aristocratic equanimity cracked only when he thought that the *bhikshus* had misunderstood him. He was quick to admonish a *bhikshu* in his group who thought that consciousness survived the body and reappeared in a new form of life and so was immortal. 'From whom have you heard, you foolish man,' he exclaimed, 'that I have explained the *dharma* in that way? Foolish man, have I not in many ways declared that consciousness is dependently arisen . . .'

He also seems to have lost his temper with Devadutta, one of the relatives he had accepted into the *sangha* on his first visit to Kapilavastu after his enlightenment. When Devadutta attempted to seize control of the *sangha*, the Buddha denounced him as a lost soul. Apparently, Devadutta then went on to befriend Bimbisara's son, Ajatashatru, and conspired with him to assassinate the Buddha. However, the men he sent out to kill the Buddha ended up in the *sangha*. A desperate Devadutta tried to crush the Buddha under a large boulder and let loose a wild elephant on his former mentor. He then tried to split the *sangha* by proposing tougher rules for the *bhikshus*. None of these attempts succeeded and Devadutta is said to have committed suicide.

On the whole the Buddha took abuse calmly – and much of it came his way, mainly from jealous competitors and people who felt he was seducing people away from their everyday duties. On one occasion, a Brahmin whose relative he had converted accused him of being, among other things, a 'thief, crackpot, camel and donkey'. The Buddha let the Brahmin rage for a while, and then abruptly asked him whether he ever had people over for dinner. When the Brahmin said yes, the Buddha asked him what he did with the leftover food. The Brahmin said that he kept it for himself. 'It is just the same with abuse,' the Buddha said. 'I don't accept it, and it returns to you.' He later told the *bhikshus* that he felt no resentment, distress or dissatisfaction when others reviled or abused him, and he also felt no joy or elation when others revered and honoured him.

He did not encourage people to revere him. He did not indulge the old Indian desire to see holy men or their images, the desire for *darshan* (sight), which even now forces Hindus into arduous journeys for the sake of a fleeting view of an idol or guru. He asked a sick *bhikshu* who had fervently wanted to see him, 'What use is the sight of this vulnerable body?' and told him that whoever understood his teaching also saw him at the same time.

Accustomed to solitude in his childhood and youth, he probably always found it a bit hard to train the *bhikshus* and give discourses to laymen. He confessed that he liked to wander alone 'like the rhinoceros', and there seem to have occurred long periods when he withdrew from public life.

A Spiritual Politics

THE BUDDHA SPENT EVERY monsoon for more than twenty years in the parks donated by Anathapindika and Vishakha near Kosala's capital, Shravasti, and gave many discourses there. He also spent several monsoons in the Magadhan capital Rajagriha and in Vaishali. For the rest of the year, he travelled. Since Kosala and Magadha covered most of North India between them, he and the *bhikshus* had free run of a very large territory.

The conversion of the king of Magadha, Bimbisara, now appears a crucial event in the history of Buddhism. Freethinkers like the Buddha and people of the *sramana* movement could expect a responsive audience in the smaller states. The Buddha had probably got too used to the atmosphere of rational discussion and tolerance that prevailed in the small self-governing republics on the margins of the Indo-Gangetic plain, such as the one he had belonged to. But for anyone hoping to preach his message and gain a greater following, the large kingdoms posed new challenges and uncertainties.

Benares wasn't the only unfriendly place in the heart of the plains, where the Brahmin orthodoxy was still dominant, and which derived much of its power from royal patronage. As the rumours against him proved, there was also some opposition to the Buddha in Rajagriha, even after Bimbisara became his lay disciple. In these circumstances, the Buddha did well to secure influence over the ruler of Magadha, which was one of the two biggest and most efficient kingdoms in North India. In many ways, this was a bigger achievement for the Buddha than the conversion of the Kashyapa brothers, who had followed the sacrifice-based religion of the Aryan settlers of India.

The Buddha seems to have known that the *bhikshus* could not move around and expect to survive on the kindness and generosity of alms-givers without a minimum of political support. Later, he also became a friend and advisor to Bimbisara's rival, Prasenajit, the philosophically minded king of Kosala.

Prasenajit, who had been educated at the university of Taxila, was the same age as the Buddha. On first meeting the Buddha, he challenged him, saying that he could not believe anyone so young could be an enlightened being. The Buddha told him that there were four things that should not be despised because they are young: a warrior, a snake, fire and a monk.

Though Prasenajit became a friend and lay follower of the Buddha, he did not give up his practice of blood sacrifices. He was fond of rich food; he had four wives, including one from the Buddha's former clan, the Shakyas. But he donated generously to the *sangha*, and sought the Buddha's advice on personal, political and philosophical matters. He was also capable of taking, it seems, a bit of ribbing about his girth. Once when he came to see the Buddha he was panting hard. The Buddha said,

> A man who always lives with care,
> And shows restraint while taking food,
> His sensuality's reduced,
> He grows old slowly, keeps his strength.[1]

Prasenajit immediately asked his attendant to remind him of this verse at every mealtime.

Although the Buddha's concern for the welfare of the *sangha* made him support the leading monarchies of his time, he seems to have preferred another model of political organization: the small tribal republics or oligarchies, such as the one he had belonged to in Kapilavastu, or that of the Licchavis, whom he had helped, which knew nothing or little of personal or autocratic rule, and where decisions affecting the community were made through collective deliberation.

By the time the Buddha died, these republics had grown fragile and were confronted with big and hungry kingdoms like Kosala and Magadha on their borders. Towards the end of the Buddha's life, Bimbisara's aggressive son, Ajatashatru, threatened to overrun an important confederation of republics called the Vrijjis. On his last journey across North India, the Buddha was in Rajagriha when an emissary of Ajatashatru came to see him. This Brahmin minister told him of Ajatashatru's plans for conquering and annexing the Vrijjis. It was then that the Buddha listed the seven principles he thought necessary for the well-being of the Vrijjis.

The Buddha probably sensed the fate of the Vrijjis. But he still tried to prescribe the rules that he thought the

Vrijjis needed to follow in order to maintain their independence:

1) Hold regular and frequent assemblies.
2) Meet in harmony, break up in harmony, and carry out business in harmony.
3) Do not authorize what has not been authorized, but proceed according to what has been authorized by their ancient tradition.
4) Honour, respect, revere and salute the elders among them, and consider them worth listening to.
5) Do not forcibly abduct others' wives and daughters and compel them to live with them.
6) Honour, respect, revere and salute the Vrijjian shrines at home and abroad, not withdrawing the proper support made and given before.
7) Make proper provision for the safety of the *arhats*, so that such *arhats* may come in future to live there, and those already there may dwell in comfort.[2]

It seems from the list that the Vrijjis formed a small community with a low level of technology and a relatively simple government that allowed direct participation of ordinary citizens in the management of public affairs. It is clear that the Buddha was concerned to ensure the welfare of women, elderly men and *sramanas*. His emphasis on following custom and tradition marks him, in this instance at least, as a conservative. But the priority he gave to regular assemblies reveals his belief in politics as a necessary activity undertaken by human beings, not purely as means to an end but as a participatory process of deliberation and decision-making.

He used more or less the same prescriptions as the basis for the Buddhist *sangha*. As a member of the ruling class in his home state, he had some experience of political and legal matters. He put it to good use in formulating rules for the *sangha*. His model for the internal structure of the *sangha* was the small republic in which communal deliberation and face-to-face negotiation were possible. A full assembly of monks took important decisions, reaching them by debate and consensus rather than vote. Any monk or novice was entitled to express his view of the matter under discussion. The debate went on until agreement was reached.

The Buddha was confident that 'as long as the monks hold frequent and full assemblies the *sangha* will prosper, and not decline'. He did not think of himself as leading the *sangha*. Nor did he encourage any of his disciples to assume the burden after his death. He saw consensus as of the utmost importance to the life of the *sangha*. The Buddha also stressed the need for each local *sangha* to remain united. He allowed for differences of opinion, but he did not wish them to undermine the structural unity of a *sangha* and vitiate the experience of everyday life. Controversy, whenever it arose, could be settled by the method of the dissenting individuals removing themselves and forming a new group.

This distinguished the *sangha* from democracy, in which majority opinion is binding on everyone, and minority opinions are subordinated to the efficient functioning of the polity. The Buddha's early effort to accommodate dissent, and acknowledge the plurality of human discourse and practice, later saved Buddhism from the sectarian wars that characterize the history of Christianity and Islam; and the Buddha's emphasis on practice rather than theory kept his teachings relatively free of the taint of dogma and fundamentalism. The Mahayana and Theravada movements are separated by a difference in emphasis: the former stresses compassion for others over personal liberation. They have never experienced the violent conflicts that have marked relations between Catholics and Protestants and between Shia and Sunni Muslims.

The Buddha encouraged individual *bhikshus* to become exemplars for the society of laymen; he may even have wished the organization of the *sangha* to become a model of a higher politics and morality. With its rules and its respect for consensus and tradition, the *sangha* does seem a prototype for the close-knit political organization – something that could conceivably serve as an alternative to the unmanageably large states in which two new human categories were coming into being: the rulers and the ruled.

But the Buddha knew that the monarchies could not be wished away, and that the *sangha* was far from becoming the whole of human society. This made him pragmatic rather than a revolutionary. He concerned himself with maintaining the conditions in which his teaching could take root and influence more and more people. And so he befriended the powerful monarchs of the day. He also reached out to the common man, with teaching modulated to appeal to him.

The picture of the common man that emerges from Buddhist texts is not a flattering one. He is a slave of his senses and addicted to pleasure; he craves and welcomes fame and praise, but resents obscurity and blame. He is greedy and lustful, easily provoked to morally unwholesome deeds. Pain overwhelms and bewilders him; he dislikes the sight of disease, old age and death. Old age crushes him, and his death is a sorry affair. All this happens because he fails to see things as they really are.

Not surprisingly, the Buddha reserved the most complex parts of his teaching for individuals who expressed a very strong urge to cease being common men. At the same time, he was sanguine about the common man's abilities to transcend his lot and to achieve, if not enlightenment, then a decent rebirth. He gave lessons in morality to lay people. There were the usual rules: do not take life, steal, be unchaste, lie or take intoxicants. In a comprehensive homily called *Sigala*, he prescribed six sets of reciprocal duties between parents and children, pupils and teachers, husbands and wives, friends and companions, masters and servants, and householders and members of the *sangha*.[3]

Good behaviour was ensured by attentiveness, by a constant awareness of what one did and thought. Virtue lay in acting in a way that helped not only oneself but others. The Buddha deemed generosity and compassion essential for the layman, particularly in respect to the *bhikshus*. Giving alms to the *bhikshus* put one in a charitable frame of mind, but it also helped the *bhikshus* appease their hunger. On the whole, to be kind and gentle and honest to others was not only to cultivate moral wholeness but also to encourage the cultivation of similar attitudes in others.

For *bhikshus* a mind so cleansed of negative attitudes was an essential prerequisite for meditation. But for the lay people it was an end in itself, much as it was for the

Stoics, for whom there was no higher form of spirituality than an active self-awareness. In the unexamined life that the common man lived, the Buddha introduced not the hard-to-achieve goal of *nirvana*, but the task of achieving self-knowledge through spiritual vigilance. As Marcus Aurelius put it:

> Everywhere and at all times, it is up to you to rejoice piously at what is occurring at *the present moment*, to conduct yourself with justice towards the people who are *present here and now*.[4]

Although the Buddha believed in what the Greeks called the 'unwisdom of the multitude', he looked for ways to mitigate it through the *bhikshus*. The *bhikshu* had liberated himself from the greed, folly, conceit and ignorance of the ordinary mass of people. He now discharged his responsibility towards the mass of society that fed him by restraining the common man from evil action, directing him towards honourable ends, sharing his knowledge, dealing with his difficulties and doubts, and showing him the way to heaven. Higher insight involved the *bhikshu* deeper in the life of society rather than placing him above it as ruler or recluse. This Buddhist notion was realized, if fitfully, in Sri Lanka, Thailand and Burma, where the Theravada tradition dominated, and where the *sangha* had much influence over the monarch and the state.[5] In Tibet, where a quarter of the male population had become monks, a monastic order effectively ruled the country from the seventeenth century through the office of the Dalai Lama.

Although the Buddha did not talk directly about politics, or offer the kind of theories of democracy and citizenship that Plato and Aristotle are known for, he followed closely the political events of his time, and drew several implications from them. For the Buddha as much as for Plato, life in society was the inescapable obligation faced by human beings. There was no private salvation waiting for them. In fact, as the Buddha defined it, liberation for a human being consists of entering a non-egotistical state, where he felt the conditional and interdependent nature of all beings.

But the Buddha did not distinguish between contemplation and action in the way Plato did, creating a hierarchical difference between the wise rulers who think and their ignorant subjects who act without thinking. In his view, contemplation and speech and action were inseparable links in the same mental and physical process; they could not be isolated or set above each other, or distributed among different groups of individuals. What mattered in all aspects of human existence – political, economic, social – were awareness and moral skilfulness. The ruler was no more immune to the law of *karma* than the ruled.

As Plato found out during his lone foray into politics in Sicily, the philosopher as king was more attractive in theory than in practice.[6] Disillusioned with his own utopia, he then wrote the *Laws*, in which he explained meticulously the intent and purpose of laws necessary for a stable political realm.

Unlike Plato in Syracuse and Athens, the Buddha seems neither to have given much political advice to the major rulers of his time, the kings of Kosala and Magadha, nor to have criticized the political systems they presided over. But his lack of theoretical passion came from a wider and deeper political experience. In his travels across North India, he seems to have known more political forms – republics, monarchies, and then, just before his death, empire – than Plato, who was familiar only with the polis.

He preferred to address the question of what constitutes the ruler's right to rule. He is unlikely to have assumed that the philosopher earned this right through some exclusive and permanent access to forms of truth, beauty and justice. What made the exercise of power legitimate for him did not exist in some transcendent realm or in nature. The ideal ruler was a *chakravarti*, the political equivalent of the Buddha, who ruled in accordance with the morality of *dharma*, with the norms of compassionate justice, and whose realm was free of oppression and hospitable to all classes of society, townsmen as well as villagers, religious teachers as well as birds and beasts. As the many stories in the *Jatakas* about the ideal king and government attest, righteousness served as the only proper basis for the ruler's authority.

In this the Buddhists differed sharply from the Indian theorists who claimed divine sanction for kingship. The Buddhists saw the king as originally a human being like any other, who had been exalted by other human beings and his own actions, and who had more duties than rights. It was essential for him to possess generosity, honesty and integrity, gentleness, self-control, forbearance. And personal righteousness wasn't enough. *Dharma*, or Buddhist principles of compassion, had to be applied to the state administration. A later Buddhist text called the *Mahavastu* gave more detailed advice to kings. It told them among other things to admit large bodies of immigrants, to cultivate friendship with neighbouring kings, and to favour the poor and protect the rich.

The philosopher Nagarjuna advised a Satavahana king to support doctors, set up hostels and rest-houses, eliminate high taxes, care for the victims of natural disasters and keep profits level in times of scarcity.[7] A Buddhist text called the *Kutudanta Sutra* even outlined a social and economic ethic for the *chakravarti*.[8] In it the Buddha narrates the story of a rich and powerful king who wanted to offer sacrifice to secure his kingdom and was told by his Brahmin advisor, apparently the Buddha in a past life, that thieves and brigands were undermining the kingdom, and that neither sacrifice, nor executions and imprisonments, would solve the problem. The advisor told the king that he could best ensure his power and the prosperity of his kingdom by giving subsidies of food and seed-corn to farmers, making available investment capital to merchants and tradesmen, and paying adequate wages and food to people in government services.

Given their times, the early Buddhists seem to have proposed radical programmes for a welfare state. There were kings, such as Ashoka, who attempted to realize them, at least partly. But even the Buddha might have sensed towards the end of his life that they were too utopian. The economic revolution of North India had made the elites of large kingdoms greedy for territory. Wars of expansion seem to have become more common than welfare programmes by the time of the Buddha's death.

Roughly seven years before the Buddha's death, Bimbisara, the king of Magadha, was deposed and murdered by his own son, Ajatashatru. Ajatashatru was wary of the

Buddha, whom he had met only once or twice. His ambitions were for empire. Kosala was floundering under the inefficient Prasenajit. The smaller states or chiefdoms, such as those Buddha had come from, looked more and more vulnerable. Ajatashatru moved fast after usurping the throne of Magadha. He attacked Kosala and humiliated Prasenajit in battle. He then began to plan his moves against the Vrijjis.

The Buddha was aware of these events. Although Prasenajit was his follower, he spoke neutrally of his defeat by Ajatashatru. He warned of the vengefulness that humiliation creates: 'Victory breeds hatred; the defeated live in pain. Happily the peaceful live, giving up victory and defeat.'[9]

Prasenajit didn't give up. He fought and won a second battle with Ajatashatru and confiscated his weapons and army. The Buddha was once again cautious. His comment was:

> To the slayer comes a slayer
> To the conqueror comes a conqueror
> To the abuser comes abuse
> Thus by the evolution of *karma*
> He who plunders is plundered in turn.[10]

This was proved when Ajatashatru struck again. This time he defeated Prasenajit comprehensively and overran Kosala. Prasenajit was deposed by his own son Vidudhaba.

The more successful Ajatashatru was, the weaker grew his moral inhibitions. While meeting the Buddha, Ajatashatru reported to him what a *sramana* called Purana Kassapa from the Ajivika sect had said to him:

Your majesty, by the doer or instigator of a thing, by him who mutilates, burns, causes grief and weariness, agitates, takes life and robs . . . no evil is done. Even if with a razor-sharp discus he were to make the beings of this whole earth one single mass and heap of flesh, there would be no evil as a result of that . . .

That a king should echo this advice, hoping for philosophical legitimacy for his realpolitik, suggests that such views had some currency at the time. The Buddha was much agitated by the Ajivika denial of *karma*. He denounced Makkhali Gosala, the leader of the Ajivikas, as a 'madman' who had brought 'harm, damage and misfortune' to many people.

For the Buddha, any kind of aggression, whether justified or not, always led to more violence. He was immune to the cult of the warrior. Once asked by a professional soldier whether a soldier goes to a special heaven after falling in battle, he remained silent at first and then, when pressed again, replied that the soldier was reborn in hell or as an animal.

He specifically warned merchants against the arms trade. Centuries would pass before the making of arms became a powerful industry in Europe, and helped turn the First World War itself into an industrial process, calling for the total mobilization of a country's population and resources. The Buddha's own experience of war was limited to what he saw in North India. But he could see signs of danger in the large states: how the kingdoms emerging out of tribal republics had already concentrated power in the hands of a few remote rulers and deprived their subjects of control over their lives.

Empires and Nations

Soon after the Buddha's death, Ajatashatru defeated the republic of Vrijjis and sacked their capital, Vaishali. Not much is known about Ajatashatru after the Buddha's death. His successors are even more obscure. But when Magadha re-enters history in the third century BC, through the record of a Greek ambassador called Megesthenes, it is the supreme power in North India. Its capital is the fabulous city of Pataliputra, which was founded by Ajatashatru just south of the old Magadha capital, Rajagriha. It controls most of the territory around the Ganges with its fertile lands and river ports. The smaller states have vanished, or have been reduced to subjection.

Such empires were coming into fashion, at the cost of smaller states and tribal republics, around the Buddha's time. Magadha was the first such Indian empire. In Persia, just sixteen years before Bimbisara's accession, the man who would later be known as Cyrus the Great had come to power. He had quickly suppressed Greek cities on the Aegean Sea, conquered Babylon, the greatest city of the ancient world, and then turned his attention to Central Asia. The Achaemenian empire he founded was the greatest there had ever been. Cyrus had many admirers even among the enemies of the Persians, including the Greeks. Herodotus wrote glowingly of him. Xenophon, a disciple of Socrates and a severe critic of Athenian democracy, presented Cyrus in his *Cyropaedia* as the ideal ruler, powerful, tolerant, generous, one the Greeks ought to emulate.[1]

Ajatashatru is very likely to have heard of the rising empire to the near west. But if he emulated Cyrus the Great, it was not by being tolerant and generous. Nor were the lessons of Cyrus fully learned by the Macedonian prince, who followed self-consciously in his footsteps and whose exploits earned him the title 'Great'.

Alexander the Great was the first famous western figure to whom I was introduced at school. The history books often referred to him by his Persian name, Secunder, and said that he had conquered much of the known world in just twelve years. In 326 BC, he had come as far as the Punjab, looking as if to invade the Magadha empire, and fought one of his greatest battles against an Indian ruler called Porus. He had established Greek colonies and founded new cities in north-west India.

No cultural monuments marked the first known contact between Greece and India, although in Macedonia, Alexander's tutor had been Aristotle himself, and some Greek philosophers, apparently including Pyrrho, even accompanied him to India. The Greeks were very struck by the ways of the people they called the *gymnosophists* (naked men of knowledge) – probably the *sramanas*, the homeless wanderers with which India became identified in the West. These Indians lived the kind of life the Hellenistic philosophers themselves recommended: they were immune to ordinary desires and ambitions, and indifferent to conventions or other people's opinion of them. Pyrrho apparently chose to live a life in seclusion because he heard an Indian confess that he had become incapable of teaching after frequenting royal courts.

Much later I came upon another story about Alexander's Indian adventure.[2] According to the Greek historian Plutarch, who presented Alexander as a philosophical conqueror bringing civilization to lesser breeds, Greek soldiers captured ten *gymnosophists* and brought them before Alexander. He asked each of the ascetics a question and said he would execute them if they answered incorrectly.

The ascetics were brave. When Alexander asked one of them what a man should do to be exceedingly beloved, he was told that he must be very powerful without making himself too much feared.

Obviously impressed by such plain talking, Alexander sent one of his court philosophers to the oldest and most famous of the ascetics, Dandamis, introduced himself as the son of Zeus, and invited him to become a camp follower, like the historians and philosophers he had brought from the West.

Dandamis replied that he was as much a son of Zeus as Alexander, and that he was content with 'those leaves which are my house, these blooming plants which supply me with dainty food, and the water which is my drink'. In the same spirit of renunciation, he also asked the Greek messengers why Alexander had undertaken so long a journey.

Alexander's answer is not known. Later historians such as Plutarch would point proudly to the long-term consequences of his conquests. The Greeks had largely been people of the Mediterranean. Alexander opened them up to the wider world, beyond Persia and Egypt. Like Napoleon, he set out on his conquests with surveyors, engineers, architects and chroniclers, seeking to memorialize himself in every way possible. The Greek colonies he founded stretched from the Mediterranean to Central Asia, encouraged trade and cultural interchange, and formed a global civilization that provided the basis for the Roman and Byzantine empires. The Egyptian city of Alexandria, founded by Alexander, became the intellectual capital of early Christianity. In the third century BC, Megesthenes compiled the first partly realistic European account of what had been a setting of fable and myth. The Greek colonies in north-west India brought Greco-Roman art to India and laid the grounds for the Buddhist visual art known as Gandhara, of which the towering statues of the Buddha that the Taliban government of Afghanistan destroyed in 2001 were a late example.

Plutarch presented Alexander as a cosmopolitan creator of a great civilization, the benefactor and civilizer of the brutish peoples he conquered. Successive historians modified Plutarch's idealized image of Alexander, and celebrated his success in terms borrowed from the vocabulary of military strategy and realpolitik. Yet to look at Alexander's life and personality is to wonder about the human costs of conquest; also, about his exalted place in history, and the moral prejudices of historians.

When in 335 BC, the first year of Alexander's reign, the Greek state of Thebes rebelled against him, he razed the city, killed six thousand people and sold the survivors into slavery. Such arrogance and brutality became routine with him as he set off eastwards in 334 BC. At Persepolis he looted and burnt the grand palace of Xerxes, who in the previous century had launched a massive invasion of Greece. Then, after defeating Darius, he began to fantasize about a ruling class consisting of Persians and Macedonians; he and his officers later married eighty Persian women in an effort to breed this master race. Suspicious of Parmenio, his powerful second-in-command, he executed him, then killed his retainers.[3]

Success made him worse. As he got closer to India, he killed one of his closest commanders with his own hands during a drunken quarrel. He adopted Persian royal dress and demanded that everyone coming into his presence perform the elaborate obeisance of Persian courts. When Callisthenes, a historian and a nephew of Aristotle, refused to abase himself, Alexander had him imprisoned, and probably murdered.

From India, he returned with his exhausted army to the West, and continued his policy of arbitrary executions and massacres. In Persia, he dressed as Dionysus and participated in a week-long drunken revel. Always keen on gods, he demanded recognition of his divine status from his Greek subordinates, who obliged reluctantly and ironically: 'Since Alexander wishes to be a god,' the decree in Sparta read, 'let him be a god.' Confirmation of divinity did not bring any relaxation in his savage wars. In 323, he was in Babylon, where after a bout of drinking he fell ill and died ten days later, at the young age of thirty-three.

This was the man, marked by a progressive mental deterioration, whom some Indian ascetics, probably Buddhists, met and admonished. According to the historian

Arrian who reported the encounter, the ascetics beat their feet on the ground as Alexander passed them. When asked about the gesture, they said that Alexander occupied, despite his conquests, no more ground than that covered by the soles of his two feet. Like everyone else, he, too, was mortal, 'except that you are ambitious and reckless, traversing such a vast span of land, so remote from your home, enduring troubles and inflicting them upon others'.⁴

Alexander wasn't without admirers in the India of his time, although no record of him survives in Indian texts. Plutarch mentions a young Indian named Sandrocottus who offered his help to Alexander in defeating the then ruler of the Magadha empire. This was Chandragupta Maurya, apparently a young man of humble origins, who early in his life had set his sights on the Magadha empire. Soon after Alexander returned to the West, Chandragupta overthrew the ruler of Magadha and annexed part of Central India. He then advanced against the Greek general Seleucus Nicator who after Alexander's death was trying to recover the Indian part of his empire. Chandragupta defeated Seleucus in battle, imposed a treaty of peace on him and ended the Greek challenge in the north-west. His already considerable empire stretched further to include parts of what is now Pakistan and Afghanistan.

Like Alexander, Chandragupta won his empire through military strength and skill. Maintaining it, however, through sheer force was much harder, as Alexander would have found out had he lived longer. The bigger the empire, the greater its cultural and economic diversity, and the more restive the small political communities it had suppressed. Chandragupta, who was advised by a shrewd

Brahmin called Kautilya, wished, no less than Alexander, to hold absolute and centralized power while sitting in his capital, Pataliputra.

To achieve this, he maintained a large army and built up a ruthlessly efficient bureaucracy and network of spies. It is not clear how far he succeeded with what later became the conventional means of statecraft. Perhaps, not very far. Megesthenes, the Greek ambassador to his court, reported that although Pataliputra was a fine city, and Chandragupta lived in a luxurious palace, he was shadowed constantly by fear of assassination. Peace still eluded his empire by the time his grandson, Ashoka, took over about 269 BC.

It was Ashoka who, while grappling with his imperial inheritance, offered a radical new vision of both conquest and empire: he made the first large-scale attempt to apply Buddha's ideas to statecraft, and to implement the Buddhist ideal of the *chakravarti*.

Ashoka's initiation into politics came at a time of crisis. He was sent by his father to put down a revolt in the northwestern city of Taxila, now in Pakistan, which, conquered by Alexander, had briefly become a Greek colony before being annexed by the Magadha empire. Ashoka seems to have been lenient with the people who were protesting against the oppressive officials of the Magadha empire. He was sent next to the city of Ujjain in central India. This experience as viceroy or pro-consul must have helped him when his father died and he took over as emperor.

But empire demanded fresh resources, and generated new enemies, which meant more conquests and suppressions. Following this imperative, in the ninth year of his reign, Ashoka attacked the state of Kalinga, now Orissa on the eastern coast of India, possibly looking for a sea route for trade. According to the thirteenth Major Rock edict, the most famous of Ashoka's edicts, which he had engraved on pillars and rock faces all across India, 150,000 people were deported, 100,000 were killed and many times that number died in the successful battles for Kalinga.

It was during the conquest of Kalinga that Ashoka confronted for the first time the human devastation of war: how brutally it disrupts social and individual relations built carefully over decades and centuries, and the customs and traditions which give dignity and meaning to human existence even during times of adversity, without which man lapses into barbarism.

The thirteenth edict declared:

> When an independent country is conquered . . . those who dwell there, whether Brahmans, *sramanas*, or those of other sects, or householders who show obedience to their superiors, obedience to mother and father, obedience to their teachers and behave well and devotedly towards their friends, acquaintances, colleagues, relatives, slaves, and servants – all suffer violence, murder and separation from their loved ones. Even those who are fortunate to have escaped and whose love is undiminished suffer from the misfortunes of their friends, acquaintances, colleagues and relatives.[5]

Such concern for the fate of ordinary lives caught up in war was rare in India. The epic *Mahabharata* records a violence that is chillingly impersonal: the deaths of hundreds of thousands of nameless people, all of whom were deemed expendable by men pursuing power. But Ashoka could see how war brings about the 'participation of all men in suffering'. His contrition, as expressed in the edicts, was profound:

> Today, if a hundredth or a thousandth part of those who suffered in Kalinga were to be killed, to die, or to be taken captive, it would be very grievous to (Ashoka) . . . (who) desires safety, self-control, justice, and happiness for all beings . . . (and) considers that the greatest of all victories is the victory of *Dharma*.

Accordingly, Ashoka made imperative the practice of honesty, truthfulness, compassion, mercifulness and non-violence in his administration. He claimed to set 'no store by fame or glory'. As the first pillar edict put it, 'this world and the other are hard to gain without great love of righteousness, great self-examination, great obedience, and great circumspection, great effort'.

Wishing to rule by righteousness alone, he declared himself available to his subjects:

> At all times, whether I am eating, or am in the women's apartments, or in my inner apartments, or at the cattle-shed, or in my carriage, or in my gardens – wherever I may be, my informants should keep me in touch with public business . . . must promote the welfare of the whole world, and hard work and dispatch of business are the means of doing so.[6]

He relaxed the severe rules that his grandfather, the empire-building Chandragupta, had introduced. In his edicts, he declared his regard for slaves and servants and his respect for teachers. He advocated concord and courteous dialogue between religions and communities. He planted trees, dug wells and constructed rest-houses for travellers. He told his officials to attend closely to the sufferings and joys of his subjects, particularly the poor.

However, contrary to what Buddhist texts claim, Ashoka did not convert immediately to Buddhism after the conquest of Kalinga. Nor did he renounce empire and become a monk. Buddhism, which was still one of many religious and philosophical sects in India, did not even become the official state religion. Ashoka came to the Buddha's teachings gradually, over two and a half years, and then applied them selectively.

His *dharma* had much in common with the virtuous conduct the Buddha preached. But it was mostly Ashoka's own invention, certainly part of his response to the suffering he saw in Kalinga, but also a way of popular liberal governance. He made the state incarnate a higher morality in the hope that it would appeal equally to his multi-religious, multicultural subjects, appease them into peace and brotherhood in this life and hold out the prospect of heaven in the next.

Ashoka also saw *dharma* as the way to a world empire. He apparently sent missionaries to Sri Lanka and Central Asia. According to Sri Lankan legend, his son Mahinda brought the Buddha's ideas to the island around 240 BC and established the first monastery; and his daughter brought a cutting of the Bodhi tree that was planted at the monastery. In one of his edicts Ashoka claimed that *dharma* had conquered the Hellenic kings of Syria, Egypt, Macedonia, Cyrene and Epirus. This was wishful thinking. The successors of Alexander couldn't have been much inclined to listen to the voice of moderation coming from distant India. Ashoka was barely able to persuade his immediate successors, none of whom seem to have followed his example. They sought glory in violent conquest, following the classical Indian texts that exalt war and aggression as the proper business of kings. While Alexander's reputation endured, Ashoka sank into obscurity, and was lost to history until British amateur scholars deciphered his edicts in the nineteenth century.

In any case, Ashoka was only part Buddhist and couldn't have been otherwise while holding down an empire. It is not surprising that Ashoka did not abolish capital punishment, or reduce his army, or federalize his empire. In fact, he instituted a new centralized bureaucracy ('officers of *dharma*') to supervise his Buddhist reforms.

In exhorting both himself and his subjects to moral effort, he was much more pragmatic than the sentimental humanitarians of modern times who believe that democracy and freedom can be imposed upon people individually seething with every kind of desire, discontent and unhappiness. But in trying to apply the Buddha's ideas to such an essentially un-Buddhistic entity as empire, he was at best a noble failure.

Ashoka himself may have been aware of this. 'It is hard to do good,' he admitted. And it was also easy to grow smug in the awareness that one was and did good. He confessed in one of his pillar edicts:

> One only notices one's good deeds, thinking, 'I have done good,' but on the other hand one does not notice one's wicked deeds, thinking, 'I have done evil,' or 'This is indeed a sin.' Now, to be aware of this is something really difficult.[7]

The efforts of Ashoka stand at the beginning of Buddhist

civilization, which flourished for a whole millennium, spreading across Asia and influencing many indigenous cultures. The Bayon temple built in the twelfth century at the centre of the Angkor Thom city complex in Cambodia, the eleventh-century pagoda at the Burmese city of Pagan, the great ninth-century Borobudur *stupa* in Java, Indonesia – these great monuments attest to the appeal and persistence of Buddhist ideals that first travelled from India during Ashoka's reign. The ideas of the Buddha dramatically changed the society and culture of the Tibetans, who were known in the seventh and eighth centuries as particularly ruthless warriors and expansionists. Even today the king of Thailand performs an elaborate ceremony in honour of the famous Emerald Buddha image in Bangkok, which apparently originated in India, with a jewel possessed by Nagasena, the monk and interlocutor of the Greek king Menander.

Ashoka's real successor in India was Kanishka, the ruler of north-west and central India and a devout Buddhist, during whose reign in the first century AD trade with China and Central Asia flourished and the first known Buddhist missionaries left for China through the Karakoram route in Kashmir.

Nagarjuna, the greatest of Buddhist philosophers, seems to have been supported by the Satavahana kings who ruled central and south India in the second century AD. Other Buddhist philosophers, Asanga, Vasubhandhu and Dignaga, whose work travelled through a vast cosmopolitan network of monasteries and universities to China, Korea and Japan, lived under the Gupta dynasty, during whose reign in the early fourth to mid-sixth century the great *stupa* and carvings of Sanchi were completed, and the university at Nalanda in present-day Bihar founded.

The Chinese pilgrim Hiuen Tsang, who visited India in the seventh century and reported on the decline of Buddhism in many of its old centres in north and north-west India, was impressed by the liberal social and political climate maintained by the emperor, Harsha, who honoured both the Buddha and the Shiva, hosted a philosophical conference, built monasteries and *stupas*, and subsidized the university of Nalanda. Even as late as the nineteenth century, there is an example of a Buddhist king attempting to realize the Ashokan ideal of righteousness: King Kirti Sri Rajasinha, who was a devotee of Shiva but revived the Buddhist *sangha* in Sri Lanka and forgave the head of the *sangha* who supported an assassination plot against him.

The policies of many of these Buddhist-influenced rulers acknowledged the plurality of human belief and discourse and the importance of dialogue and non-violence. The lessons of the Buddha have not been so keenly embraced by Buddhists in the modern era. In the 1980s in Sri Lanka, many Buddhist monks supported Sinhalese nationalists in the violent civil war with Tamil Hindu separatists. Most egregiously, Buddhists in Japan in the early twentieth century supported the militarists who led their country into a genocidal imperialist campaign in Asia and then eventually into a disastrous conflict with the United States.

After centuries of isolation, Japan had opened up to foreigners in the mid-nineteenth century and had immediately found itself faced with the rapidly growing empires of the West. The solution of its Meiji rulers was the same as the one that ruling elites in most Asian countries would later reach: they declared the past corrupt and weakening; they stressed the need to modernize institutions and peoples and give them a central purpose. Japan after 1868 moved faster than any other Asian country to catch up with the West by embracing science and technology, strengthening the state and embarking on imperial expansion.

The Meiji rulers of Japan initially denounced Zen Buddhism, which had travelled to Japan from China in the eighth century AD. Buddhism was apparently backward, part of the feudal past that Japan had to outgrow. But then a generation of Buddhist intellectuals sought to deflect such criticism by placing themselves and their Buddhism at the vanguard of growing Japanese power. Many Buddhist monks became ideologues of the new nationalism. They claimed that Zen Buddhism was in complete accordance with *bushido*, the spirit of the warrior. Zen Buddhism became by the twentieth century the mascot of a progressive, rational and politically unified Japan, a sign of its spiritual and cultural superiority over the rest of Asia.

The most important feature of Japan's newly found modernity was an increasingly militarized state, which won stunning victories against first China in 1895 and then Russia in 1905, and then expanded into Manchuria, Taiwan and Korea. Many Buddhist leaders had little trouble endorsing Japanese imperialism. The Zen teacher Shaku Soyen, who had represented Zen Buddhism at the World Parliament of Religions at Chicago in 1893 and who helped introduce Zen to America, was even more nationalistic than his Asian counterparts in Chicago: Vivekananda and Dharampala. He refused to join Tolstoy in condemning the Russo-Japanese war in 1905. In 1906,

speaking before an American audience, he described how
Japanese Buddhists distrusted individuality and how they
proposed to 'sacrifice their lives for a cause' and develop 'a
nobler interpretation of death'.

He sought to defend Japanese aggression against
Manchuria in 1912. He claimed that

> war is not necessarily horrible, provided that it is fought
> for a just and honourable cause... Many material
> human bodies may be destroyed, many human hearts be
> broken, but from a broader point of view these sacrifices
> are so many phoenixes consumed in the sacred fire of
> spirituality, which will arise from the smouldering ashes
> reanimated, ennobled, and glorified.[8]

Four years later, when Rabindranath Tagore, the Indian
poet, visited Japan on a lecture tour, he sensed the spirit of
imitative nationalism that had seized large parts of the
Japanese intelligentsia. Tagore was then in his mid-fifties,
and a much travelled man. His poem *Gitanjali*, though
florid in English translation, had won him the Nobel Prize
in 1913, and brought him the admiration of W. B. Yeats
among many other European artists and intellectuals. With
his long flowing beard and penetrating dark eyes, he was
to many Europeans the embodiment of Indian or eastern
spirituality.

When he set out in 1916 for his lecture tour in Japan
and the United States, two decades after Vivekananda had
mesmerized his audiences, his admirers probably expected
a bit of high-flown abstraction from the beatific sage from
the mysterious East. Tagore spoke instead of the problems
he thought the world faced, particularly the competing

nationalisms of Europe that had exploded into a world war.

Writing in the 1880s, at a time of increasing competition among European nations for colonies, empires and markets, Nietzsche had warned against the mass politics of nationalism, against the 'national scabies of the heart and blood poisoning with which European peoples nowadays delimit and barricade themselves against each other as if with quarantines'.[9] European nations had conducted their rivalries in Asia and Africa, at the expense of weaker peoples, while preparing for war with each other without really expecting it. The long peace that ended in 1914 had been maintained by European statesmen practising realpolitik, the 'pallid hypocrisy administered by mandarins' that Nietzsche had raged against.

It was clear by 1916 that the quick victories each nation expected would not come. Armies had faced each other across trenches for months; there seemed no way to stop the vast machinery of death the European nations had constructed. War itself had turned into a form of mechanized factory work; it had, as the German writer Ernst Jünger, who fought in the war, saw it, the 'precise work rhythm of a turbine fuelled by blood'.[10]

With the help of the latest advances in science and technology, the war killed, wounded and displaced countless millions, inaugurating a new kind of reckoning with human depravity and horror – statistics became the common measure of the suffering caused by the wars (Spain, the Second World War, Korea, Vietnam), massacres (Armenians, Jews, Cambodians) and uprootings (Indians, Germans, Greeks, Russians) that marked the twentieth century.

In Japan, Tagore praised the West for its liberty of conscience, of thought and action. But he also spoke of the 'grave questions that western civilization had presented the world but not completely answered':

> the conflict between the individual and the state, labour and capital, the man and the woman; the conflict between the greed of material gain and the spiritual life of man, the organised selfishness of nations and the higher ideals of humanity; the conflict between all the ugly complexities inseparable from giant organisations of commerce and state and the natural instincts of man crying for simplicity and beauty and fullness of leisure.[11]

In Japan, Tagore spoke to a largely sceptical audience of the dangers inherent in their national mood. He said that Japan's 'social ideals are already showing signs of defeat at the hands of politics'. He mentioned the irony that Europe had not respected Japan until the latter militarized. He spoke of the political civilization that the West had created in which the state is an abstraction and the relations among men are utilitarian. It was 'based on exclusiveness', eager to keep aliens at bay or to exterminate them. He said that 'what is dangerous for Japan is not the imitation of the outer features of the West, but the acceptance of the motive force of western nationalism as her own'.

Tagore feared that the idea of the nation state had acquired existential roots within the culture of Japan. What was originally a concept had turned under the imperatives of greed and conquest into a sacred and exclusive cosmic order. It created homogeneity within and excluded foreignness from without, dividing the world into 'us' and 'them'. It claimed a monopoly on truth and goodness, and attempted to become the sole source of identity, meaning and purpose in human lives – something that men could easily be persuaded to die for.

Speaking in the midst of the war, Tagore knew that the European masses had largely welcomed it at first – perhaps out of relief from the wearying routine of mechanized work that they had been forced into. Ernst Jünger later confessed how, 'having grown up in a period of security, we all felt a desire for the unusual'. 'The war,' he wrote, 'was supposed to offer us, finally, great, strong, solemn things.' People everywhere were swept away by patriotic fervour. As Simone Weil wrote, the 'state, the object of hatred, repugnance, derision, disdain, and fear' demanded absolute loyalty, total self-abnegation, the supreme sacrifice, and obtained them, from 1914 to 1918, to an extent which surpassed all expectations.[12]

In America, to which he travelled from Japan, Tagore claimed with more relief than concern that India 'has never had a real sense of nationalism'. He asserted that 'India shouldn't compete with western civilization in its own field'. He wryly mentioned the Japanese newspaper that had editorialized about Tagore's speeches against Japan's imitation of the West: how they were 'the poetry of a defeated people'.

Subsequent events proved that Tagore was wise in not minding such defeats. The mood of triumph he had sensed was to turn Japan into an efficient military-imperial state through the 1920s and 1930s. In its attempt to counter the influence of Britain and the United States, it invaded and conquered China and after the fall of France moved into Indo-China. Finally, in 1941, it attacked the United States, which four years later ended the most serious challenge to the western dominance of the world by dropping nuclear bombs over the Japanese cities of Hiroshima and Nagasaki.

Tagore, rightly nervous of Japanese nationalism, proved to have been too optimistic about India. The example of Ashoka's humane reign was of mostly rhetorical value in an India striving after independence to be a modern nation state. For much of the time after 1947, the Nehru-Gandhi dynasty presided over a system of administration left behind by British colonials. Impersonal bureaucrats had combined with autocrats into a heavily centralized state that claimed to promote democracy and economic development and set itself up as a supreme arbiter in the lives of its citizens.

The government of free India often responded more ruthlessly to dissent than even the old colonial state. Its violence – usually carried out in the name of democracy and national security – had become most visible in Kashmir, the Muslim-majority Himalayan valley at the northernmost extremity of Ashoka's empire, which had once been the centre of Buddhism in India. It was from here that Indian translators in the centuries after Christ had taken the Buddha's ideas to Central Asia and China.

Islam had come to the valley in the fourteenth century by way of Central Asian and Persian missionaries and, blending well with earlier Hindu and Buddhist cultures, had taken on a uniquely Kashmiri character; it was to become known for the mystics, poets and saints whom both Hindus and Muslims revered. It was part of the gentleness of life in Kashmir – the fragile achievement of a small, self-enclosed community, which had lived without great wars and conflicts, and whose later violation – by Islamic fundamentalists from or trained in Pakistan, and by Indian security forces – was to appear especially brutal.

In the fall of 1987, as a teenager, I had first visited the valley of Kashmir. Growing up in the oppressively warm, dusty, flat and blindingly bright Indian plains, I imagined the bowl-shaped valley of Kashmir as containing all the marvels of the world: soft light, cool air and a gentle landscape of lakes and mountains. And on that first trip to Kashmir, the disappointment I had set myself up for never came.

There was the Kashmiri countryside, where the poplar-lined avenues seemed to run endlessly, past the apple orchards and the rice fields, past the cool streams flowing over smooth pebbles, to some place of great calm and happiness. There was the capital, Srinagar, a medieval city with its densely packed alleys and wooden mosques, the butcher stalls with hanging flesh and the small dark shops where papier mâché toys sat in orderly rows and nimble hands unrolled bright rugs of fine Persian design.

Around the Dal lake were the seventeenth-century terrace gardens created by Mughal emperors, where water ran through elaborately carved pavilions, and where on the peanut-littered grass young Kashmiri men and women met on surreptitious dates, not kissing, touching or even talking much, but simply being happy together.

I didn't take much notice of the Kashmiris except to wonder at their exotically pale skins and long woollen cloaks, and the slight resentment they seemed to harbour towards Indian visitors. I didn't think much about them afterwards. It was as if the shawl and rug sellers, the drivers of taxis and shikaras, the countless touts and the red-cheeked children standing outside huts with rose-laden mud roofs existed merely to sustain my nostalgia for Kashmir.

Years passed before I could wonder at my political innocence. India and Pakistan had fought two wars over Kashmir. Pakistan, which had come into being as a separate homeland for Indian Muslims during the partition of British India in 1947, had always claimed the Muslim-majority valley of Kashmir.

I had visited Kashmir in the last peaceful days it would know for the next fifteen years. By 1987, a better-educated and more articulate generation of Muslims had begun to chafe at the lack of democracy and economic development in the valley. The Indian government did little to help. Indeed, its representatives saw the distinct culture of Kashmir as something that had to be undermined before the state could join what they called the 'national mainstream'.

The backlash was not long in coming: what a colonized people fear most is the possibility of being swallowed up by the dominant alien culture in their midst. As in Algeria, Iran and Egypt, anxiety about modernization, about cultural influences from elsewhere and rampant unemployment turned, in Kashmir, into an anxiety about religion: the notion that not only Muslims but Islam itself was in danger.

In the spring of 2000, I returned to Kashmir for the first time since 1987 to report on the Pakistan-supported anti-India insurgency. More than thirty thousand people – militants, soldiers and civilians – had died by then. I stayed in a big hotel, formerly a palace of the Maharajah of Kashmir, overlooking the Dal lake. I was the only guest.

Less than a mile away, a bomb had exploded in a bazaar, killing seventeen civilians. Machine-guns poked out of almost every vehicle on the road. Army men had turned the hotels on the boulevards into bunkers. Srinagar was full of spectacularly ruined houses and new graveyards. Kashmiris appeared sullen and tense and it was only in closed unheated rooms that they poured out their rage and grief.

I left the hotel on the day I learnt about the building next to it. It had been one of the more dreaded Indian interrogation centres, called Papa 1, where, among other things, burning and dripping tyres were hung over the naked backs of suspected militants. The screams of the prisoners, a journalist told me, often reached the hotel.

I had been in Kashmir for a week when some unidentified men massacred thirty-five Sikhs in a remote Kashmiri village called Chitisinghpura. The killers, dressed in army fatigues, had come late in the evening. At two separate places in the village, they had asked the men to line up and then opened fire on them.

The village lay in a little hollow muffled by pine, walnut and chenar trees, divided by a brisk stream of cool clear water. A bathing cabin of rough timber stood beside the meadowed bank, where cows grazed among the leafless willows. The villagers were apple, almond and rice farmers. Some of them turned out to own transport businesses – there was enough money around for the village to have two gurudwaras, domed prayer halls with courtyards, one for each side of the village.

Chitisinghpura, which seemed at first sight so self-sufficient and serene, reminded me of Mashobra. But now this remote Himalayan village had been dragged into international geopolitics. The Indian government and media described the killers as Pakistani or Pakistan-backed Islamic fundamentalists. Journalists and strategic experts on television were speculating that the fundamentalists had killed the Sikhs in order to send some sort of message to the American president Bill Clinton, who was arriving in India on a state visit that very morning, and who had described Kashmir as the 'most dangerous place in the world'. They had gone on to speak of India as a victim of Islamic terrorism.

Later that morning, while journalists and politicians continued to arrive in the village, I met a middle-level officer from the Border Security Force, one of the paramilitary organizations fighting the anti-India insurgency in Kashmir. He was a Hindu, a short, paunchy and courteous man. He had refused to talk to the Kashmiri journalists who accompanied me. He told me that he preferred to talk to a fellow Hindu; the Muslim journalists were unreliable. He had been in Kashmir for a long time; he knew about the treachery of Muslims. He told me that he wasn't worried about the prospect of large numbers of Sikhs fleeing Kashmir after the massacre in the way the Hindus had done after being targeted by Muslim separatists. In fact, he wanted them to leave.

'Isolate the Muslims in Kashmir,' he said, 'and then we'll have a free hand to deal with them.' He thought all pro-Pakistan separatists were traitors and Pakistan's henchmen deserved no mercy. He himself hadn't let go of any of the separatists he had captured in the six years he had spent in Kashmir: it had been torture and then execution for them. He couldn't compromise, he said, on what he called India's 'national integrity'. The separatists had to be brought into line, preferably by violence, so as to end the rebellion against India.

A day after President Clinton's departure from India, the Indian government announced that the Pakistani murderers of the Sikhs had been killed in a military operation in a village called Panchalthan in a remote valley in Kashmir. The next day, the Indian newspapers carried black and white photos issued by the government of the partially charred bodies in Indian army fatigues.

The Pakistanis were quickly buried; so it seemed was the whole matter. But a few days later some Kashmiri villagers discovered, near the graves of the five alleged terrorists, the personal effects of several of their relatives who had been kidnapped from their homes soon after the killing of the Sikhs. When exhumed, the bodies were found to have been badly mutilated; one of them was headless. But the local villagers had little trouble in identifying them as their relatives.

When I climbed up the hill one late afternoon in Panchalthan where the bodies were exhumed, the villages of hay-topped houses down the valley seemed peaceful. Across shimmering rice fields, women in colourful headscarves sang traditional songs as they planted the paddy. Then, as dusk fell, they sat cross-legged upon little Kashmiri rugs and sipped salty tea from samovars.

It was from villages such as these that Indian security officials had kidnapped four of the five men. They had taken them to a shepherd's shelter on a steep hill, and shot them there in cold blood. Placing the necks of the corpses on logs, they had beheaded and dismembered them. They had then soaked the bodies with petrol and set them alight before presenting them to the world media as Pakistani terrorists or Islamic fundamentalists.

I had met the police officer most Kashmiris suspected of kidnapping and murdering the villagers. Sitting in an executive chair behind a large table strewn with maps, he had struck me as an amiable, frank man; and I had spent much of my meeting trying mentally to square this person, with his quick smile and graceful manners, with the stories I had heard of his ruthlessness.

The police officer was a Kashmiri Muslim. He came from a village not unlike the ones I had visited, and had worked his way up the administrative hierarchy. I expected him for this reason to be sympathetic to fellow Kashmiri Muslims. When I said so to a friend, a local Kashmiri journalist, whom I knew to be a devout Muslim, he replied, 'He is a careerist. Careerists have no religion.'

But the careerists had another kind of faith. The Muslim police officer, like the Hindu military officer at the Sikh massacre, had spoken to me of the need to preserve 'national integrity'. There were other officials who when I asked them about the rising costs of Indian rule over Kashmir – the tens of thousands of dead, maimed, widowed and orphaned people – spoke of the need to protect Kashmir from the malevolent designs of Pakistan, a patriotic duty that sometimes required acts of violence. Sometimes they pleaded that they were only men obeying orders sent to them from above.

Most of these men had a reputation for honesty; the corrupt ones were easier to understand. They had families in distant India, worrying about their safety. Photos attesting to the domestic happiness they were cut off from often sat in wooden frames on their large tables. In their armoured jeeps, among automatic rifles, machine-guns and hand grenades, they carried tapes of melancholy Hindi film songs, the songs about love and loss they shared with the people they tortured and killed. How had they allowed themselves to destroy other human beings in the name of a nation or state? How had they come to ally themselves with such meaningless abstractions as 'national integrity'?

Describing the modern state in his notebooks as 'organized *immorality*', Nietzsche had wondered, 'How is it achieved that a *great mass* does things the *individual* would never consent to do?' His answer, which he hoped to elaborate upon in a book, was unambiguous: 'by the division of responsibility; of commanding and carrying out commands; by *intercalating* the virtues of obedience, of duty, of the love of prince and fatherland; upholding pride, severity, strength, hatred, revenge'.[13] Still, as Simone Weil asked after the First World War, how had the state managed to 'set itself up as an absolute value in this world, that is, as an object of idolatry?'

In the last century, these questions, new and urgent in India, had been asked many times in Europe, before as well as after six million Jews were killed in the most vicious state-sponsored crime in history. And the irony too had been noted: that the omnipotent state was born in Europe ostensibly to protect the interests of a new kind of citizen – individuals who were supposedly able to pursue their own interests and to make choices for themselves.

This idea of the individual, still new in a traditional society like India's, had arisen relatively late even in Europe. Alexis de Tocqueville was certain that 'our ancestors lacked the word individualism, which we have created for our own use, because in their era there were, in fact, no individuals who did not belong to a group and who could regard themselves as absolutely alone'. For centuries since the spread of Christianity, family, church or local community had limited the horizons of human beings. Their rights and duties were communally determined; most people were bound firmly to pre-existing relations of status and kinship.

What was true of much of Europe before the political and economic revolutions of the nineteenth century was true of India even as late as 1947, when middle-class nationalists claiming to represent the Indian people inherited control of a vast administrative machinery from the British. In India, where the ascetic and the renouncer had been the first individuals of any kind, there was little individualism in de Tocqueville's sense of the word. Most people were defined through their membership in caste and community; few of them enjoyed the freedom of choice that was supposedly the essence of the modern individual.

This state of affairs was what a westernized ruling elite proposed to change after seeing off the British. Men like Nehru were offended by the passive Indian acceptance of poverty and what seemed to him to be feudal oppression sustained by the prestige of religion. Nehru believed that the poorest and most downtrodden Indians could be modernized into European-style rational individuals through mass secular education and a socialistic economic system.

He had little doubt that given sufficient time and incentive most Indians would shed their previous identities and become like Europeans: i.e. wear modern clothes, work in a factory or office, live in an urban setting, raise nuclear families, drive a car, vote in regular elections and pay taxes. The example of Europe had proved that such autonomous and secular individuals alone could form a modern democratic nation. But since few of them existed in India at the time of independence, it was the state's responsibility to create them – to produce, in effect, its citizens.

Five decades later, the Indian state could still claim plausibly to be saving its citizens from themselves in places like Kashmir. But who was this autonomous and secular individual whom the state required for its existence – the person who lived merely for the sake of increasing and satisfying his material needs? There were hardly any precedents in India's own intellectual and spiritual traditions. And, here, a particular version of European history became important for modernizers like Nehru – the history whose innate assumptions I grew up with and accepted without being aware of them.

This history began with the Reformation. Calvin and Luther had condemned the idleness and opulence of the church. They had held up a remote and mysterious creator God, who had already predestined men to salvation or damnation, but for whose glory men had to work and seek to create his kingdom on earth. The reformed Christian was humble, ascetic, hardworking. He was also the progenitor of free enterprise and economic individualism.

In this history, when the medieval forms of life in Europe broke up, partly under pressure from the rising bourgeoisie seeking worldly success as a sign of salvation, a new universe of personal choices opened up before human beings.[14] To accept these choices was to plunge into the adventure of individuality. In the centuries that followed, there emerged accordingly a new vocabulary for human character that was defined by personal choice and desire and the capacity of self-transformation.

The European Enlightenment was another step towards what Kant had called 'man's emergence from his self-incurred immaturity'. Philosophers like Hume, Locke and Adam Smith assumed that man had a natural right to independent existence, to the fulfilment of personal desires, to the pursuit of things, or to activity for its own sake. For them the problem was to explain how such separate individuals could live together; how the autonomous self related to other autonomous selves in the pursuit of its interests.

The new world view presumed that man was motivated by self-interest, or, in so far as he cared about others, by *enlightened* self-interest. Modern government had emerged in order to convert individual interests into a system of rights and duties, and to prescribe laws, which would apply equally to all individuals. It was a single, sovereign power, because by concentrating all authority in itself, it could quicken the escape of the individual from his various allegiances to family, guild, church and local community. At the same time, it had weakened itself enough in western Europe and America to allow the individual the full enjoyment of his individuality. By constraining itself through democratic procedures, the making of law through consultation between ruler and the ruled, it had guaranteed him his freedom.

There seemed something very grand about the concept of freedom, about the individual's liberation from the constraints of traditional society, and his freely chosen right to movement, occupation, speech, religious belief and property. It was why an Indian of my background could not easily challenge the idea that the modern nation state, absolute and impersonal, could be the liberator of the new individual from his old chains.

Indeed, to look at the seventeenth, eighteenth and nineteenth centuries in Europe was mainly to admire intellectuals like Hume, Voltaire, Diderot and Marx who had upheld the potential of the human being to master circumstances instead of being a slave to them. The fate of the world seemed to have been happily settled somewhere in the assertions of the two major figures of the Scottish Enlightenment, David Hume and Adam Smith.

But there was a special irony here for those Indians who were enamoured of the new secular assessment of human possibility arrived at in distant Europe, and hoped to realize it to the full in postcolonial India. For India had already suffered some of the less anticipated consequences of the endless striving for growth. The moral climate in which the multiplication of human needs was seen as good, private happiness was posited as the highest aim, and activity for its own sake turned into a principle, was also one that had legitimized the conquest and subjugation of strange peoples around the world.

It wasn't clear to most of us who revered the great thinkers of Europe that many of them had anticipated and outlined the type of politics, economics and philosophy that the all-conquering bourgeoisie needed to extend its power over the earth. Nor did we know much about the complex doubts these men had revealed about the character and motives of the free and ambitious individual even as they celebrated his emergence.

Marx had ideological reasons to fear what the endlessly renewed needs of the individual might lead to. He thought that 'modern bourgeois society, a society that has conjured up such mighty means of production and exchange, is like the sorcerer who can no longer control the powers of the underworld that he has called up by his spells'.

But even Adam Smith, the proponent of free trade, had wondered early in his life if power and wealth, 'those great objects of human desire', can make one immune to 'anxiety, fear, sorrow, diseases, danger and death'. He had considered the idea that happiness could be secured through desiring more things than one needs a deception and had eventually concluded that it is 'well that nature imposes on us in this manner. It is this deception which rouses and keeps in continual motion the industry of mankind.' After all,

> it is this which first prompted them to cultivate the ground, to build houses, to found cities and common-wealths, and to invent and improve all the sciences and arts, which ennoble and embellish human life; which have entirely changed the whole face of the globe, have turned the rude forests of nature into agreeable and fertile plains, and made the trackless and barren ocean a new fund of subsistence, and the great high road of communication to the different nations of the earth.[15]

Smith believed that any society which restricted its needs would endanger its poorest members. He asserted that free trade would conquer scarcity and create abundance and leisure wherever it was allowed. He envisaged a system of natural liberty in which individuals were free to create and compete for wealth.

Smith's influential vision of human growth and competition, which had been transformed into the ideology of imperial conquest, and which still drives much of international politics, had not gone uncontested in Europe. Its greatest critic was Rousseau, whom I knew only as the intellectual father of the totalitarian state. He had despaired of the lack of virtue in a society built upon the unfettered pursuit of desire. For him the state was necessary precisely to regulate this emerging society of commerce and money, of envy and inequality, in which he thought individuals would be hostile strangers to each other.

As he saw it, mankind might have lived once in a state of simplicity and equality, but the discovery of agriculture and metals had trapped men into more and more complicated relationships. Then, the idea of private property had introduced men to strife, envy, jealousy and exploitation; it had made man, who was naturally good and compassionate, more dependent on other men, which always involved hypocrisy and corruption and made man more uncertain and fearful than he had ever been.

Rousseau wished to bring man the genuine individual freedom he had known outside society. Strangely, for Rousseau this could only be achieved by the state. He was clear that 'it is only by the force of the state that the liberty of its members can be secured'.[16] The state embodied what he called the 'general will' of the masses. It represented the will of the political organism, which was above all the individual interests that constituted it, a general surrender to which formed the social contract. 'Each citizen' could only be 'completely independent of all his fellow men' by being 'absolutely dependent upon the state'.

In his wish to secure an imagined absolute autonomy for the individual, where he would presumably be free to enjoy his individuality, Rousseau turned the state into an absolute suprahuman, mystical reality. The state was the liberator of man from society; it was the prerequisite for his moral development. What was needed was 'an absolute surrender of the individual, with all of his rights and all of his powers'.

As he wrote:

> It is good to know how to deal with men as they are, it is much better to make them what there is need that they should be. The most absolute authority is that which penetrates into a man's inmost being, and concerns itself no less with his will than with his actions.[17]

It was with such abstract ideas – of a hypothetical equality, of the state as the guarantor of virtue and the engineer of human souls – that Rousseau, however inadvertently, set the stage for the terrors of not just the French Revolution or Hitlerism and Stalinism, but also of the well-intentioned regimes of the twentieth century, which destroyed human beings while claiming to remake them – the regimes which with their atrocities provided in dismal detail the answer to the question posed by Nietzsche, when he defined the state as 'organized *immorality*' and wondered how it was achieved 'that a *great mass* does things the *individual* would never consent to do'.

But this wasn't the history I knew in India: one in which revolutions weren't usually triumphs of the oppressed and the virtuous, and the slogans of liberty, equality and fraternity often led not to peace and brotherhood on earth but to greater and more complicated forms of oppression.

There seemed something so beautifully neat about the Marxist assumption that man was a materialist, evaluated by what he produced through his labour, who could use technology to increase his mastery over nature, end his slavery to factory work, and build an efficient modern society where all, and not just a few, citizens shared equally the benefits of a controlled economy.

I did not suspect when I first came across them that such elaborate schemes were pure optimism on the part of a brilliant intellectual in exile in London. The dialectic was so impressive in its design: the bourgeoisie overthrowing the feudal lords, and then being overthrown in turn by the proletariat. It gave to human beings a central role as makers and shapers of their collective destiny. It affirmed the individual in his ability to change the world, and made it easy to believe Marx when he asserted that history explained the past, foretold the future, revealed the cunning of reason, and showed why one part of the world was superior to the other.

It didn't bother me that Marx had little to say about 'the anxiety, fear, sorrow, diseases, danger and death' that even Adam Smith had worried about; and that he had simply taken over a sanguine modern vision in which man no longer needed to be burdened with his own sense of imperfection, and didn't have to struggle in his inner life towards the good because he *was* good, simply by being human and playing his role in history.

I didn't notice that Marx had offered no morality beyond that of the self-serving group, or class: the laws of history explained why the working class should eventually triumph without giving any reason why the values of this class or the group of revolutionaries should better serve the individual than those they overthrow.

The cunning of reason had long failed to work out in the way Marx had predicted. Here, Nietzsche was more prescient, predicting at a time when socialism was merely a dream that it 'needs the most submissive subjugation of all citizens to the absolute state, the like of which has never existed', and which was likely to maintain itself through 'the most extreme terrorism'.

In 1922, while denouncing Buddhism as a nihilist religion and a bad influence on Europe, the Russian poet Osip Mandelstam had wished for a return to the 'schematic intellect and spirit of expediency' of the French rationalist philosophers of the eighteenth century. Mandelstam wasn't alone in his hopes. In the early 1920s, the nine million people killed in the First World War still weighed on the many artists and intellectuals in the West who thought that the Russian Revolution was inspired by the universal and secular values of the Enlightenment, which by reorganizing society on scientific lines would help, as Mandelstam hoped, undermine the power of old irrationalisms like Buddhism.

For many of them, their hopes seemed close to fulfilment when in the 1920s Stalin began, with a schematic intellect and in the spirit of expediency, his Five Year Plans and programmes of collectivization and industrialization, in an ambitious attempt to modernize Russia.

The worst consequences of overly rational thinking – mass murder, forced labour and migrations, all deemed necessary by a bureaucratized state for the cause of a better future – were visible by the late 1930s when Mandelstam, transported to a labour camp in Siberia, became one of the millions of victims of Stalin. But this kind of news travelled late to places like India.

The distrust of science, and the idea of history and progress, which deepened in Europe from the beginning of the twentieth century, reached India even later. An artilleryman called Franz Rosenzweig had been one of the millions trapped in the mud and the filth of the trenches of the First World War. Writing on postcards during the war, he had accused 'reason' of having 'devoured' man and proclaimed that 'it alone exists':

> Let man creep like a worm into the folds of naked earth before the fast-approaching volleys of a blind and pitiless death; let him sense there forcibly, inexorably, what he otherwise never senses: that his *I* would be but an *It* if he died; let him therefore cry his very *I* out with every cry that is still in his throat against the merciless one from whom there is no appeal and who threatens man with such unthinkable annihilation.[18]

'In the face of all this misery,' Rosenzweig wrote, 'philosophy only smiles its vacuous smile.' Writing after the war, which shattered the longest peace and greatest prosperity Europe's recorded history had ever known, the French poet Paul Valéry was only one of the many European writers and intellectuals to suspect that the complacent European faith in history, rationality and science had brought about a new scale of devastation:

> With our own eyes, we have seen conscientious labour, the most solid learning, the most serious discipline and application adapted to appalling ends. So many horrors

could not have been possible without so many virtues. Doubtless, much science was needed to kill so many, to waste so much property, annihilate so many cities in so short a time; but moral qualities in like number were also needed. Are Knowledge and Duty, then, suspect?[19]

The Buddha seems far away from the world-historical events that preoccupied men like Rousseau, Smith, Marx and Valéry: the rise of the individual in a market society; the scramble for profits by the new individuals created by the break-up of old moralities; the creation of centralized states; the conquest and organized exploitation of peoples and their resources around the world; the violent revolutions based on the seizure of state power and private property.

In Indonesia one day, walking around Borobudur, I read a pamphlet a Thai monk was passing out. It contained the famous passage on the Buddhist sentiment of loving-kindness that the Buddha enjoined as a mental habit upon the laymen he spoke to:

Whatever beings may exist – weak or strong, tall, broad, medium or short, fine-material or gross, seen or unseen, those born and those pressing to be born – may they all be without exception happy in heart!

Let no one deceive anyone else, nor despise anyone anywhere. May no one wish harm to another in anger or ill-will!

Let one's thoughts of boundless loving-kindness pervade the whole world, above, below, across, without obstruction, without hatred, without enmity![20]

I read the lines, and couldn't help wondering what, if anything, the Buddha would have thought of a place like

East Timor where entire village populations were lined up and machine-gunned. Old age, disease, death, desiring and clinging – the most natural processes individuals know – proved to him the fact of suffering. To what extreme diagnoses and prescriptions would he have been provoked had he witnessed the twentieth century, the high intensities of suffering human beings inflicted and continue to inflict on other human beings, the wars, the massacres, the famines, the Holocaust, the Gulag? It was easy to imagine the Buddha from a simpler time who stressed the need for loving-kindness, and who could only be utterly bewildered in a historically more complex age by the enormous ordeals of human beings.

But there was plenty of suffering during the Buddha's time too – and people had fewer distractions with which to dull the pain. There was the suffering of people uprooted from their native habitats and forced into cities. There was the suffering of loneliness caused by the breakdown of the old social order. There was also the suffering caused by wars of conquest: the large new armies of the big kingdoms of Kosala and Magadha overrunning the smaller republics. The Buddha's own clan, the Shakyas, were slaughtered in one such war a few years before his death.

Organized greed, war, genocide – they were not unknown to the Buddha. They seem to have led him to his suspicion of the amoral individualism which was rapidly emerging in the India of his time, and which was reflected in the politics and the philosophical speculation of his peers. Their presence partly explains the obsessive way in which he tried to undermine the idea that there was anything like an autonomous or stable individual self.

Liberation from old bonds of caste and community was

not the same as freedom for the Buddha. It could just as easily lead to nihilism, as the rise of discontented European masses proved. These masses, whose old certainties of belief, occupation and status had been destroyed in the process of enthroning the bourgeois individual, felt personal identity not as a relief but a burden. Their frustration and resentment channelled themselves into demands for greater equality, or levelling down; into violent revolutions. Seeking anonymity and uniformity, these uprooted and underdeveloped individuals became the primary ingredient of the totalitarian states of Europe and, later, Asia.

In his own time, the Buddha saw the men created by the new social and economic forces of North India. His primary audience existed in the urban centres where people felt most acutely their new individuality as a burden and were attracted to nihilism as preached by the new thinkers, such as the Ajivikas, who attacked the moral laws of *karma*. He could sense the dangers inherent in men freed from traditional morality and claiming to be self-directed individuals.

It is partly why he questioned the very premise of the autonomous self-directed individual: that he is someone who chooses and pursues his own desires, and thereby comes to possess his individuality – the hypothesis which lies even now, in an age where mass manipulation is a respectable industry, at the basis of modern civilization.

Like many modern thinkers, the Buddha, too, had begun with anatomizing the person driven and defined largely by desire, the habits of craving, or *trishna*, which did not normally cease until death. But he did not think that individuality or happiness could be achieved through these habits.

Trapped in its subjectivity, the self recognized each image of the world as something to be made use of or exploited. This is how it entered into a purely instrumental relationship with nature as well as with other human beings, whose subjectivity it did not acknowledge. In pursuit of its desires, it reduced everything in the world to the level of 'things', which were either an aid or a hindrance to the fulfilment of desire. The occasional fulfilment of desire strengthened the belief that one was a self, distinct from others; and such a belief fixed one further into the grid of such emotions as greed, hatred and anger.

The Buddha tried to reverse this process by advocating a form of mental vigilance that undermined the individual's sense of a distinctive unchanging self with its own particular desires. To observe even temporarily the incessant play of desire and activity in the mind was to see how the self was a process rather than an unchanging substance; how it had no single identity across time; and when assumed to be unchanging could only cause suffering and frustration.

He hoped to bring about a fundamental change in the attitudes of men savouring their individuality: to prove to them that everything in the world is part of a causal process and cannot exist in or by itself; that things are interdependent, and that this is true as much for human beings as for physical phenomena.

Even Adam Smith feared that the market society driven by desire and the multiplication of needs would degenerate into chaos and violence if its citizens did not exercise self-control. He hoped that the individual living in it would be able to distinguish between what he wants and what he needs. But this was more an expression of optimism than a practical method to unravel altogether what Smith himself recognized as the deception of desire.

The Buddha, too, began with a biological image of man as ruled by impulses and desires – the same image that inspired Adam Smith and Hobbes. But he might have been puzzled by the assumption that the private satisfaction of these impulses and desires would not only somehow bring about an ideal state and society but also eventually make the individual more self-aware. His own attempt was to reveal how unchecked desire led to the individual's alienation from both nature and human society.

It is partly why he did not try to envision the moral and political order that could accommodate such autonomous individuals and their desires. He wished to establish what Rousseau called 'the reign of virtue'. But he did not see it coming about through an abstract political organization. Although he stressed that the ruler be righteous, he balked at making a faceless entity such as the state the supposed arbiter between allegedly solitary and fearful individuals, who preyed upon each other and so were in need of a remote master. The same delusion that made men suppose themselves to be solid and independent individual selves could also make them see such changing, insubstantial entities as state and society as real and enduring, and subordinate themselves to them.

Given his experience, the Buddha would not have disagreed with Rousseau's diagnosis: life was indeed simpler when men had little to work with and lived in small groups, preoccupied almost entirely with the tasks of survival. He would have agreed that the idea of private property set men against each other and created a state of inequality. But he would also have accepted the change as inevitable in the light of technological innovations and the growing human need for comfort and space. Although, in practice, the *sangha* held property in common, the Buddha did not preach against private property.

His preference was for small political communities where the power of decision-making was distributed among all the members. Even as large states emerged in North India, he hoped to preserve the small bonds and solidarities that protect the individual and prevent him from being ground down by vast impersonal forces. By establishing the *sangha*, he wished to reintegrate uprooted people in a mode of life, a tradition and a form of spiritual practice.

He did not detach even so apparently private a sphere as the spiritual from the larger human world; the *bhikshus* didn't live in forests but in retreats close to urban centres, and were bound to laymen by an ethic of social responsibility. He is unlikely to have had much time for the modern idea that freedom was something the individual enjoyed in private after discharging his obligations to his society and state.

Like Rousseau, the Buddha disliked selfishness, and upheld the value of compassion. But his compassion was different from that which the revolutionaries of France and Russia claimed to be driven by, based on solidarity with an abstract mass of lonely and angry individuals who had not been allowed to pursue their self-interest. The Buddha's compassion presupposed no gulf of class or caste between persons; it sprang from his concern with the mind and body of the active, suffering individual. It sought to redirect individuals from the pursuit of political utopias to attentiveness and acts of compassion in everyday life.

As he saw it, without the belief in a self with an identity, a person will no longer be obsessed with regrets about the past and plans for the future. Ceasing to live in the limbo of what ought to be but is not here yet, he will be fully alive in the present.

The Buddha's insistence on inhabiting the here and now prevented most Buddhists from lapsing into the utilitarianism of those who sought to build better worlds and ruthlessly sacrificed the present for the sake of a hypothetical future. But it didn't save Buddhists from the consequences of the search for political utopias that blighted the twentieth century.

The Vietnamese Buddhist monk Thich Nhat Hanh, who was born in 1926, grew up to see his country divided among and ravaged by Marx-inspired nationalists and their pro-American opponents. Amid a civil war that killed millions of Vietnamese and thousands of Americans he upheld non-violent methods of negotiation and dialogue, and eventually was forced to leave Vietnam for America in 1966.

Buddhists often became the victims of the degraded forms of Marxism that spread across large parts of Asia. Tibet, a mainly Buddhist country in which about 20 per cent of the population consisted of ordained monks and nuns, had already shown its vulnerability to the organized forces of the modern world in 1904, when British-led invaders massacred hundreds of poorly equipped Tibetan defenders and forced the Dalai Lama to flee to Mongolia. In 1951, the Chinese Communists invaded Tibet and began a still ongoing process of brutalization: hundreds of thousands of Tibetans have been killed, and thousands of monasteries destroyed, in the course of what the Chinese describe as an attempt to end medieval feudalism in and bring modernity to Tibet.

Buddhists also suffered greatly in Cambodia, where out of the chaos created by heavy American bombing in the early 1970s emerged the Khmer Rouge, the most radical Communists yet. The leader of the Khmer Rouge, Pol Pot, dreamed of a Rousseauian utopia where each person would have his own little farm. In a perverse parody of the Chinese Cultural Revolution, his cadres destroyed hospitals and schools, and forced anyone who looked like a doctor, teacher or engineer into menial work in the villages. In just five to six years, up to three million Cambodians died from starvation, overwork, torture and execution. Before their overthrow by the Vietnamese army in 1979, the Khmer Rouge destroyed more than three thousand Buddhist temples, and only three thousand out of fifty thousand monks survived their murderous fury.[21]

The Buddhist response to such unprecedented modern atrocities may at first seem unrealistic. The Buddhist monk Maha Ghosananda, who lost his entire family in the Cambodian killing fields and who became a major figure in the reconstruction of his country, insisted on including the Khmer Rouge at UN-sponsored talks on the future of Cambodia. He claimed to want an end to antagonism, not to antagonists. He said, 'We must condemn the act but we cannot hate the actor. The unwholesomeminded must be included in our loving-kindness because they are the ones who need loving-kindness the most.'

Over more than four decades of exile, the Dalai Lama continued to insist on non-violent opposition to the brutal Chinese rule over Tibet. He threatened to resign his leadership of the Tibetan community in exile if Tibetans ever resorted to a violent insurrection against the Chinese. Similarly, the Buddhist democrat, Aung San Suu Kyi, refuses to lead an armed struggle against the military rulers of Myanmar who have kept her under house arrest on and off for more than a decade.

These modern-day Buddhists derived their scruples from the Buddha. But they claimed to draw their immediate inspiration, and courage and optimism, from a man who, though not a Buddhist himself, appears to have consistently applied Buddhist principles to the murky world of politics.

Mourning his death, Albert Einstein asserted that 'generations to come will not believe that such a man walked the face of the earth'. But Mohandas Karamchand Gandhi provoked such incredulity in his own lifetime. A confidential government report in South Africa, where he organized a small and frequently trampled-upon Indian minority against racial discrimination, said that 'the workings of his conscience . . . his ethical and intellectual attitude, based as it appears to be on a curious compound of mysticism and astuteness, baffles the ordinary processes of thought'.

Rabindranath Tagore called him Mahatma – great-souled. The word implied that Gandhi was a sage, part of a long Indian tradition of spirituality. So he was in many ways; but he was also an activist. As Gandhi himself put it, 'the quest for truth cannot be prosecuted in a cave' – a sentiment the Buddha would have approved. His life-long attempt, as the leader of the Indian anti-colonial movement, was to infuse morality into the realm of politics where falsehood and violence had become widely accepted norms.

Born in 1869, half a century after the British consolidation in India, Gandhi grew up in an India where the traditional forms of community, though under assault from British colonialism, still existed in various tribes, sects, castes and clans. He died in 1948, when India was free and on the brink of rapid modernization; and, as with the Buddha, his life and insights emerged out of an intimate experience of a fast-changing world.

Many of his contemporaries were much more optimistic about the healing power of political independence. Many of his more westernized followers, such as Nehru, despaired at his seemingly quixotic rejection of the industrial revolution and other aspects of western modernity. But for Gandhi, liberation from British rule meant nothing if it wasn't preceded by self-appraisal and introspection by individual Indians. This often made him withdraw altogether from the freedom movement and for years immerse himself in social work with peasants, women and untouchable Hindus.

Like the Buddha, he was partial to the small-scale self-governing political unit. He was wary of nationalism; and he distrusted the over-centralized state of the kind the British had created in India and which Indians were to inherit in 1947. This was not just personal whimsy. Gandhi was among the first western-educated Indians to realize how thoroughly the imposition of alien ways had bewildered and demeaned Indians. He spoke less of administrative and legal reforms than of the need for spinning wheels, cow protection and village democracy, all the things that he thought Indians needed to achieve true self-government. He would have agreed with the Russian Christian thinker Nikolai Berdyaev, who asserted that 'the concept of man as a citizen obscured the concept of man as a free spirit belonging to another order of being and also obstructed the vision of man as labourer and producer'.[22]

He felt it important for a conquered people to look for fresh identity and dignity in their own traditions. India, he felt, must find its own way instead of imitating western models of the nation state, military and economy. To attempt to beat the West at its own game, as Japan was then doing, was already to admit defeat.

For the enemy were not the British, or the West, but the immemorial forces of human greed and violence that had received an unprecedented moral sanction in the political, scientific and economic systems of the modern world.

Appropriately, his political method, *satyagraha* (non-violent persuasion), which went on to inspire Martin Luther King and Nelson Mandela, attempted to change the rules of the game. Spiritual awareness and self-control are of the utmost importance. The activist has the option of retaliation when faced with violence. But he actively chooses to forgo it. He works to purify his mind, ridding it of anger and hostility right in the midst of conflict – as with the Buddha, what was in the mind was as important as the specific action in which it resulted, if not more so. By doing so, the activist tries to win the respect of his oppressor, and to turn him into an equal interlocutor, a partner in the political process.

As Gandhi saw it, a political movement against the British could not be, as national liberation struggles usually were, a zero-sum contest, with clearly defined winners and losers. He exhorted Indians not only not to demonize their British rulers but to make them participate in a process of self-questioning and self-purification. He hoped for *satyagraha* to bring about an inner transformation within the British, to the point where they themselves would share with their victims an awareness of the profound evil of colonialism: how the suffering created by organized exploitation touched both exploiter and victim. Such awareness, reached individually, could alone create the possibility of reconciliation between peoples and nations who would otherwise remain locked in mutual distrust and hostility – a method tried most recently in South Africa by the Truth and Reconciliation Commission which followed the end of the apartheid regime.

With his Buddhistic insight into suffering as something universal and indivisible, Gandhi made compassion the basis of political action. In the process, he rejected the idea of politics as an occasionally grubby means to a predetermined end (independence, revolution, regime change), something that an elite of experts carried on among itself for the sake of some imagined good for society. He didn't only infuse it with ethical responsibility, he tried to make politics an ongoing public and private process, a matter of individual conscience rather than of an arbitrarily decided general will.

For Gandhi, *satyagraha* or non-violence was not merely another tactic, as terrorism often is. It was a whole way of being in the world, of relating to other people's and one's own inner self: a continuous project of spiritual self-awareness. He knew, as Václav Havel wrote in a collection of essays titled *Living in Truth*, that 'the less political policies are derived from a concrete and human "here and now" and the more they fix their sights on an abstract "someday", the more easily they can degenerate into new forms of human enslavement'.[23]

Gandhi practised what Václav Havel, living under a totalitarian regime, once described as 'anti-political politics', that is, 'politics not as the technology of power and manipulation, of cybernetic rule over humans or as the art of the useful, but politics as one of the ways of seeking and achieving meaningful lives, of protecting them and serving them'.

In this vision, politics was inseparable from the spiritual life of individuals. It was an arena of action where human beings nurtured those basic dimensions of their humanity that the impersonal power structures of the modern world had exiled into the private realm: 'love, friendship, solidarity, sympathy and tolerance' which, as Havel wrote, 'were the only genuine starting-point of meaningful human community'.[24]

Regardless of the regimes they lived under – British or Indian, capitalist or socialist – individuals always possessed a freedom of conscience: the freedom to make choices in everyday life. To exercise this choice correctly – to work with what the Buddha called right view and intention – was to live a moral as well as a political life. It was also to take upon one's own conscience the burden of political responsibility and action rather than placing it upon a political party or a government.

Gandhi knew as intuitively as Havel was to know later that the task before him was not so much of achieving regime change as of resisting 'the irrational momentum of anonymous, impersonal, and inhuman power – the power of ideologies, systems, apparat, bureaucracy, artificial lan-guages and political slogans'. This was the fundamental task that Havel believed 'all of us, East and West' face, and 'from which all else should follow'. For this power, which took the form of consumption, advertising, repression, technology or cliché, was the 'blood brother of fanaticism and the wellspring of totalitarian thought' and pressed upon individuals everywhere in the political and economic systems of the modern world.

It was why Havel once thought that the western cold warriors wishing to get rid of the totalitarian system he belonged to were like the 'ugly woman trying to get rid of her ugliness by smashing the mirror which reminds her of it'. 'Even if they won,' Havel wrote, 'the victors would emerge from a conflict inevitably resembling their defeated opponents far more than anyone today is willing to admit or able to imagine.'

Gandhi knew that 'a genuine, profound and lasting change for the better can no longer result from the victory of any particular traditional political conception which can ultimately be only external, that is, a structural or systemic conception'. Writing after a century of cruelly botched rev-olutions, Havel was convinced that

> such a change will have to derive from human existence, from the fundamental reconstitution of the position of people in the world, their relationship to themselves and to each other, and to the universe. If a better economic and political model is to be created, then perhaps more than ever before it must derive from profound existential and moral changes in society.

But the examples of the Buddha and Gandhi lacked

sufficient force to prevent India from embracing the clichés of modern politics. A few months after India's long-delayed independence in 1947, a Hindu nationalist called Nathuram Godse assassinated Gandhi.

Godse turned out to be one of the many rationalists and advocates of realpolitik exasperated and bewildered by Gandhi's attempt to combine politics with morality. In a remarkably coherent statement in court, he explained that he had killed Gandhi in order to cleanse India of such 'old superstitious beliefs' as the 'power of the soul, the inner voice, the fast, the prayer and the purity of the mind'.[25] He had felt that non-violence of the kind Gandhi advocated could only 'lead the nation towards ruin'. With Gandhi out of the way, India, Godse said, would be 'free to follow the course founded on reason which I consider to be necessary for sound nation-building'. It would 'surely be practical, able to retaliate, and would be powerful with armed forces . . .'

More than half a century after Gandhi's assassination, I met Nathuram Godse's younger brother, Gopal Godse, in the western Indian city of Pune. Godse spent sixteen years in prison for conspiring with his brother and a few other Hindu nationalists to murder Gandhi. In his tiny two-room flat, where the dust from the busy shopping street outside thickly powdered a mess of files and books and the framed garlanded photographs of Gandhi's murderers, Godse, a frail man of eighty-three, at first seemed like someone abandoned by history.

But recent events in India seemed to Godse to have vindicated his Hindu nationalist cause. The massacre by Hindu nationalists of over two thousand Muslims in

Gujarat had proved that the Hindus were growing more militant and patriotic. The Muslims were on the run not just in India but everywhere in the world. India had nuclear bombs and was willing to use them; it was growing richer and stronger while Pakistan was slowly imploding. Only recently, Godse reminded me, the deputy prime minister Advani had advocated the dismemberment of Pakistan.

India had turned its back on Gandhi, Godse claimed, and had come close to embracing his brother's vision. His brother, Nathuram Godse, had not died in vain. He had asked for his ashes to be immersed in the Indus, the holy river of the Aryan settlers of India, which flows through Pakistan, only when Mother India was whole again. For over half a century, Godse had waited for the day when he could travel to the Indus with the urn containing his brother's ashes; and he now thought he wouldn't have to wait too much longer.

Western *Dharmas*

M Y JOURNEYS OUT OF India took me out of what I
began to think of as a stagnant and limited world.
I found attractive the prospect of travel, of exposing myself
to new places and peoples – the prospect that I had once
dreaded. The opportunities came in the form of small journalistic assignments, which also paid well, allowing me to
feel finally free of the financial worries I had lived with for
so long.

They involved me with more and more people; kept me
out of Mashobra for long stretches, and took me back there
only for very brief periods. I often returned just long enough
to write my articles in the silence and seclusion of my cottage.

I hadn't signed a lease or contract for my house with the
Sharmas. I wouldn't have known how to go about it. I paid
them a flat sum occasionally, based on the figure Mr Sharma
had first quoted. As years went by, I increased the amount.
They themselves never brought up the matter of rent. Mr
Sharma always looked slightly embarrassed while accepting
the money I gave him. He often said on such occasions that
he hadn't built the house in order to make money and

repeated that it was meant as a place of retreat for scholars and writers. But I continued to think, especially when I was away from Mashobra, that I depended too much on his goodwill, which I feared could run out at any moment. I wondered whether Mr Sharma, who didn't appear very rich, would some day be compelled to put the house on the market.

Even after many years in Mashobra I couldn't quite believe in my good fortune of having found a place of my own; never ceased feeling the fragility of my claim upon it; and I returned to the village at the end of each winter burdened with a grim sense of foreboding.

On one of my trips I found that Daulatram had married and had come to live with his wife, Girija, beneath my cottage, in the small room where apples were previously stored. Mr Sharma built them a tiny bathroom. He bought them a double bed, a gas cylinder and stove, a pressure cooker and some pieces of crockery. Crammed with these domestic things, the room took on a new hopeful aspect.

As the days passed, the hiss of the pressure cooker, the fragrance of burning spices, the subdued voices of Daulatram and Girija, and the old film songs on All India Radio, rising from below, became familiar and comforting.

Returning to Mashobra one summer for a short stay I learnt that Mr Sharma's mother had died the previous week. Mr Sharma and his father, Panditji, had just returned from immersing her ashes in the Ganges at Hardwar. They spoke of the unpleasantness they had faced on the plains. The Brahmins officiating at funeral ceremonies had cheated them. Policemen at a checkpost had demanded bribes and

Panditji had had to contact his political friend, the former king of Rampur, in order to smooth his way.

Thirteen days after her death, Mr Sharma hosted a feast on the lawn facing his house. Many people from the village joined his relatives under the bright tent, the shopkeepers dressed nervously in their best clothes. The next issue of *Divyajyoti* was dedicated to the memory of Mr Sharma's mother. The cover had a photograph of her, taken one bright summer afternoon with my camera. Inside, there were tributes from her husband, son, daughters, sons-in-law.

Her husband spoke of her support and energy during the difficult period of poverty he had known in the 1920s and 30s when he was trying to find a job as a Sanskrit teacher. Other contributors offered similar instances of her generosity and kindness. I read them, surprised by the number of people whose lives she had touched, even altered, in significant ways. It made me see how much solid endeavour and achievement even a life as restricted hers could contain.

There were other changes, although I wasn't then much aware of them. People I knew had got married, or found work elsewhere and moved away. Wildflower Hall, where I often went walking, burned down in a fire. One evening I went to see the charred ruins. The flowerbeds still bloomed in the blackened lawns, and tourists wearing Himachali folk-dress posed for pictures amid them.

Mr Sharma, who had acquired a new set of teeth, looked much older. Older still, his father, whom I saw meditating on the balcony, rarely left the house. Mr Sharma came with his nephew Vayur before dusk to help Daulatram milk the cows. While Vayur returned to the main house with a brass pail full to the brim, Mr Sharma dropped in. He was still incurious about my travels and my long and frequent absences from Mashobra. He spoke of how little or much it had snowed the previous winter and what it portended for the apple harvest later that year. He spoke again of the growing unpredictability of the weather; and blamed it often on modern society and its constant need for progress, for new shiny things.

As the years passed, I saw less and less of Mr Sharma. I had always thought of my time in Mashobra as preparation for the larger world, where I hoped that a professional career as a writer awaited me. And now, almost imperceptibly, the writing commissions steadily accumulating, my ambition had been realized.

In London, where I had started to spend some months each year, my life as a freelance writer was placid. I worked most of the day. Occasionally, I would meet publishers, editors, agents and other writers. Sometimes I joined various academics, think-tank experts and journalists in the studios of the BBC to comment on international events – the news, usually bad, emanating from what seemed from London to be the remote and dark places of the world.

My illusions about the writer's life diminished. To be a writer wasn't, as I had imagined, to arrive at a plateau of wisdom; it wasn't even to possess a special anguish, or to assume a critical attitude towards the social and political arrangements of the day. I was disconcerted when men I considered successful and confident suddenly revealed anxieties about the sales, publicity and distribution of their books, and began resentfully to compare them with the publishing records of other writers. Writing had become (or had always been) a profession like any other, pursued in solitude but contaminated by many of the jealousies and tensions of the public workplace.

I couldn't complain much. I had worked hard to be in London, the very heart of the empire that had shaped my life and the primary source of the modernity whose cold hand touched my father even in his remote village, and whose finer achievements I could see around me: efficiency, the rule of law, a tolerance of diversity.

I cherished the freedom of the freelance writing life – the kind of fringe vocation that could not have been possible outside the metropolitan world, which required information about the world outside and so spent its surplus wealth on maintaining individuals like myself: freelance writers, academics, journalists, think-tank experts. I compared my situation not to that of other writers but to those of the people I had first seen at European and American airports, pursuing the richness of the world, the Arabs, Africans, Iranians and South Asians, who in London seemed trapped in their small shops, kiosks and minicab cubicles.

And, without the idea of a literary life, and the sense of being supported by a culture of writing and reflection, I would have felt too exposed to the young Bangladeshis in long beards who preached radical Islam in the streets near my flat in the East End, or their secular counterparts, the aggressive white boys wearing the hoods of their sweatshirts over their heads.

I was content to anchor myself to my desk, to work with what was familiar rather than to try to break through the inscrutable surface that faces, gestures, clothes and houses presented – the strangeness that had dissolved slowly since my first day in London when I saw Sophiya among the crowd of ashen faces emerging from the underground station.

As always, I had thought that history could be my guide, and for several years I kept seeking out books about London. No city appeared to have been more written about. It had its own prolific chroniclers – Dickens, Mayhew – and then almost every Indian or Asian visitor in the last two centuries had felt compelled to record his or her admiration, awe and even, occasionally, fear and repulsion.

The reputation was still overwhelming. It had been the capital of a great empire. Millions of men had left its protective light in order to bring the remotest parts of Asia, Africa and the Caribbean into the web of trade and industry. Millions had arrived in the city seeking security and prosperity. There was hardly a part of the world that had not known its language and laws. Kipling's words, 'The Thames has known everything,' had gone round in my mind when from the plane I first saw the river curving across London, and the grand buildings in the narrow streets and alleys of the City, near where I lived and where I knew that a few bankers and traders had once decided the fate of India, had seemed to possess the same oppressive air of experience and omniscience.

This imperial past reared up frequently in the statues standing in squares of colonial administrators or military officers, whose names I associated easily with a place or event – the building of a North Indian canal, the quelling of the 1857 Mutiny. It existed in the bearded, slightly brutal faces of the men in the National Portrait Gallery, and in the mock-imperial Gothic of the Parliament building and St Pancras station. But the grand avenues and vistas, and the imposing monuments that were meant to overawe the natives in Calcutta and New Delhi, were absent from London itself. And the past that was still alive for me was unrecognizable for most English people my age.

The books I read made me approach London as a historical abstraction. They placed the city in the light either of empire or the industrial revolution, of the drastic transformations – the destruction of small crafts and trades, the growth of population and slums, the steady and savage impoverishment of millions of people – that England, specifically London, had undergone before any other place in the world. They made it easy to enter the attractive fantasy of London as a series of linked villages, nothing but open fields between Oxford Street and Hampstead.

The fantasy didn't last long. Ever-growing London had managed to relegate even its modern past – the scars of the industrial revolution and of the Blitz – to its museums. In the cramped rooms of Georgian houses in the East End, all traces of an old meanness had been banished by the developers outfitting them for investment bankers. The tenements of the East End had been turned into studio apartments for rich conceptual artists, and the monuments constructed out of the wealth of industry and empire – the National Gallery, the Albert Hall, the Royal Academy, Buckingham Palace and the many separate town halls with Grecian facades – co-existed uncomplainingly with the watering-holes – McDonald's, Pizza Hut – of another, even more commercially minded empire.

In India, the past never went away, or, being ever present, never became the past. But in Europe it was mainly tourists with cameras and Walkmans who gathered in the shadows of cathedrals; the monks, knights and troubadours had been absorbed into the heritage industry. The individual figures I had admired in India – Montaigne, Flaubert, Proust, Tolstoy, Emerson, Nietzsche – people who had been marginal within their own societies, alienated from, and often actively opposed to, their main political and economic tendencies, had, in a prosperous and confident age, been reincarnated as representatives of western civilization, their solitude, melancholy, bitterness and passion turned into the cold artefacts, the classics, of high culture.

'Original', 'inventive' and 'individual' were the words often used for them – the terms of praise also used for discoveries in the sciences, which seemed the more prestigious realm of human endeavour. It was as if a society prodigiously organized for expansion and consumption could absorb everything, even the few individuals who had once stood opposed to it.

Seen from the vantage point of a glamorous present, the past with its potentially endless store of events was simplified easily into a series of stages on the long road of progress. Indeed, to be an intellectual was partly to abstract, like the scientist, a few 'facts' from a larger whole, and to set them in a sequence of sorts. As for questions of ethics, which had preoccupied human beings for over two millennia, history had already provided most of the right answers.

In the radio studios of the BBC, the think-tank experts, pundits, academics and journalists would earnestly discuss how much or little Islam, India, the Middle East, or, simply, the East had travelled through the phases – Reformation, Enlightenment, Industrialization, Nationalism, Democracy, Corporate Capitalism – that led to the summit of affluence occupied by a handful of western nations.

Black cabs waited outside when I emerged from this warren of analysis. As I went home, past the shoppers who moved as if in a trance on Oxford Street, the voices of the experts in the studio – the voices I had once listened to in India and admired for their rich timbre and modulation, their suggestions of knowledge, even wisdom – would go round my head, and sometimes I would think about their ancestors, who had conquered the world and sought to remake it in the name of civilization, progress, history, socialism, the free market, secularism, development and science. What had brought them out of their own world? Half surprised at my ability to formulate the question in this way, I would wonder what new meaning they had brought to the idea of being human in seeking to remould a diverse humanity in their own image. Compared to the ancient Greeks, Chinese and Indians, what kind of spiritual image of man had they evolved in the course of their recent history – the history of conquest and violence in which they saw their own greatness, and which they presented to others as a guide to happiness.

I felt more at ease in America, free of a prettified past, better able to withdraw into myself and in New England, Virginia, California, to indulge my love of solitude and landscape. I knew this feeling for America as a ridiculous pang in my heart as the plane banked for the final approach at JFK airport and the towers of the city at the edge of the vast entranced continent rose serenely into view.

It was easy to denounce that American vision of endless space and well-being and leisure as a deception; to accuse it of obscuring the inner cities and drugs and violence, and the ruthless suppression of remote and near enemies. But to people from tormented societies, America was the country whose nation-building traumas seemed to lie in the remote past, and where many individuals could afford to look beyond the struggles for food, shelter and security that still weighed upon people elsewhere.

It was in America that I began to think again about the Buddha and Buddhism, almost a decade after my visits to the Buddhist Himalayas had first awakened my curiosity. Just as European travellers had once alerted me to the India the Buddha had belonged to, so American Buddhists made me see the new role the Buddha had acquired in the modern world.

In late 2000, I spent a few days at a Zen meditation retreat centre near San Francisco. I was then in the midst of a long stay in England and America, working as usual, but increasingly feeling the strain of the ambition that had driven and defined much of my adult life. I had fallen into a habit of thinking about the carefree days of reading and daydreaming I had spent in Benares and Mashobra.

In San Francisco, this nostalgia made me seek out Helen, my neighbour and friend from Benares. The last time I had seen her in Sarnath, I'd tried to duck behind a tree. Then, I had seen her as one of the many western travellers in India, people indulging their privilege – the unique licence offered to them by the power and wealth of their countries – to be whatever they wished to be: Buddhists, Hindus, Missionaries, Communists. Later, I had remembered Helen's various kindnesses to me, and I now felt ashamed at my cowardice and self-righteousness.

By then, I had come to know better the impulse that came over people when they decided to leave their highly organized societies – the impulse that was no less deeply felt even when it was indulged, as often happened, in apparently absurd ways. The constant striving for achievement, for the fulfilments that were small and brief and in retrospect appeared empty, the effort needed to simply maintain a way of life that affirmed one's identity, the hardening of social roles – all of this I had begun to see in my own life and understand more clearly.

I had begun to understand, too, the peculiar forms the spiritual life could take in America: how the excesses and disappointments of a materialist society – broken families, drugs, an unresponsive legal system, an unjust economy and cynicism about politics – could lead many people to apocalyptic forms of religion, mostly fundamentalist Christianity; and how the spiritual impulse had to negotiate many traps before it reached any place close to fulfilment.

It was still awkward to see Helen in San Francisco, dressed in maroon robes in the middle of the busy shopping district, amid a flamboyantly diverse Californian crowd. At the Starbucks café we went to I was much more conscious than she of the occasional curious glance in our direction. She was surprised to see me order chai; she didn't know that American coffee bars offered a good approximation of the milky sticky-sweet tea sold on the ghats of Benares. We talked about Benares, and I remembered the raw, unmade person who had looked upon the peanut butter and olive oil in her room as emblems of a distant exotic world. In an ironic reversal of roles, I was now more at home in this world than she was. Writing had brought me to the secure, stolid, middle-classness – the world of work, leisure, consumption – which was her inheritance, and which she had sought to move away from.

She took me to her parents' home in Sausalito, a long

luxurious house overlooking a bay crammed with yachts. There were candles and incense sticks on the dining table; the food was vegetarian, and the ciabatta bread, Helen told me, had come from a famous Buddhist-run bakery. Before eating, we held hands across the table while Helen uttered a short prayer in Tibetan. Her father, a lawyer, probably hoping to get over his unease, questioned me at length about the legal system in India. Her mother said that she was getting into meditation; a friend of hers had found it a good substitute for psychotherapy. She thought of herself as a Buddhist. Helen, barely picking at her food, smiled and winked at me across the table, and later told me how accepting her parents had been one of the radical changes in her life.

I didn't see her again after that evening. She was busy for the rest of that week. Being a Buddhist nun for her hadn't meant, as I had once presumed, renunciation of and seclusion from the world. If anything, it appeared to have involved her even more deeply with it. She worked with a group that ran a hospice for AIDS patients, and another group that cared for homeless people. She also worked with a forum that promoted peace and justice on a Buddhist model.

Buddhism, she said, had helped her see that striving for political and social change could not be separated from a striving for inner transformation. There was little point in trying to restructure societies if individual minds were still cluttered with greed, anger and delusion. She gave me brochures and books about the ecological and political groups she was working with. I read them, surprised by the large claims they so briskly made.

One of them spoke of the natural fit between Buddhism

and ecological ideals and quoted the Beat poet Gary Snyder describing as 'cancer' the world view in which 'men are seen as working out their ultimate destinies (paradise? perdition?) with planet earth as the stage for the drama – trees and animals mere props, nature a vast supply depot'. It also quoted E. F. Schumacher praising the Buddha for having shown a 'Middle Way between materialist heedlessness and traditionalist immobility'.

Another brochure asserted that destruction caused by man pursuing his self-interest with the help of modern technology had become more visible around the world in the shrinking of forest cover, the falling of acid rain, the creation of the ozone layer and the contamination of food.

It went on to claim that biological and ecological discoveries of the relationships between living beings had proved that nothing could exist in itself and by itself. It spoke of interdependence revealed by the working of multinational corporations: how western consumers making small choices as to coffee, jeans, shoes affect the invisible labourer in Honduras and Bangladesh; how everyone is implicated in the global system of labour and trade, especially the hugely lucrative western arms trade kept going by innumerable small wars or military stand-offs in Asia and Africa. It ended with an appeal to pay more attention to the seemingly simple Buddhist idea that greed, hatred and delusion were the source of unhappiness, discontent and violence.

In the small bookshop at Simla, where many years before I had begun reading about the Buddha, there had been many such publications. There were books with titles beginning with *The Zen of* . . . or *Buddhism and* . . . and usually ending with *Psychoanalysis* and *Science* and *Ecology*. The foreign visitors to the bookshop tended to be more interested in them. They had little or nothing to say about the Buddha's life. And the ones about Buddhism and the environment sounded too much like Mr Sharma.

Although I was intrigued by magazine articles on Buddhism by writers and artists whose work I followed or knew of – the composer Philip Glass, the writer Charles Johnson, the academic critic bell hooks, the painter Francisco Clemente – who were also Buddhists or had affinities with Buddhism, I did not learn much about the new forms of Buddhism that had emerged during my own lifetime in the West.

I discovered much later that Buddhism, though among the oldest of religions and the latest to become a world religion, had in the twentieth century spread more rapidly than either Christianity, which, beginning in a remote province of the Roman Empire, had waited for over a millennium and a half before becoming, with the help of European imperialists and colonists, a global religion, or Islam, which was spread by traders and conquerors, and had taken an equally long time in expanding across the world.

In all my time in England and America, I had never gone to a meditation retreat. I had always found odd the idea that one needed to take time off and go somewhere in order to meditate, or that one needed to receive expert instruction in how to sit still with an empty mind. It seemed to be a peculiarly western way of dividing time – like the idea of confining leisure to the weekends.

But suddenly one day the longing for rest, silence and solitude came over me; and when I arrived at the retreat near San Francisco one foggy morning it seemed that the same longing had brought most of the others there, too.

*

There were rules everywhere in the retreat; and the severe-looking monks in black robes seemed to be in charge of enforcing them. You had to enter the meditation hall with your left foot forward. Then, while walking to your place in the hall, you had to stop and bow before the monk-instructor. After meditation you had to bow to the floor nine times. You were then asked to recite the prayer printed on a piece of paper that had been handed out. It began with these words:

> Avalokiteshvara Bodhisattva, when deeply practicing prajna paramita, clearly saw that all five aggregates are empty and thus relieved all suffering . . .

The prayer ended:

> Therefore, know the prajna paramita as the great miraculous mantra, the great bright mantra, the supreme mantra, the incomparable mantra, which removes all suffering and is true, not false. Therefore we proclaim the prajna paramita mantra, the mantra that says: 'Gate Gate Paragate Parasamgate Bodhi Svaha.'

The ritual with its incomprehensible words reminded me of my childhood, of the ceremonies attending birth, marriage and death. I did not understand a word of the Sanskrit mantras the presiding pandit recited. Nor, it appeared, did anyone else. But everyone looked solemn, and satisfied with mere incantation.

These rituals demanded a collective surrender to old mysteries. I couldn't but feel their irrelevance to the world I was growing up in. I had lived much of my adult life without them, and so, at the Zen retreat in California, I found it hard to stop after entering the meditation hall with my left

foot forward and bow to an empty seat. I gave only a per-
functory nod in the direction of the monk-instructor before
walking on and taking a seat towards the back of the vast
hall. I moved my lips wordlessly during the prayer. The
American monk who walked through the rows of meditating men and women, checking and commenting on their
postures, stopped where I sat, and seemed to appraise me
sceptically.

The place had, in addition to white Americans, people of
Vietnamese, Thai, Korean, Chinese and Japanese ancestry.
They were from around the Bay Area, upper-middle class
people in their late thirties or forties, with large cars, even
sports utility vehicles, in the parking lot. Most of them did
not appear to have visited a retreat before. They had trouble adopting the classic meditation posture and had to use
cushions to support their knees and backs. But they were
eager to learn, quick to fall into line, and to approve and
admire. They laughed heartily at the small witticisms of the
monk who formally welcomed us, and between long stints
of meditation they filled the dining room with a polyglot
cheerfulness.

I couldn't help wondering about their presence at a Zen
meditation retreat. The people with East Asian ancestry
would have known the particular Buddhisms of their original homelands. There had been Buddhist temples in
California since the late nineteenth century when Japanese
immigrants began to arrive in America. The later arrivals
from Vietnam, Thailand and Cambodia had brought their
faiths with them. These national Buddhisms had their own
temples and rituals, where people came together periodi-
cally and affirmed their sense of community in the way their

ancestors once had in the towns and villages of South-east Asia.

But the well-to-do participants at the meditation retreat seemed to be looking for something more than the security of shared ethnicity the temples and rituals offered. It was as if the religion of their ancestors could not fulfil the special needs they had developed while living in America – the needs that only an Americanized form of Buddhism could appease.

It was on this visit to California that I first began to learn about the many kinds of Buddhisms available in America. They had different names – Zen, Vipassana, Tibetan, Engaged – each of them had its own sects and sub-sects, with different leaders claiming separate spiritual lineages. The Asian Americans followed a more ritual-based Buddhism than the white Americans, who considered meditation the central practice of Buddhism. And the range of Buddhisms on display was matched by the ingenuity with which they reached out to their potential audience.

The Zen Buddhists who ran the retreat centre also owned a famous vegetarian restaurant in San Francisco and another retreat in the mountains close to the Pacific Ocean. Even the large chain bookstores in San Francisco were full of books on Buddhism and Eastern religion and the magazines called *Dharma Life* and *Shambhala*, whose ads for 'Buddhist vacations' and 'Buddhist investment advice' I had once looked through curiously while in India. There were many Buddhist bookshops as well as stores specializing in Buddhist 'accessories' (expensive cushions, mats, incense, music CDs), where the muzak featured Tibetan gongs and

chants, and on whose crowded notice boards new meditation and Yoga retreats vied with new Zen bakeries.

It was as if California, specifically the Bay Area, had
most of what Nietzsche once defined as the 'precondition'
of Buddhism:

> a very mild climate, very gentle and liberal customs, *no*
> militarism; and that it is the higher and even learned
> classes in which the movement has its home. The supreme
> goal is cheerfulness, stillness, absence of desire, and this
> goal is *achieved*.[1]

I also learnt on this trip about the scandals which had
made many people suspect that the American forms of Buddhism, though followed by up to four million people, were
less than perfect. The American Buddhist who had set up
the meditation retreat centre and the bakery in San Francisco had driven around in expensive cars, and had
conducted an affair with a married woman. The American
head of a Tibetan Buddhist sect had lived a promiscuous life
while infected with AIDS.

Faced with public criticism and scorn, Buddhist sects
and groups had had to democratize and invest leadership in
collectives rather than individuals. They had to accommodate women in the small monastic movement, and accept
gay, lesbian and bisexual people as Buddhists. Since the
renunciations required of monks were deemed too rigorous,
Buddhism teachers in America had to reorientate themselves to lay people, and to reconcile themselves to the
absence of monastic communities such as those that tradi-
tionally existed in Asia. It was as if Buddhism in America
had to adjust itself to a set of cultural assumptions fundamentally inimical to it.

The incongruities certainly seemed deeper than those
that had shadowed Buddhism elsewhere. As Alexis de
Tocqueville had noticed in the early 1830s, individual self-
interest was the very basis of the brand-new commercial
and industrial society that Europeans had created in the
seemingly unlimited spaces of the New World. The related
ideas of the autonomous individual, of man as the maker of
history, the carrier of progress and civilization, had first
taken strong root in America. The American Revolution
had preceded the French in upholding the rights and liber-
ties of individuals, and in positing the ideal of a common
humanity, held together by such inalienable rights as the
right to life, liberty and the pursuit of happiness. America,
Tocqueville thought, was the first place where the 'moral
and intellectual activity of man' had been diverted to the
'production of comfort and the promotion of general well-
being'. Tocqueville, who was in America primarily to learn
the lessons of the French Revolution, which had degener-
ated into violence and terror, followed by a highly centralized, semi-dictatorial government, predicted, accurately,
that Europeans would in time embrace the change in human self-perceptions brought about by their all-conquering
kinsmen in America.

Tocqueville's admiration for the achievements of the
American Revolution was deep. It was also, as events in the
next century and a half were to prove, remarkably prescient. America, which was to accommodate multitudes of
persecuted peoples from across the world, and lead decisive
battles against the totalitarian political systems of fascism
and communism in Europe, could persuasively claim a high
moral purpose as a nation at the end of the twentieth century. After two world wars and a cold war which had

undermined the European imperial powers of the previous century, Germany, Britain and Russia, America seemed not only the most capable defender but also the greatest representative of western civilization.

Nowhere else was the human intellect harnessed more exhaustively for practical use in industry, commerce and politics. Progress was nowhere else more visible than in America where scientists first split the atom, sent man to the moon, won important victories over disease and began to unravel, through the discoveries of DNA, the secret of life itself. And happiness and freedom – the special promises made by the West in the previous two centuries – nowhere seemed easier to pursue than via the endless highways, the cheap gasoline, the big cars and houses, the music and the slick films of America.

Buddhism in America might have surprised the Buddha only because he hadn't expected the *dharma* to survive this long. He thought it impermanent, like all mental events and physical states, with no unchanging essence, and had, in fact, predicted its disappearance. But he would have agreed that his ideas, too, were subject to specific causes and conditions, and so could assume a very different form in America from the one they had in China and Japan. After all, they had first gained resonance partly because they emerged at a mature phase in the civilization of North India. They had then travelled variously and found different forms everywhere else they went.

The Buddha himself, while travelling across the different societies and cultures of North India, was inclined to modulate his teachings for the sake of his audience. He gave one of the most famous of his discourses to the Kalamans, a people living apparently on the margins of the Indo-Gangetic civilization. The Kalamans were part of an independent republic not unlike the one the Buddha was born in. Like all other republics, they were being drawn into the larger world of kingdoms through conquest, commerce and better communications. Their simple, close-knit society with its clearly defined code of morality was slowly disintegrating. This explains their vulnerability to the new forms of wisdom preached by the *sramanas* who passed through their territory, and explains why a group of Kalamans approached the Buddha while he was resting in a village during one of his regular tours.

They told him about the various wandering ascetics and Brahmins who had visited them recently, presenting their views and attacking others. There were many of these itinerant teachers, each with his own form of knowledge. But the Kalamans did not know whom to believe.

The Buddha, who had described the overheated intellectual atmosphere of his time as the 'jungle of opinions', told the Kalamans that they should not rely

> on hearsay, on tradition, on legends, on learning, nor on mere inference or extrapolation or cogitation, nor on consideration and approval of some theory or other, nor because it seems fitting, nor out of respect for some ascetic.

The Buddha then recommended individual judgement to the Kalamans. But he wasn't upholding only pure reason as the best means of knowledge. Reason could emerge only out of a moral regimen. The individual had to reflect thoroughly on the consequences for both himself and others of his deeds and the intentions behind them. Here, the Buddha's favourite notion of *kusala*, or skilfulness, was crucial;

it applied to both skill in meditation and to moral discipline. To be morally skilful was to know that what was good and bad was good and bad for both oneself and for others. Only then could the choices confronting the individual be narrowed down:

> When you know for yourselves that this is unskilful and that skilful, this blameworthy and that blameless, this deprecated by the wise because it conduces to suffering and ill, and that praised because it conduces to well-being and happiness . . . when you know this for yourselves, Kalamans, you will reject the one and make a practice of the other.

There was nothing startlingly original about the conclusions the Buddha hoped that the Kalamans would reach through moral reasoning; they were akin to the prescriptions he gave to lay people: do not kill, do not take what is not given, or incite others to their harm. But the Buddha realized that since moral rules could no longer derive their sanction from tradition and custom they had to be inferred from actual individual experience. In the larger world, which increasingly absorbed small groups like the Kalamans and where tradition and custom had lost force, the individual had to rely upon his newly discovered rational faculty. Normally deployed in the pursuit of self-interest, it could also be used to cultivate the mental skills and attitudes necessary to a moral life in society.[2]

The self-governing individual with moral self-discipline was what had struck Tocqueville on his tour of New England townships, and it was what he wished would appear in France where he thought religious faith had been too hastily undermined. 'How is it possible,' he asked, 'that society should escape destruction if the moral tie is not strengthened in proportion as the political tie is relaxed?' Tocqueville claimed that although the early Americans were unselfconscious followers of Descartes who had exhorted individuals to rely on their own judgement, they had managed to combine the spirits of religion and freedom. He saw religion as a necessary ethical and spiritual influence upon individuals in a mass society devoted to individualism and materialism. Buddhism in modern America often seemed to have, still in an extremely limited way, the same role Tocqueville thought religion had once played in early American civil society.

The peculiarly modern vision of the Buddha, which presupposed the individual, and his capacity for reason and reflection, had proved extremely portable from the very beginning. Free of dogma, it could travel across political and cultural boundaries, just as the Buddha himself had, and adapt itself to local needs. When in the first centuries after Christ, traders and merchants took the Buddha's teachings to Central Asia and then to China, they blended with the powerful pre-existing religion of Taoism.

Monks and scholars began to make the Buddha available to a Chinese elite in the fourth and fifth centuries AD. Mahayana Buddhism became the pre-eminent religion of China under the T'ang dynasty in the seventh and eighth centuries, when rich Chinese built Buddhist temples and retreats in extravagant styles in an attempt to gain good *karma*. From China, a version of the Ch'an lineage went to Japan, where it came to be called Zen. A Japanese teacher called Dogen returned from China in the thirteenth century and revived Zen in Japan. And now, more than a thousand years after their first major efflorescence, the Buddha's ideas had moved beyond their old Asian frontiers and into the vast areas of the New World where members of another elite, by far the most powerful and wealthy in history, seemed to use it to re-enchant the modern world.

Even as early as the 1830s, Tocqueville had diagnosed – in almost the Buddhistic sense of *trishna* – the peculiar restlessness of people living in a democratic and materially abundant society:

> The inhabitant of the United States attaches himself to the goods of this world as if he were assured of not dying, and he rushes so precipitately to grasp those that pass within his reach that one would say he fears at each instant he will cease to live before he has enjoyed them. He grasps them all but without clutching them, and he soon allows them to escape from his hands so as to run after new enjoyments.[3]

De Tocqueville spoke, too, of how the pursuit of equality leads people into envy and resentment. It explained to him the 'disgust with life that sometimes seizes them in the midst of an easy and tranquil existence'. He claimed that in democratic societies people enjoyed life more keenly and in greater numbers. By the same token, 'hopes and desires are more often disappointed, souls are more aroused and more restive, and cares more burning'.

Such restlessness led many middle-class people in the 1960s to experiment with drugs, sexuality and the Eastern religions and philosophies found in such unexpectedly popular books as the *I Ching, Tao Te Ching*, the *Bhagavad Gita* and *The Tibetan Book of the Dead*. Artists and intellectuals were instinctively drawn to Buddhism, particularly to Zen, which was linked with psychotherapy by the books of D. T. Suzuki, a Japanese scholar, as well as those of Alan Watts, an English writer on Asian religions. Buddhism, which had first arrived in America with the trappings of Protestant rationalism, was now seen as emphasizing spontaneity and creative self-expression and exhorting the rejection of authority and convention.

As Jack Kerouac wrote in 1954:

> Self be your lantern/self be your guide –
> Thus spake Tathagata
> Warning of radios
> That would come
> Some day
> And make people
> Listen to automatic
> Words of others.[4]

Ginsberg and Kerouac had met Suzuki in New York, where the latter lectured for six years in the 1950s at Columbia University before audiences that included the composer John Cage and the psychoanalyst Erich Fromm. In 1956, Anchor Books published Suzuki's book *Zen Buddhism*, with an introduction by William Barrett, author of books on existentialism, who suggested Zen as a way out of the trap of modern existence in which neither science nor western metaphysics had provided certainty or meaning.

In 1958, Kerouac published his novel, *The Dharma Bums*, which spoke of a 'great rucksack revolution, thousands or even millions of young Americans . . . all of 'em Zen lunatics who go about writing poems that happen to appear in their heads for no reason'. His novel introduced young Americans to quasi-Buddhist ideas of a spiritual liberation. The same year *Time* magazine announced in an article on Alan Watts that 'Zen Buddhism is growing more chic by the minute'.

Much of the early American interest in Buddhism came through a highly idiosyncratic form of Zen, in which Buddhism could be personalized, embraced without responsibilities, mixed with drugs and psychotherapy, and pursued without self-discipline or institutions. Some of these accretions survived, but as the 1960s ended, Americans came to know many more kinds of Buddhism – brought to America by a fresh wave of immigrants from Thailand, Korea, Japan and Vietnam after the changes in immigration law in 1965.

The idea of an 'engaged Buddhism' took deeper root as Tibetan refugees fleeing the Chinese Communist takeover of Tibet began to arrive in the West in large numbers in the 1960s and 70s. Among these refugees were young masters, such as Allen Ginsberg's controversial later mentor, Chogyam Trungpa, who went on to have a large western following as teachers of Buddhism. But it was the Dalai Lama who, as the head of the Tibetan diaspora, helped give Buddhism a political edge in the West.

Buddhism assumed another form in America as the Tibetan presence expanded. On the whole, Buddhism in the 1960s, particularly Zen, still addressed itself to the individual, responding to his need for a purely personal and particular escape from the oppressiveness of the hyper-rational world. The Buddhism that entered mainstream culture through a profusion of sects, and the mass media, in the 1980s and 90s was still orientated towards lay persons. But rebirth and *karma* ceased to have the central role they had in Asia. For many American converts, Buddhism came, as one influential book put it, 'without beliefs'; it was an 'existential, therapeutic, and liberating agnosticism'.[5]

In his discourse to the Kalamans, the Buddha envisioned the individual who though forced to live in a confused world whose vagaries he little understood was still able to monitor his own habits and motivation. Americans attempting to design a suitable Buddhism for themselves found this particularly useful. As Gary Snyder wrote in an essay published in 1969, 'Meditation is going into the mind to see this (Buddhist wisdom) for yourself – over and over again, until it becomes the mind you live in. Morality is bringing it back out in the way you live, through personal example and responsible action, ultimately toward the true community (*sangha*) of all beings.'

Meditation, particularly *Vipasyana*, became the central practice of Buddhism in America. The Buddha's emphasis on meditation may not have been the only reason for this. Meditation was one of the few viable forms of practice still available to modern man. As an ancient form of mystical experience, it offered him release from the nervous, irritable, disciplined and information-heavy consciousness he was required to possess in his everyday world of work and responsibility. At the same time, it did not sunder him from the sources of his livelihood – a lesson learned by the New Age gurus who offered it as a substitute for psychotherapy and by the corporate managers who introduced meditation to their employees.

Overcoming Nihilism

BUDDHISM IN AMERICA COULD be seen to meet every local need. It had begun as a rational religion which found few takers in America before being transformed again, during the heady days of the 1960s, through the mysticism of Zen, into a popular substitute for, or accessory to, psychotherapy and drugs.

Towards the end of the twentieth century, it had begun to appear, tentatively, in the mainstream of American life. It attracted not just white or Asian Americans but also, increasingly, African-Americans and Hispanics. It had been infused with political protest and ethical responsibility. At the same time, it had been commercialized and commodified.

It often appeared a refined form of self-help, with meditation as its most widely available and practised technique. Few people explored its metaphysics and epistemology, partly because the key Buddhist ideas of *karma* and reincarnation were fraught subjects for people brought up to believe that all human beings are born, or at least should be considered, equal in all respects.

Buddhism in America ran up not only against deeply

internalized political ideologies but also against many obdurate psychological and emotional habits. On one of his first visits to America, the Dalai Lama was bewildered to hear some students at Harvard confess that they suffered from 'self-hatred'. The Dalai Lama, who was brought up in a tradition much less keen on individualism, did not know what the word meant and had to consult the more westernized men in his entourage.

It wasn't clear what form if any Buddhism would settle into in America, where much of the discontentment with secular modernity was channelled into conservative politics and fundamentalist Christianity. But its quietly paradoxical and growing presence in a culture which exalted individual energy and optimism and action already seemed one of the most interesting events in its two and a half millennia-long history.

It was Nietzsche who, towards the end of the nineteenth century, had seen most clearly how Buddhism would attract the peoples of the West precisely in the wake of their great success, after science and progress had abolished their belief in a transcendent world, in God and God-enforced values.

Nietzsche also had the clearest foreboding of the cost of this success: the destruction of old moral and religious certainties, the rise of mass societies along with new forms of control and domination through the state and technology, and the beginning of an 'era of monstrous wars, upheavals, explosions'.

He called the end of religion 'the most terrible news', and predicted that 'rather than cope with the unbearable loneliness of their condition, men will seek out their

shattered God, and for his sake they will love the very serpents that dwell amid his ruins . . .'

Nietzsche claimed to have identified these serpents that
gave Europeans the consolations of belief: progress, history, reason, science. He denounced progress as a 'false
idea'; he dismissed Hegel's vision of history as charlatanry.
He doubted if increased theoretical knowledge about the
world could heal the 'wound of existence'. He saw modern science – an article of faith for secularized Europeans
– as an aspect of the nihilism that he feared was blighting
the world – a view that became commonplace after the
First World War, which proved that science was unre-
strained by ethics and could be put to the most destructive
uses.

Nietzsche also saw the obsession with economic
growth, which had greatly increased in his lifetime, as con-
cealing the futility of life and the diminishment of human
beings. Utilitarianism to him was one of the empty substitute religions of the nineteenth century:

> What I attack is the economic optimism which behaves as
> though, with increasing *expenditure* of all, the *welfare* of
> all would also necessarily increase. To me the opposite
> seems to be the case: the sum total of the expenditure of
> all amounts to a total loss: *man is diminished* – indeed
> one no longer knows what purpose this immense process
> has served in the first place.[1]

For Nietzsche, life and the world had no value in themselves; human beings adorned them with meaning by using
such concepts as god, history, progress. Nothing was given
as real to us except our 'world of desires and passions'
and that 'we can rise or sink to no other reality than the

reality of our drives'. As he saw it, men needed to destroy
their self-invented values before beginning the strenuous
task of embracing their fate in a world which is without
evident meaning but which, in the absence of beliefs in
god, history, science, etc, 'might be far more valuable than
we used to believe'.

Contemptuous of all modern faiths, Nietzsche concerned himself with finding out how Europeans could
recover this valuable world that he thought two thousand
years of Christianity and its secular replacements – the
ideals of progress and science – had obscured. But he suspected that their despair and weariness would make
Europeans vulnerable to religions and philosophies that
preached 'passive nihilism' and helped people reach a private reconciliation with the general malaise.

He believed that the Buddha offered a temptation to
exhausted Europeans. He considered Buddhism a 'danger'
partly because he admired it himself. He described the
Buddha as a 'physiologist', administering to a depressed
people, to *late* human beings . . . races grown kindly,
gentle, over-intellectual who feel pain too easily'. He gave
a succinct account of how he thought the Buddha dealt
with the spiritual weariness caused by the collapse of old
beliefs and the rise of nihilism in his time:

> with life in the open air, the wandering life; with moder-
> ation and fastidiousness as regards food; with caution
> towards all emotions which produce gall, which heat the
> blood; *no* anxiety, either for oneself or for others. He
> demands ideas which produce repose or cheerfulness –
> he devises means for disaccustoming oneself to others.
> He understands benevolence, being kind, as health-
> promoting . . . His teaching resists nothing *more* than it

resists the feeling of revengefulness, of antipathy, of *ressentiment* ('enmity is not ended by enmity': the moving refrain of the whole of Buddhism . . .)[2]

Nietzsche's own solution to nihilism was the self-creating superman in a meaningless world, who not only lives in but also learns to love a world without value, direction and purpose. He spoke frequently of hardness, loneliness and struggle. From his intimate knowledge of physical and emotional pain, he concluded that life acquired meaning only through the odds it overcame.

This was salutary given the naive assumption Nietzsche struggled against in his time: that man was essentially good, if a bit mediocre, and that his happiness could be guaranteed through an improved state or technological innovation. But, proudly solitary himself, Nietzsche couldn't see how the superman would live in a human community. If Marx overemphasized the social at the expense of the individual, Nietzsche did the opposite in proposing the superman as release from the soullessness and mediocrity of modern life. And he did not escape the assumptions of his own time.

At one level, the superman merely incarnates the sense of the self and heightened individuality that came to be especially prized after the decline of religion in Europe. In seeking to reach out beyond himself, he also embodies the hubris of modern man: the refusal to accept limits; the attempt to become the God which a great chasm had previously divided from man. Not surprisingly, while spelling out what he meant by self-overcoming, Nietzsche expressed a banal idea of human greatness; the few examples he gave of supermen were Julius Caesar, Borgia and Napoleon.

Though astonishingly prescient, he couldn't foresee how his own ethic of the superman – overreaching, strenuousness, spirit of sacrifice, contempt for traditional morality – would, in an era where God is dead and everything is permitted, be enlisted in authentically nihilistic ideologies: how Hitler and Stalin would emerge as the real supermen, mobilizing everything – men, labour, natural environments, vast bureaucracies of death and destruction – in order to impose their will upon the earth. He also couldn't see how technology with its destructive capacities, rather than individuals, would incarnate the will to power that he thought underlay all life, and, as an endless process without clear value, direction or purpose, make nihilism a universal, rather than a western or European, phenomenon.

Just before his collapse, Nietzsche was trying obsessively to undermine what he called man's 'erroneous articles of faith', foremost among which was the notion of a stable and enduring individual identity – the ego that separated itself from the world, analysed and experimented upon it, and reduced it to formulas in a deluded effort to alter it.

In Nietzsche's Buddhistic vision, 'death, change, age . . . growth, that all are becoming' i.e. in process.[3] Since man wanted power and control over the chaos that is both himself and the world, he spun a web of 'conceptual mummies'. He used reason to posit unity, substance and duration where there is only constant flux and change; these errors helped him make his world intelligible and bearable.

He praised Heraclitus for discovering

> the eternal and exclusive process of becoming, the utter
> evanescence of everything real, which keeps acting and
> evolving but never *is*, as Heraclitus teaches us, is a ter-
> rible and stunning notion. Its impact is most closely
> related to the feeling of an earthquake, which makes
> people relinquish their faith that the earth is firmly
> grounded. It takes astonishing strength to transpose
> this reaction into its opposite, into sublime and happy
> astonishment.[3]

Nietzsche never ceased to think of the Buddha as a passive nihilist, and so failed to see that the Buddha, far from
wallowing in Oriental nothingness, had offered a practical
way of achieving such a sublimation: how human beings,
beginning with mental skilfulness and meditation, could
reach a perception of *trishna*, the state of endless desire,
insecurity and frustration, and control and transmute their
basic strivings into a recognition of impermanence. In his
freedom from *ressentiment*, greed and hatred, the Buddha
was like the superman who had liberated himself from the
'morality of custom' and acquired 'a power over oneself
and over fate', which has 'penetrated to the profoundest
depths and become instinct'.

Like Nietzsche, the Buddha too had attempted to
reaffirm the natural dignity of human beings without
recourse to the ambitious schema of metaphysics, theology, reason or political idealism. Nietzsche himself
recognized as much when he wrote:

> The spiritual weariness he (the Buddha) discovered and
> which expressed itself as an excessive 'objectivity' (that is
> to say weakening of individual interest, loss of centre of

gravity, of 'egoism'), he combated by directing even the spiritual interests back to the individual *person*. In the teaching of the Buddha, egoism becomes a duty: the one thing 'needful', the 'how can *you* get rid of suffering' regulates and circumscribes the entire spiritual diet.[4]

This was the Buddha's own project of self-overcoming. It was based on his unillusioned insight into what human beings, though bound by society, by impersonal forces they barely understood, could still do: realize within their own being and share with others the conditioned nature and interdependence of things, and the need for an ethical life – all the aspects of the Buddha's teaching that were not only rediscovered by Buddhists in the West but also echoed by some of the great spiritual and intellectual figures living through the extraordinarily violent century prophesized by Nietzsche.[5]

The Last Journey

THE BUDDHA LIVED VERY long – about eighty years, at a time when most people died before thirty. He lived carefully – midday siestas, no evening meals. He bathed frequently in hot springs. But towards the end of his life he developed several diseases. He had back pains and stomach upsets. He had exhorted the *bhikshus* to meditate on the body, its fragile and repellent quality. He felt his own decay acutely, speaking once of how the body was kept going only by being bandaged up. His contemporaries, including his close disciples, died before him. Bimbisara, the king of Magadha, was murdered by his own son. The successor to Prasenajit, the king of Kosala, massacred the Buddha's clan, the Shakyas, and razed Kapilavastu to the ground.

The Buddha's farewells have an exhausted quality; they seem to be those of an essentially solitary man who has done, said and seen enough since that night in Bodh Gaya forty-five years earlier when he sat under the pipal tree and felt himself to be possessed of a liberating insight. Yet there is something grandly real and moving about his slow last journey across North India.

For more than twenty years, the Buddha had spent the monsoon months near Shravasti, at a monastery in a park donated to him by his rich lay follower, the merchant Anathapindika. He was there in his last year when the new king of Kosala, the successor to Prasenajit, sacked Kapilavastu. It had been a brutal affair. According to one source, the Shakyas were packed tight in pits dug into the ground and then trampled by elephants. The Buddha is said to have received the news silently.

He then heard that Sariputra, his closest disciple, had died. Sariputra's younger brother brought to him the dead man's alms-bowl, robe and some ashes wrapped in the fine cloth monks used as a water strainer.

The Buddha had a small relic shrine made for these remains. When the rains stopped, he left Shravasti and travelled southwards. He hadn't gone far when he heard that his other great disciple, Maudgalyayana, had died near Rajagriha, probably killed by mercenaries hired by rival *sramanas*.

At Rajagriha, he stayed at the hill with the vulture's ledge that he had visited when he first left home, with the views of the green hills and the small caves, where he had met Bimbisara, meditated and preached, and where his envious cousin Devadutta had hurled the stone that wounded him.

Here the Brahmin minister of the king of Magadha, Ajatashatru, visited the Buddha. The Brahmin told him that Ajatashatru planned to attack the confederation of Vrijji tribes living north of Rajagriha. The Buddha revealed to him what he had said to the Vrijjis about the seven conditions of their well-being: as long as the Vrijjis followed them they were unlikely to be conquered by Ajatashatru.

The minister went away convinced that Ajatashatru would not succeed until he managed to find a way of creating dissent among the tribes. After he had gone, the Buddha gave the same discourse to the monks and added some more conditions that he thought would be vital to the integrity and longevity of the *sangha*.

He then moved on to the village on the banks of the Ganges, where the ministers of Magadha were building a fortress in preparation for the war against the Vrijjis. He ate with the Brahmin minister who had visited him in Rajagriha, and made a prophecy about the great city, Pataliputra (now Patna), which he thought would emerge there.

He crossed the Ganges and travelled to a village called Kotigama, where he addressed the monks on the four noble truths of suffering. Nearing Vaishali, he stopped in the mango grove of Ambapali, a famous courtesan. Ambapali, whose son had become a *bhikshu*, heard of his arrival and travelled to see him and to invite him to her house in Vaishali the next day for a meal.

While returning from her successful meeting with the Buddha, she ran into a convoy of eminent citizens from Vaishali who were planning to ask the Buddha to a meal the next day. They asked her to withdraw her invitation, but she refused. The Buddha told the citizens that he had already been invited. At her home, Ambapali prepared a fine meal and donated her grove to the *sangha*.

The Buddha stayed in this grove for a while. When the rains began that year, he asked the monks accompanying him to find their own retreats. He wished to be alone with Ananda, his attendant, and devote himself to meditation. But soon after arriving in a village called Beluva on the outskirts of Vaishali, he was attacked by a severe sickness.

When he got a little better, he told Ananda that, 'It would not be fitting for me to attain *nirvana* without having addressed my attendants, and without having taken leave of the *sangha*.' When Ananda replied that he was relieved that the Buddha would attain *nirvana* only after having determined something about the *sangha*, the Buddha replied:

> Why does the order of Monks expect this of me? I have taught the *dharma* making no distinctions of 'inner' and 'outer' . . . (and have) no teacher's fist (in which certain truths are held back). If there is anyone who thinks: 'I shall take charge of the order', or 'the order is under my leadership', such a person would have to make arrangements about the order. But the tathagata does not think, 'I will lead the order', or 'The order looks up to me'. When then should the tathagata determine something about the order?

He added:

> Ananda, I am now old, worn out, venerable, one who has traversed life's path, I have reached the term of life, which is eighty. Just as an old cart is made to go by being held together with straps, so the tathagata's body is kept going by being strapped up. It is only when the tathagata withdraws his attention from outward signs, and by the cessation of certain feelings, enters into the signless concentration of mind, that his body knows comfort.[1]

He wanted his teaching to lead the *sangha*. He was

clear about what he expected Ananda and the monks to do after his death:

> You should live as islands unto yourselves, being your own refuge, seeking no other refuge; with the *dharma* as an island, with the *dharma* as your refuge, seeking no other refuge . . .

He recovered enough from his illness to go begging for alms in Vaishali. He had spent much time in the city and its shrines, and one afternoon, sitting under a mango tree he described them as 'delightful' to Ananda, he said that the world was so delightful that one might want to live in it for a century or more.

He asked Ananda to bring the monks living in Vaishali to Beluva. When they had assembled, the Buddha exhorted them to stay faithful to his teachings so that the religious life may last longer and announced that he would die in three months.

He went for alms to Vaishali the next day. He knew that it was his last trip to the city, and while returning from it, he stopped, turned round and gazed nostalgically at the city for a while.

At villages along his way, he gave discourses to monks. He probably wished to die in Shravasti. In a village called Pava, he stopped in the mango grove which belonged to a smith called Cunda. As was customary, the smith insisted on serving him a meal. Suspicious for some reason, the Buddha asked him not to serve one part of food to anyone but himself and throw the remainder into a hole after he had eaten. He thought that no one other than himself could digest it. But he ate it anyway, hoping not to offend his generous host.

Soon after the meal, the Buddha suffered an attack of bloody dysentery. Though exhausted, he insisted on walking on to the town of Kushinagara. He stopped to rest under a tree and asked for water. Ananda said that the nearby stream had been fouled by the passage of ox carts. But the Buddha told him to go and check and when Ananda did so he found the water miraculously clear and pure.

While the Buddha rested under a tree, a man called Pukkusa came along. He turned out to be a follower of Alara Kalama, the very first teacher the Buddha had approached after leaving Kapilavastu. Pukkusa saw the dirty robes the Buddha and Ananda were wearing and sent his servant to fetch a pair of gold-coloured robes, which he promptly presented to the Buddha and Ananda.

They kept walking and at a river called Hiranyavati the Buddha took his last bath. He worried that Cunda might be blamed for poisoning him, and told Ananda to persuade Cunda that his good intentions had earned him much good *karma*, and save him from guilt and remorse. The Buddha waded through another river and reached the sal grove of Kushinagara. Here he told Ananda that he was suffering, and asked him to prepare a bed with the head to the north. As he lay down on his right side, his feet placed on top of each other, flowers fell from the sal trees.

The Buddha knew he was not going to get up again. He gave his final instructions to Ananda: the monks could visit the four places, where he was born, enlightened, preached his first sermon and attained *nirvana*. When asked about his funeral arrangements, the Buddha told Ananda not to worry about them but to devote himself to his liberation: he said that believing that laymen and others would take care of his funeral.

Ananda was suddenly full of grief, and began to speak of how much he still had to learn from the Buddha – the man who had been so compassionate to him and who was about to die:

> Enough, Ananda, do not weep and wail! Have I not already told you that all things that are pleasant and delightful are changeable, subject to separation and becoming other? So how could it be, Ananda – since whatever is born . . . is subject to decay – how could it be that it should not pass away?[2]

Ananda asked him not to pass away in Kushinagara, which he described as a 'miserable little town of wattle-and-daub, right in the jungle in the back of beyond'. He had hoped, he said, that the Buddha would attain *nirvana* in one of the big cities, where a funeral in proper style could be held.

The Buddha replied that Kushinagara had been a great city in the past, and then told Ananda to inform its inhabitants of his impending death. The news, spreading fast, brought many more griefstricken people to the grove where the Buddha lay. Careful not to disturb the Buddha, Ananda announced them by their family names as they shuffled past.

A *sramana* called Subhadra also arrived and asked Ananda for a private audience with the Buddha. Ananda refused, but the Buddha overheard him and asked him to let Subhadra in. Subhadra asked him which of the Buddha's famous contemporaries, the six *sramana* teachers, had attained enlightenment. The Buddha told him not to worry about such matters and taught him the *dharma*. Subhadra then became the last man to be accepted into the *sangha* by the Buddha.

The Buddha again stressed that his teaching, not an individual monk, was going to lead the *sangha*. Finally, he asked the monks who had assembled around him if they had any 'doubts or uncertainty about him, the *dharma*, the *sangha*, or about the path or the practice'. He told them that they shouldn't feel remorse afterwards, thinking that they had their teacher before them but failed to ask him face to face.

The monks were silent. The Buddha repeated his words a second and a third time.

Then he said that if the monks respected him too much to speak directly to him, they could put their questions through a fellow monk.

But the monks remained silent. It was late at night when the Buddha spoke to the monks again. 'All conditioned things,' he said, 'are subject to decay – strive on untiringly.' These were his last words.

When I read the *Mahaparinirvana Sutra*, the account of the Buddha's last journey, I thought of Gandhi. These two Indians had much in common: middle-caste men from regions peripheral to where they made their name, charismatic public figures who had renounced the calling of their ancestors and stressed individual awareness and self-control at a time of increasing violence.

Their melancholy last days also had much in common. In 1947, a few months before India's independence, and his own assassination, Gandhi, with a growing sense of futility and helplessness, had moved through parts of the same region where the Buddha had travelled. The Hindu–Muslim animosity against which Gandhi had worked all his life had exploded into savagery as the partition of India approached. Muslims and Hindus murdered and raped each other, not even sparing small children, whom they often hacked to pieces. In Bengal and then Bihar, Gandhi, then a frail man of seventy-seven, walked from village to village, where the bodies lay heaped in burnt houses or in wells, or in bamboo groves awaiting vultures.

He sought out both perpetrators and victims, asking them to admit their guilt and to renounce revenge. He was usually met with hostility. On the narrow pathways on which he walked, villagers would often spread human excrement. Once a Muslim spat in his face. Gandhi wiped the spit off and kept walking. People spoke of the danger to his life. His feet bled; he suffered from high blood pressure. He was tormented by his failure, and half longed for death – he spoke more than once of being killed. But he still persevered. He started early each morning and walked all day, often singing with his few companions the haunting song Tagore had written:

> Walk alone.
> If they answer not thy call, walk alone;
> If they are afraid and cower mutely facing the wall,
> O thou of evil luck,
> Open thy mind and speak out alone.

Committed to Becoming

> The world, whose nature is to become other, is committed to becoming, has exposed itself to becoming; it relishes only becoming, yet what it relishes brings fear, and what it fears is pain.

Years ago, returning from the first of my trips to the Buddhist Himayalas, I had thought of writing a historical novel about the Buddha, something that I thought would help me learn about India's past and also help me acquire some much-needed ancient wisdom. I accumulated books and notes, and travelled to Buddhist sites.

But other things held me more strongly as I emerged from my secluded life in Mashobra, and the Buddha began increasingly to appear an unpromising subject; there seemed something fixed and sterile about it, like the specimens in the museums to which Europe had confined its past.

Then, one warm afternoon in London in the spring of 2001, while I lay in a park, feeling lost and homesick, the idea returned.

I had just got back then from Afghanistan and Pakistan.

I had gone there partly to look for traces of Buddhism and also to learn more about the political situation in Afghanistan. It was not a good time to be doing so. Some months previously the Taliban had defaced the tall statues of the Buddha in the Bamiyan valley and destroyed the Indo-Greek statues of the Buddha remaining in the museum of Kabul. In the streets of Peshawar, where gaunt Afghan refugees sold drugs and guns, and mosque preachers railed against various infidels, there was no memory of Asanga and Vasubhandhu, the fourth-century Buddhist philosophers who had lived in this ancient town; and only fleetingly, amid the lonely ruins of Takht-e-Bhai and Taxila, was I able to imagine the Greek colonies, the Buddhist monks, the universities, the travellers from China and Central Asia – the whole cosmopolitan life of Buddhism that had so irrevocably vanished from even its greatest centre in the Indian subcontinent.

In the same place, a new kind of multinational religion and politics had grown in recent years. In squalid madrasas, where the Taliban had been given the most rudimentary education in the Koran, and where another generation of young men prepared themselves for jihad, men spoke calmly of how the oppressed Muslims of the world had come together in Afghanistan to destroy one superpower – the Soviet Union – and would, with the grace of god, also take care of America and Israel if they did not relent in their persecution of Muslims.

I went to an international conference of radical Islamists near the border with Afghanistan, where 200,000 men – many of them from North Africa, the Middle East and Central Asia – listened to speeches on similar themes. The atmosphere there was of a medieval desert fair: thousands of men walking urgently around the sprawling township of tents under a vast cloud of dust, past the pushcarts with fresh sugarcane juice and piles of chewed-up canes, past the stalls selling beautifully illustrated copies of the Koran in Urdu and Arabic, along with posters of Osama Bin Laden, who was clearly the star of the event.

Many of the older men attending were Pakistani peasants who I later discovered had been paid, in the Indian subcontinental way, to swell the gathering. But the larger part of the crowd was made up of young men in their late teens and early twenties. These were students from the madrasas in the region south of Peshawar that borders Afghanistan. They had travelled to the conference in a variety of vehicles, crammed in cars, buses, pick-up trucks, three-wheeler tempos and even horse-drawn carts, flying the black-and-white striped flag of the organizers, a fleeting touch of colour and excitement among the mud villages in the flat drab landscape around the Grand Trunk Road. In the speeches, they were referred to, more than once, as the reserve army of the Taliban, ready to martyr themselves in the noble task of jihad.

On the first day a ferocious dust storm blew down some of the tents. The long white shirts of the men flapped and rippled in the wind as they ran out from under the dangerously swaying tents; the new Afghan rugs lost their bright colour and blended into the dust-white ground. But the speeches remained fierce: speaker after speaker recounted a long history of humiliation and atrocity, the Crusades, Granada, Iran, Palestine, Kashmir, and urged Muslims to join the worldwide jihad against the United States and its allies.

*

It took me some time to sort out my own responses to all this. I knew about the corruptions of jihad; of the leaders grown fat on generous donations from foreign and local patrons, sending young men to poorly paid *shahadat* (martyrdom) in Kashmir and Afghanistan. But I hadn't expected to be moved by the casual sight in one madrasa of six young men sleeping on tattered sheets on the floor. I hadn't thought I would be saddened to think of the human waste they represented – the young men, whose ancestors had once built one of the greatest civilizations of the world, and who now lived in dysfunctional societies under governments beholden to, or in fear of, America, and who had little to look forward to, except possibly the short career of a suicide bomber.

The other kind of future once laid out for them had failed. This was the future in which everyone in the world would wear a tie, work in an office or factory, practise birth control, raise a nuclear family, drive a car and pay taxes. There were not nearly enough secular schools to educate these young men in the ways of the modern world – and few jobs awaited those who had been educated.

The forward march of history was to include only a few of them. For the rest, there would be only the elaborate illusion of progress, maintained by a thousand 'aid' programmes, IMF and World Bank loans, by the talk of underdevelopment, economic liberalization and democracy. But the fantasy of modernity, held up by their state, and supported by the international political and economic system, had been powerful enough to expel and uproot them from their native villages.

This had also been the fate of my father and countless

others like him. But the journey from the old to the new world had become harder over the years for most people. Now this journey seemed never-ending, and it seemed to consume more and more people as it lengthened: hundreds of millions of stupefied and powerless individuals, lured by the promise of equality and justice into a world which they had no means of understanding, whose already over-strained and partially available resources they were expected to exploit in order to hoist themselves to the level of affluence enjoyed by a small minority of middle-class people around the world.

To the more frustrated among them modernity already appeared as a tall mountain where a few people occupied the summit, watching others inch up the steep slopes, occasionally throwing down a tattered rope but, more often, giant boulders. They knew that there remained no unknown lands and peoples for them to conquer, control and exploit. They could only cut down their own forests, pollute their own rivers and lakes, and seek to control and thereby oppress their own people, their women and minorities.

Having lost the protection of their old moral order, their particular bonds and forms of authority, they hoped to stave off chaos and degeneration by joining such authoritarian movements as Hindu nationalism and radical Islam, by surrendering their dreams to demagogues like Bin Laden.

It was obvious at the fundamentalist gathering that neither the angry speakers nor their fervent audience knew, or could know, much about America. Out of fear and confusion, they had built an arbitrary notion, to which they ascribed their own suffering, and all the evils in the world.

And, armed with the idea of the enemy, they had begun to dream the old western dream of revolution: the swift and complete transformation of society in all its aspects, economic, legal, political, religious and cultural, the making from scratch of a pure state and society which alone could guarantee human happiness and virtue, the utopia that could only come about after its corrupt adversary had been laid low. The dream of revolution came with an additional religious romanticism: of an Islam which had supposedly offered security and justice in the past, and which now held a blueprint for the ideal future.

Uprooted men from societies that were once small and close-knit trying to organize themselves into large collectives; a people falsifying their past and turning a privately and diversely followed faith into political ideology; focusing their rage against such imagined entities as 'America' and the 'West'; and working to rouse people the world over for the sake of revolution – it was hard not to see these men as trying to find their being within history and only floundering in vast empty spaces.

But on that afternoon in London, a few weeks after my return from Pakistan, when I thought again of the Buddha, I had become aware too of the futilities in my own life. For the previous few months I had been living near the East End, writing a series of long articles about the political situation in Afghanistan and Pakistan. During the long days, when the harsh light and crowded streets and parks robbed London of its sombre air, there had come over me a homesickness which did not open out into nostalgia, and which in its heaviness was almost a kind of grief.

I was in my early thirties. I had written a few things. I had travelled a bit. Given my modest beginnings, it was hard not to see all this as a kind of achievement. For much of my life, I had been oppressed by the shame of being poor and ignorant and belonging to a backward-looking community, of not fully possessing a language, and of not having any clearly defined gift or talent.

I had in time overcome these fears, partly by learning the ways of the modern world, picking up its primary language, English, and educating myself through the immense literature available in it. I had become one of the privileged few who had overcome their disadvantages and found a provisional home in the West. In time, all that had initially struck me in England as inscrutable – faces, gestures, clothes, houses, accents – had lost its power to alienate. I spent much of the year in London. I had never ceased to consider my presence there as a small miracle – something I couldn't have imagined living in Mashobra. I still remembered that first day when I emerged from Heathrow into a bright autumn day and found a calm green land, overlaid in places with broad concrete strips on which cars glided with toy-like precision.

Yet this strange journey had also made a strange man of me. When I looked back, I saw many different selves: the callow student in Allahabad hoping for revolution, and also seeking to buy a baseball cap in Nepal; the young man in the Himalayas, reading the *Milindapanha* and thinking ambitiously about a book on the Buddha; the self-righteous and fearful journalist turning away from Helen, the weary person learning from her about Buddhism in

America. In few of these restless, grasping selves, these nexuses of desires and impulses that had spread themselves around the world, could I find as much as a trace of humility, or compassion.

Far from being unique or individual, as I had once imagined, my desires contained nothing of any vital importance or consequence. And I couldn't always suppress the quiet panic at the thought that the intellectual and spiritual vagrancy I had come to know was all I had to look forward to, no matter how much I knew or travelled.

I thought then, as I had on many occasions, of returning to Mashobra. During my years there, I had come to know no one in the village well. My memories of it were private, awakened occasionally, in very different landscapes, by long summer evenings, the sound of rain on the roof, a smell of resin. But in my fantasies it had begun to serve as home, the place to return to, where I could reliably find familiar faces and friendliness and generosity, and the illusion, perhaps necessary to uprooted people, of changelessness, of a stable and coherent past.

For years now I had arrived in Mashobra in the evening after a day's journey from Delhi and stood uncertainly with my bags on the road where I had first seen the broad view of the mountains and the valley and noticed a path running down to a house with a red roof.

And then to walk down to the house and to see Mr Sharma's mother sitting at the open windows, to watch Mr Sharma slowly come down the stairs with the keys jangling in his hands, to walk through the apple trees wearing their first blossoms, to enter the house and walk into the stale darkness and smells of the previous winter, to open the door onto the balcony and see the hills and the valley with their shifting shadows, the sickly lump of snow wasting away in the shade of pine trees and the cows looking well-fed and healthy, was to return to a feeling of relief and quiet elation.

It was raining this time when I arrived in Mashobra. Clouds and mist drifted around the valley, veiling the high mountains. When they lifted I went walking again and found new houses and hotels in the village. Real estate speculators with alleged Middle East connections had built condominiums, offered them at very high prices and sold them to suspiciously rich army officers. A five-star hotel stood in place of Wildflower Hall. Mr Sharma was building a new house just above mine; he had also installed a telephone in my cottage. Cable had reached Mashobra, with white wires strung tightly across electric poles penetrating even the flimsiest shack in the village.

A young entrepreneur at Daojidhar, who had once shared with me his schemes for transforming Mashobra into a tourist destination, had died abruptly. Tall monsoon grass stood in place of the brightly coloured tents he had put up on his property; excited singing voices no longer drifted in from the east.

Mr Sharma's big house felt empty. The second-floor window, where Mr Sharma's mother had sat on sunny afternoons, lay open as before, but the void there now brought a pang each time I walked past it. I noticed grief beginning to work upon Mr Sharma's face, deepening the melancholy in his eyes, lining his mouth.

He came once, to ask about my book. I told him that I was working hard on it. I didn't tell him that I had yet to resolve an important question about the Buddha in my mind.

For many years now I had read and thought about the Buddha's life and teachings. I was far from calling or thinking myself a Buddhist – I hadn't even attempted the hard and continuous self-scrutiny required of serious Buddhists. But I had got over many of my initial difficulties with the more metaphysical aspects of Buddhist teachings. I had come to understand that the Buddha had offered an internally coherent set of ideas, in which abstruse-sounding theories were never far apart from practice, and I had given up much of my scepticism about them.

It was probably true that greed, hatred and delusion, the source of all suffering, are also the source of life, and its pleasures, however temporary, and that to vanquish them may be to face a nothingness that is more terrifying than liberating. Nevertheless, the effort to control them seemed to me worth making. I could see how, whether successful or not, it could amount to a complete vocation in itself, as close as was possible to an ethical life in a world powered mostly by greed, hatred and delusion.

But I was still uncertain where the Buddha's teachings stood in relation to the unmanageably large political and economic conflicts that increasingly decided the fates of most human beings. They may have helped Ashoka and other absolutist rulers. But I couldn't see how they could be applied to the conduct of modern nations and empires, the clash of ideologies that had shaped much of the contemporary world, and the globalization that reflected an actual state of economic and political interdependence.

What did the Buddha, who had lived in a simpler time,

have to offer people fighting political oppression, social and economic injustice, and environmental destruction? It was easier to say what he hadn't promised. He had never conceived of the radical, large-scale social engineering that almost all modern ideologies on the right or left – socialism, free-market democracy, radical Islam, Hindu nationalism, and liberal imperialism – advocate. His indifference to ambitious political projects was part of his belief in individually achieved, rather than collectively organized, redemption. An early Dalai Lama had said that the meditator faced with an intractable world starts with repairing his own shoes instead of demanding that the whole planet be covered immediately with leather. But how did this assuage the political impotence felt by many people in the world today?

I had been in Mashobra for a month, imprisoned by rain and mist, reading about the Buddha and making notes, when one evening the telephone rang. It was a friend in Calcutta; he told me about the extraordinary scenes from New York unfolding on his TV screen.

I knew that Mr Sharma rarely switched on his television set. Nevertheless, I walked through the orchard as the light begun to fade and knocked on his door. Opening the window on the first floor, he was surprised to see me. I tried to convey to him the strange urgency of the moment; I told him that suspected terrorists had crashed planes into two of the tallest buildings in the world. He did not seem to understand. Then he said that it was his prayer time.

I listened to the radio; talked on the phone to friends in New York. Terrible images arose in my mind, images that seemed to have accumulated over the last twenty years, during the several militant uprisings in India, scenes from the aftermath of the tens of thousands of murders and hundreds of suicide attacks on individuals and institutions. They obscured what I struggled to articulate to myself: that the brutality of the world I had grown up in had come to America.

It was some days later that I watched the images of the burning and collapsing towers on a small, grainy black and white screen in the tin shack of the hunchbacked peasant who worked in the orchard below my cottage.

By then, the machinery of war had begun to grind. Leaders with emotional speeches and meticulous dossiers – the scientific evidence of evil – were preparing their frightened masses for fresh subjection to the state. The realpolitik experts, academics, and journalists were out in strength on CNN, advocating the end of states and the change of regimes, trying hard with their big words – Islamic fundamentalism, terrorism, fascism, totalitarianism, democracy, freedom, humanity – to seize a sense of reality, to somehow arrest and crystallize the ceaseless flow of events.

I sensed the labourer standing behind me. I had never spoken to him. I did not even know his name; and when I went up to him in the orchard to ask if I could watch TV in his shack he had become very shy, nodding his bent head and then quickly turning away.

His large family was busy cooking a meagre meal over a kerosene stove in one corner, amid a litter of dented aluminium plates and bowls and a smell of peanut oil. They were made nervous by me, as if not sure why the man who lived in the big cottage and seemed well off was present in their cramped dingy quarters, watching intently something they had already seen and quickly forgotten.

Once, during one of the replays of the collapsing towers, the labourer said, his quiet voice almost drowned out by the excited men on CNN, but chilling in its heartfelt conviction, 'This is all God's will,' and for a disturbing instant of perfect lucidity I saw what he meant on the screen, where the mighty work of man was being brought down to earth by a power which had been made devastating by modern technology, and which suddenly appeared, in what it had achieved, to have been abetted by a malevolent divinity.

The previous day I had heard on the radio about a speech that the US Defense Secretary had made at a memorial service for the victims of the attacks. He had spoken of the attackers as believers in the 'theology of self', and in the whispered words of temptation: 'Ye shall be as gods.' I had thought then about the young jihadis in Pakistan and Afghanistan: how quickly they would have moved from their sense of besiegement and impotence to exultation at the sight of the rich and proud superpower brought to grief and anger.

The sons of peasants in remote, backward countries, too, had come to possess the technical secrets that had made other men presume to divine status; and they had finally registered their arrival in the modern world, in the history that the experts said had ended, with an atrocity.

There seemed to be no refuge from the nightmares of a history that was now truly universal. The makers of this history, and its vigorous chroniclers, weren't fazed by the perplexities of a world grown too big for the human intellect to grasp. They were too infatuated by their own concepts – totalitarianism, liberalism, fundamentalism, imperialism, terrorism, etc. – to examine the crude assumptions – for instance, the belief that human beings have a single identity – that underpinned their thinking.

Ideology – democracy, freedom, Islamic virtue – gave them the moral certainty with which they spoke of the necessity of violence for remaking the world. It made them assume, almost as a matter of course – reverting on a terrible scale to the bloody rituals of tribal societies – that some must die so that others can live and be happy and free.

Given their immense power to manipulate and coerce, it was easy to see individuals everywhere reduced to spare parts of an imaginary humanity. But there was something missing in this bleak, compelling vision of individuals delivered to vast blind forces.

It was what I began to see more clearly that autumn in Mashobra: what the Buddha had stressed to the helpless people caught in the chaos of his own time: how the mind, where desire, hatred and delusion run rampant, creating the glories and defeats of the past as well as the hopes for the future, and the possibility for endless suffering, is also the place – the only one – where human beings can have full control over their lives.

The mind is where the frenzy of history arises, the confusion of concepts and of actions with unpredictable consequences. It is also where these concepts are revealed as fragile and arbitrary constructions, as essentially empty. What seems like necessity weakens in the mind's self-knowledge, and real freedom becomes tangible.

This freedom lies nowhere other than in the present

moment – the concrete present, the here and now, that the Buddha had affirmed over the claims of an abstract past and an illusory future.

To live in the present, with a high degree of self-awareness and compassion manifested in even the smallest acts and thoughts – this sounds like a private remedy for private distress. But the deepening and ethicizing of every-day life was part of the Buddha's bold and original response to the intellectual and spiritual crisis of his time – the crisis created by the break-up of smaller societies and the loss of older moralities. In much of what he had said and done he had addressed the suffering of human beings deprived of old consolations of faith and community and adrift in a very large world full of strange new temptations and dangers.

This was the human condition that Baudelaire, Kierkegaard, Nietzsche and Dostoevsky had also described, with much intellectual passion, anguish and irony. But the Buddha had not been content with vivid description or eloquent lament. He had not only diag-nosed the new intellectual and spiritual impasse faced by human beings at a time of tumultuous change: he had also tried to overcome it. In the process, he undermined many assumptions that lie behind the political and economic arrangements of the modern era.

In a world increasingly defined by the conflict of indi-viduals and societies aggressively seeking their separate interests, he revealed both individuals and societies as nec-essarily interdependent. He challenged the very basis of conventional human self-perceptions – a stable, essential identity – by demonstrating a plural, unstable human self – one that suffered but also had the potential to end its suffering. An acute psychologist, he taught a radical suspicion of desire as well as of its sublimations – the seductive concepts of ideology and history. He offered a moral and spiritual regimen that led to nothing less than a whole new way of looking at and experiencing the world.

I couldn't have understood this in the hopeful days when I first arrived in Mashobra and thought of writing about the Buddha. He was then part of a half-mythical antiquity, where I imagined myself roaming pleasurably for a few years.

I was to alter my view, but as a rigorous and subtle therapist the Buddha still belonged, in my mind, to the past. It was to take me much longer, and require more knowledge and experience, to discover him as a true contemporary.

I now saw him in my own world, amid its great violence and confusion, holding out the possibility of knowledge as well as redemption – the awareness, suddenly liberating, with which I finally began to write about the Buddha.

Acknowledgements

This book grew over a decade of travel and reading, and has accumulated many debts. I can acknowledge only a few of them here and in the notes that follow. Barbara Epstein's encouragement and support has been invaluable. Jason Epstein brought his usual intellectual rigour to the manuscript, which also benefited greatly from the close reading of Jonathan Galassi, Andrew Kidd, Sam Humphreys, John H. Bowles, Craig Murphy, Margery Sabin, John Gray, Mary Mount, Paul Elie, Jeremy Russell and Robyn Davidson. I am also grateful to Norma Bowles, J. F. Christie, my parents and sisters, and the Sharmas in Mashobra for their various kindnesses to me.

Notes

The notes are intended for the general reader who wishes to explore further the subjects I have discussed in this book. For the sake of readability, I have often altered the translations of Buddhist texts quoted.

Abbreviations

AN *Numerical Discourses of the Buddha: An Anthology of Suttas from the Anguttara Nikaya*, trans. Nyanaponika Thera and Bhikkhu Bodhi, Delhi, Vistaar, 2000.

DN *Digha Nikaya*, trans. as *The Dialogues of the Buddha*, 3 vols, by T. W. Rhys Davids, rpt. London, P.T.S., 1973.

MN *Majjhima Nikaya*, trans. as *The Middle Length Discourses of the Buddha*, by Bhikkhu Nanamoli, Boston, Wisdom Publications, 2nd edn, 2001.

SN *Samyutta Nikaya*, trans. as *The Connected Discourses of the Buddha*, by Bhikkhu Bodhi, Boston, Wisdom Publications, 2000.

The Invention of 'Buddhism'

1 Dialogue between Nagasena and Menander, adapted from *The Questions of King Milinda*, trans. T. W. Rhys Davids, 1890, rpt. Delhi, Motilal Banarasidass, 2 vols, 1965, pp. 43–4.

2   Translation of the pillar inscription in Lumbini by Thapar Romila, *Ashoka and the Decline of the Mauryas*, Delhi, Oxford University Press, 2nd edn, 1997, p. 261.

3   For more on Hiuen Tsang, see René Grousset, *In the Footsteps of the Buddha*, trans. Mariette Leion, London, Routledge and Kegan Paul, rpt. 1972. *Si-yu-ki, Buddhist Records of the Western World*, translated from the Chinese of Hiuen Tsang by Samuel Beal, 1884, Delhi, Oriental Books Reprint Corp., 2 vols, 1969. *Hui Li: The Life of Hiuen-Tsiang*, Samuel Beal, trans. 1911, rpt. Delhi, Munshiram Manoharlal, 1973.

4   For a spirited presentation of the Buddha as a critic of Brahmin ideology see Kancha Ilaiah, *God as Political Philosopher: Buddha's Challenge to Brahminism*, Kolkata, Samya, 2001. Some of Ambedkar's writings on the Buddha are collected in Valerie Rodrigues (ed.), *The Essential Writings of B. R. Ambedkar*, Delhi, Oxford University Press, 2002. Also see Sangharakshita, *Ambedkar and Buddhism*, London, Windhorse Publications, 1986.

5   Asvaghosa, *Buddhacarita*, chs. 1–17, E. B. Cowell (trans. and ed.) in *Buddhist Mahayana Texts*, New York, Dover Publications, 1969.

6   Claude Lévi-Strauss, *Tristes Tropiques*, trans. John and Doreen Weightman, London, Jonathan Cape, 1973, p. 503.

7   Osip Mandelstam, *The Collected Critical Prose and Letters*, London, Collins Harvill, 1991.

8   Jorge Luis Borges, *The Total Library: Non-Fiction, 1922–1986*, London, Penguin, 1999, pp. 3–9.

9   Visiting India in the seventh century, Hiuen Tsang saw destroyed and derelict Buddhist monasteries in Kashmir and elsewhere. For an interesting Tibetan perspective on the decline of Buddhism in India see Debiprasad Chattopadhyaya (ed.), *Taranatha's History of Buddhism in India*, trans. from the Tibetan by Lama Chimpa and Alaka Chattopadhyaya, Delhi, Motilal Banarasidass, 1990. For a Marxist view of the encounter between Brahminism and Buddhism see D. D. Kosambi, 'The Decline of Buddhism in India' in *Exasperating Essays: Exercises in the Dialectical Method*, Pune, R. P. Nene, 1986.

10 For early links between India and the West, see W. W. Tarn, *Greeks in Bactria and India*, Munshiram Manoharlal, Delhi,

1951; George Woodcock, *The Greeks in India*, London, Faber, 1966; E. M. McCrindle, *Ancient India as Described by Megesthenes and Arrian*, London, 1877, rpt. Delhi, Oriental Books Reprint Corporation, 1979; Demetrios Vassiliades, *The Greeks in India: A Survey in Philosophical Understanding*, Delhi, Munshiram Manoharlal, 2000; Donald F. Lach, *Asia in the Making of Europe*, vol.1, book 1, Chicago, University of Chicago Press, 1965.

11   Victor Jacquemont, *Letters from India*, 2 vols, 1834, rpt. Delhi, AES, 1993; vol. 2, p. 200.

12   Jacquemont, vol 1, p. 199.

13   *Ibid.*, p. 228.

14   For an account of Kennedy and Simla's origins see Pamela Kanwar, *Imperial Simla*: *The Political Culture of the Raj*, Delhi, Oxford University Press, 1990.

15   Jacquemont, vol. 1, p. 252.

16   For an overview of the scholarly British engagement with India, see P. J. Marshall (ed.), *The British Discovery of Hinduism in the Eighteenth Century*, Cambridge, Cambridge University Press, 1970; John Keay, *India Discovered: The Achievement of the British Raj*, Leicester, Windward, 1981; Philip Almond, *The British Discovery of Buddhism*, Cambridge, Cambridge University Press, 1988; Charles Allen, *The Buddha and the Sahibs: The Men Who Discovered India's Lost Religion*, London, John Murray, 2002. For a critical analysis of western and Indian suppositions about Indian religions see Richard King, *Orientalism and Religion*, Delhi, Oxford University Press, 1999.

17   On Buddhism in China see Stanley Weinstein, *Buddhism Under the T'ang*, Cambridge, Cambridge University Press, 1987; Arthur Wright, *Buddhism in Chinese History*, 1959, rpt. Stanford, Stanford University Press, 1971; K. Ch'en, *Buddhism in China: A Historical Survey*, Princeton, Princeton University Press, 1973. On contacts between India and China see P. C. Bagchi, *India and China: A Thousand Years of Cultural Relations*, 1950, rpt. Westport, Greenwood Press, 1971; Liu Xinru, *Ancient India and China: Trade and Religious Exchanges*, Delhi, Oxford University Press, 1988.

18   Macaulay's tone, as of many British people in the nineteenth cen-

tury, was set by James Mill's influential *History of British India*, 1817. Mill never visited India but lack of direct experience did not prevent him from attacking the 'absurdity and folly' of Indian religion. His son, John Stuart Mill, rejected all European claims to racial superiority but still believed that the 'East' was a backward place. For a stimulating discussion of Mill's view of imperialism see J. S. Mehta, *Liberalism and Empire: India in British Liberal Thought*, Delhi, Oxford University Press, 1999.

19 Jacquemont, vol. 1, p. 235.

20 On the German Romantics and India see W. Halbfass, *India and Europe: An Essay in Understanding*, Albany, State University of New York Press, 1988; Raymond Schwab, *The Oriental Renaissance: Europe's Rediscovery of India and the East, 1680–1880*, New York, Columbia University Press, 1984.

21 Jacquemont, vol. 2, p. 306.

22 *Ibid.*, p. 307.

23 *Ibid.*, p. 283.

24 For more on William Moorcroft and Alexander Csoma de Körös see John Keay, *Explorers of the Western Himalayas, 1820–1895*, London, John Murray, 1996; Edward Fox, *The Hungarian who Walked to Heaven: Alexander Csoma de Körös, 1784–1842*, London, Short Books, 2001.

The World of the Buddha

1 On India before Buddhism see F. R. and B. Allchin, *The Birth of Indian Civilisation*, Delhi, Penguin, 1997; A. L. Basham, *The Origins and Development of Classical Hinduism*, Boston, Beacon Press, 1989; Romila Thapar, *Early India: From the Origins to AD 1300*, London, Allen Lane, 2003; Romila Thapar, *Interpreting Early India*, Delhi, Oxford, Oxford University Press, 1992; D. D. Kosambi, *An Introduction to the Study of Indian History*, 2nd edn, Bombay, Popular Prakashan, 1975. On ancient Indian cities, see R. S. Sharma, *Material Culture and Social Formation in Ancient India*, Delhi, Macmillan, 1985; D. K. Chakrabarti, *The Archaeology of Ancient Indian Cities*, Delhi, Oxford University Press, 1992.

2 On the ancient theory of sacrifice see Georges Bataille, especially

the chapter on Tibetan Buddhism, in *The Accursed Share: An Essay on General Economy*, trans. Robert Hurley, vol. 1, London, Zone, 1989. Also see Roberto Calasso, *The Ruin of Kasch*, trans. William Weaver and Stephen Sartarelli, Cambridge, Mass., Harvard University Press, 1994.

3   For a controversial but stimulating discussion of the origins of the Indian caste system see Louis Dumont, *Homo Hierarchicus*, 1970, rpt. Delhi, Oxford, 1998. Also see B. K. Smith, *Classifying the Universe: The Ancient Indian Varna System and the Origins of Caste*, New York, Oxford University Press, 1989.

4   For social and political conditions of North India during the Buddha's time see H. C. Raychaudhuri, *The Political History of Ancient India*, 1965, rpt. Delhi, Oxford University Press, 1996; N. N. Wagle, *Society at the Time of the Buddha*, Bombay, revised edn, Popular Prakashan, 1995; B. C. Law, *The Geography of Early Buddhism*, Delhi, Oriental Books Reprint Corporation, 1979.

5   AN, p. 55.

6   The story of the Buddha is found in *Buddhist Birth Stories: Jataka Tales: The Commentarial Introduction entitled Nidana-Katha*, trans. T. W. Rhys Davids, London, George Routledge and Sons, 1925, pp. 151–4.

7   Quoted in A. L. Basham, *The Wonder That Was India*, 3rd revised edn, New Delhi, Rupa & Co., 1967. See another version of the Creation Hymn with a sparkling commentary in Wendy Doniger O'Flaherty, *The Rig Veda: An Anthology of One Hundred and Eight Hymns*, Harmondsworth, Penguin, 1981. Also see A. B. Keith, *The Religion and Philosophy of the Veda and Upanishads*, 2 vols, 1925, rpt. Delhi, Motilal Banarasidass, 1989; *The Origins and Development of Classical Hinduism*, Boston, Beacon Press, 1989.

8   In A. L. Basham, *The Wonder That Was India*, p. 250.

9   On Pythagoras and transmigration see Jonathan Barnes, *Early Greek Philosophy*, London, Penguin, 2001, p. 33.

10 For a scholarly yet accessible account of yoga see Mircea Eliade, *Patanjali & Yoga*, trans. Charles Lam Markmann, New York, Funk and Wagnalls, 1969.

11 On *karma* see Wendy Doniger O'Flaherty (ed.), *Karma and*

Rebirth in Classical Indian Traditions, Delhi, Motilal Banarasidass, 1983.

12 Patrick Olivelle, *Upanisads*, New York, Oxford University Press, 1996, p. 65.

13 *Ibid.*, p. 142.

14 Hesiod and Theognis, *Theogony & Works and Days; Elegies*, trans. Dorothea Wender, Harmondsworth, Penguin, 1973, pp. 54–5.

15 On early Indian asceticism see A. L. Basham, *History and Doctrine of the Ajivikas*, London, 1952, rpt Motilal Banarasidass, Delhi, 1982; G. C. Pande, *Studies in the Origin of Buddhism*, 1957, revised edn, Delhi, Motilal Banarasidass, 1995; Deviprasad Chattopadhyaya, *Lokayata: A Study in Ancient Indian Materialism*, Delhi, People's Publishing House, 1981.

16 The sayings of the Buddha's radical contemporaries are found in DN, vol. 1, pp. 69–70. Also see SN, pp. 991–1003. For a broad-ranging discussion of the India of the Buddha's time see Uma Chakravarti, *The Social Dimensions of Early Buddhism*, Delhi, Munshiram Manoharlal, 1987.

The Death of God

1 Friedrich Nietzsche, *Daybreak: Thoughts on the Prejudices of Morality*, trans. R. J. Hollingdale, Cambridge, Cambridge University Press, 1997, p. 54. Paul Deussen, one of Nietzsche's closest friends, was one of the most prominent Indologists of his time. But Nietzsche seems to have got much of the information about Buddhism from such books as Carl Friedrich Köppen's, *The Religion of the Buddha*, which was also read by Schopenhauer, Wagner and the French historian Hippolyte Taine, whom Nietzsche greatly admired.

2 Friedrich Nietzsche, *Twilight of the Idols/The Anti-Christ*, trans. R. J. Hollingdale, Harmondsworth, 1968, p. 141.

3 *Ibid.*, p. 137.

4 Friedrich Nietzsche, *The Gay Science*, trans. R. J. Hollingdale, Cambridge, Cambridge University Press, 2001, p. 219.

5 Quoted in Erich Heller, *The Importance of Nietzsche*, Chicago, University of Chicago Press, 1988, p. 5.

6 Nietzsche, *The Gay Science*, p. 181.

7 Karl Marx, 'The Communist Manifesto', Marx/Engels *Selected Works*, vol. 1, Moscow, Progress Publishers, 1969, pp. 98–137.

8 For a well-informed and insightful discussion of Islamic modernists see Fazlur Rahman, *Islam and Modernity*, Chicago, University of Chicago Press, 1982. Also see Albert Hourani, *Arabic Thought in the Liberal Age: 1798–1939*, Oxford, Oxford University Press, 1962.

9 On Vivekananda see Tapan Raychaudhuri, *Perceptions, Emotions, Sensibilities*, Delhi, Oxford University Press, 1999, and by the same writer, *Europe Reconsidered*, Delhi, Oxford University Press, revised edn, 2002; Amiya P. Sen, *Swami Vivekananda*, Delhi, Oxford University Press, 2000.

10 Quoted in William Radice (ed.), *Swami Vivekananda: The Modernization of Indian Tradition*, Delhi, Oxford University Press, 1998, p. 28.

11 Karl Marx, *The German Ideology*, *Collected Works*, Moscow, Progress Publishers, vol. 5, p. 27.

The Long Way to the Middle Way

1 *Buddhist Birth Stories: Jakata Tales*, trans. T. W. Rhys Davids, London, George Routledge and Sons, 1925, pp. 163–4.

2 AN, p. 54.

3 MN, p. 340.

4 MN, p. 187.

5 *Buddhist Birth Stories*, p. 173.

6 MN, p. 335.

7 MN, p. 256.

8 Allen Ginsberg, *Indian Journals*, San Francisco, Haselwood Books/City Lights Books, 1970, pp. 202–3. For another view of Ginsberg in India see Gary Snyder, *Passage Through India*, San Francisco, Grey Fox Press, 1983.

9 *Buddhist Birth Stories*, p. 180. Also see *Sutta Nipata*, trans. as *Woven Cadences of Early Buddhists*, by E. M. Hare, Pali Text Society, London, 1945, pp. 405–24.

10 On the Buddha's first teachers see MN, pp. 257–9.

11 On meditation see E. Conze, *Buddhist Meditation*, Delhi, Mun-

shiram Manoharlal Publishers, 1997. Also see Nyanaponika Thera, *The Heart of Buddhist Meditation*, London, Rider, 1969.

12 MN, p. 259.
13 MN, p. 174.
14 MN, p. 175 and p. 239.
15 MN, p. 340.

A Science of the Mind

1 *The Dhammapada*, trans. S. Radhakrishnan, Oxford, Oxford University Press, 1950, p. 110.
2 SN, p. 158.
3 Quoted from William Theodore de Bary (ed.), *The Buddhist Tradition in India, China and Japan*, New York, Vintage, 1972, p. 100.
4 For a critique of the reductive view of consciousness, see John Searle, *The Mystery of Consciousness*, New York, NYRB Books, 1997 and, by the same author, *Mind, Language and Society*, New York, Basic Books, 1998.
5 SN, p. 595.
6 Fyodor Dostoevsky, *Notes from the Underground*, trans. Constance Garnett, New York, Dover, 1992, p. 12.
7 *Ibid.*
8 For more on the Yogachara school, see A. K. Warder, *Indian Buddhism*, 1970, revised edn, Delhi, Motilal Banarasidass, 2000; Lal Mani Joshi, *Studies in the Buddhistic Culture of India*, Delhi, Munshiram Manoharlal, 1977; Jay L. Garfield, *Empty Words: Buddhist Philosophy and Cross-Cultural Interpretation*, New York, Oxford University Press, 2002.
9 Werner Heisenberg, *Physics and Philosophy: The Revolution in Modern Science*, London, Penguin, 1990. The literature on the links between Buddhism and modern science is growing fast. For an overview see B. Alan Wallace (ed.), *Buddhism and Science: Breaking New Ground*, New York, Columbia University Press, 2003.

Turning the Wheel

1   MN, pp. 261–2.

2   See MN, pp. 263–4.

3   SN, p. 1843.

4   David Hume, *Dialogues Concerning Natural Religion*, 1779, Harmondsworth, Penguin, 1990, pp. 106–7.

5   Michel de Montaigne, *The Complete Works: Essays, Travel Journal, Letters*, trans. Donald M. Frame, Stanford, Stanford University Press, 1958, p. 964.

6   *Ibid.*, p. 565.

7   *Ibid.*, p. 611.

8   MN, pp. 203–4.

9   SN, p. 1843.

10 Quoted in Nanamoli, *The Life of the Buddha: According to the Pali Canon*, Kandy, BPS, 3rd edn, 1992, p. 32.

11 SN, p. 1843.

12 Quoted in Michael Carrithers, *The Buddha*, Oxford, 1983, p. 61.

13 Erasmus quoted in Tzvetan Todorov, *Imperfect Garden: The Legacy of Humanism*, Princeton, Princeton University Press, 2002, p. 237.

14 Friedrich Nietzsche, *The Gay Science*, trans. R. J. Hollingdale, Cambridge, Cambridge University Press, 2001, pp. 162–3.

15 On science and meditation see 'The Colour of Happiness', *New Scientist*, 24 May 2003.

16 A. A. Long, and D. N. Sedley (eds), *The Hellenistic Philosophers: Vol. 1, Translations of the Principal Sources, with Philosophical Commentary*, Cambridge, Cambridge University Press, 1987, p. 155. Martha C. Nussbaum describes the Hellenistic philosophers in ways that make them seem very close to the Buddha. See her *The Therapy of Desire: Theory and Practice in Hellenistic Ethics*, Princeton, Princeton University Press, 1996. Also see A. A. Long, *Hellenistic Philosophy: Stoics, Epicureans, and Sceptics*, 2nd edn, Berkeley, University of California Press, 1986.

17 MN, pp. 1092–3.

18 The Legend of Yasa is told in the *Vinaya*. See Hajime Nakamura, *Gotama Buddha*, Tokyo, Kosei, 2000, pp. 276–85.

19 Socrates quoted in Pierre Hadot, *What is Ancient Philosophy?*,

trans. Michael Chase, Cambridge, Mass., Harvard University Press, 2002, p. 29. At the end of the book, Hadot mentions Buddhism and hopes that he has implied that the 'ancients were closer to the Orient than we are'. For Hadot's elegant attempt to rescue western philosophy from its academic cloisters see his *Philosophy as a Way of Life: Spiritual Exercises from Socrates to Foucault,* trans. Michael Chase, Oxford, Blackwell Publishers, 1995.

20 MN, p. 534.
21 *Ibid.,* p. 535.
22 Quoted in Nakamura, *Gotama Buddha,* p. 286.
23 *Ibid.,* p. 289.
24 Quoted in Stephen Batchelor, *The Awakening of the West: The Encounter of Buddhism and Western Culture,* Berkeley, Parallax Press, 1994, p. 38.

Looking for the Self

1   For the exchange between the Buddha and Vacchagotta see SN, p. 1393.
2   René Descartes, 'Meditations on First Philosophy', in J. Cottingham, R. Stoothoff and D. Murdoch (trans.), *The Philosophical Writings of Descartes,* vol. 2, Cambridge, Cambridge University Press, 1984, p. 19.
3   For a detailed exposition of Buddhist theories of the self see S. Hamilton, *Identity and Experience: The Constitution of the Human Being According to Early Buddhism,* London, Luzac Oriental, 1996; S. Collins, *Selfless Persons: Imagery and Thought in Theravada Buddhism,* Cambridge, Cambridge University Press, 1982.
4   For a clear account of the five *skandhas* see Walpole Rahula, *What the Buddha Taught*, Oxford, Oneworld, rpt. 1997.
5   David Hume, *A Treatise of Human Nature*, Harmondsworth, Penguin, 1969, p. 300.
6   *Ibid.,* p. 301.
7   Marcel Proust, *Remembrance of Things Past*, trans. C. K. Scott Moncrieff, vol. 1, London, Chatto and Windus, 1964, p. 58.
8   *Ibid.,* p. 60.
9   *Ibid.,* p.61.

10   MN, p. 927.

11   *The Voice of the Buddha*: *Lalitavistara Sutra*, trans. Gwendoline Bays, 2 VOLS, Berkeley, Dharma Publishing, 1983, pp. 175–7.

12   DN, vol. 2, pp. 53–4.

13   Quoted in William S. Waldron, *The Buddhist Unconscious*, London, Routledge, 2002, p. 68.

14   Friedrich Nietzsche, *The Gay Science*, trans. R. J. Hollingdale, Cambridge, Cambridge University Press, 2001, p. 112.

15   DN, vol. 2, p. 60.

16   For a modern interpretation of Nagarjuna's philosophy see Stephen Batchelor, *Verses from the Centre: A Buddhist Vision of the Sublime*, New York, Riverhead, 2000. Also see J. L. Garfield, *Empty Words: Buddhist Philosophy and Cross-Cultural Interpretation*, New York, Oxford University Press, 2002.

17   Claude Lévi-Strauss, *Tristes Tropiques*, trans. John and Doreen Weightman, London, Jonathan Cape, 1973, p. 503. Among other modern thinkers, Heidegger is said to have found affinities between his ideas and Zen Buddhism. Michel Foucault was deeply interested in Buddhist philosophy and felt that a philosophy of the future could only come out of the non-western world or be 'born in consequence of meetings and impacts between Europe and non-Europe'. See his dialogue with a Japanese monk in Jeremy R. Carrette (ed.), *Religion and Culture*, New York, Routledge, 1999. For a feminist view of Buddhism see Luce Irigaray, *Between East and West: From Singularity to Community*, trans. Stephen Pluhacek, New York, Columbia University Press, 2002.

The Fire Sermon

1   SN, p. 1143.

2   For a discussion of the legend of Angulimala see Richard F. Gombrich, *How Buddhism Began: The Conditioned Genesis of the Early Teachings*, London, Athlone Press, 1996.

3   On the role of women in Brahminical patriarchy see Uma Chakravarti, 'Beyond the Altekarian Paradigm: Towards a New Understanding of Gender Relations in Early Indian history' in Kumkum Roy (ed.), *Women in Early Indian Societies: Readings in Early Indian History*, Delhi, Manohar, 2001.

4 SN, p. 222. For a thorough analysis of Buddhist attitudes towards women see Rita M. Gross, *Buddhism after Patriarchy: A Feminist History, Analysis, and Reconstruction of Buddhism*, Albany, SUNY Press, 1993.
5 MN, p. 267.

A Spiritual Politics

1 SN, p. 176.
2 DN, vol. 2, p. 80.
3 See DN, vol. 3, p. 173.
4 Quoted in Pierre Hadot, *Philosophy as a Way of Life: Spiritual Exercises from Socrates to Foucault*, trans. Michael Chase, Oxford, Oxford University Press, 1995, p. 84.
5 On Buddhism in Thailand and Sri Lanka see S. J. Tambiah, *World Conqueror and World Renouncer: A Study of Buddhism and Polity in Thailand Against a Historical Background*, Cambridge, Cambridge University Press, 1984; Michael Carrithers, *The Forest Monks of Sri Lanka, An Anthropological and Historical Study*, Delhi, Oxford University Press, 1983; Richard F. Gombrich, *Theravada Buddhism: A Social History from Ancient Benares to Modern Colombo*, London, Routledge, 1988; H. L. Seneviratne, *The Work of Kings: The New Buddhism in Sri Lanka*, Chicago, University of Chicago Press, 2000.
6 On Plato's misadventure in Syracuse see M. I. Finley, *Aspects of Antiquity*, London, Chatto and Windus, 1968.
7 For Nagarjuna's advice to the king see *Nagarjuna's Letter*, trans. Geshe Lobsang Tharchin and Artemus B. Engle, Dharamshala, Library of Tibetan Works and Archives, 1979.
8 For the story about the king and the Brahmin see DN, vol. 1, p. 173.
9 SN, p. 177.
10 *Ibid.*, p. 278. For a comprehensive study of Buddhist ethics, see D. Keown, *The Nature of Buddhist Ethics*, London, Macmillan, 1992.

Empires and Nations

1   Xenophon, *Cyropaedia*, trans. W. Miller, Cambridge, Mass., Loeb Classical Library, 1989.

2   On Alexander and the ascetics see *Plutarch's Lives*, vol. 2, trans. Dryden, revised by Arthur Hugh Clough, New York, Modern Library, 1992, p. 190.

3   A. B. Bosworth presents a chilling account of Alexander's brutalities in *Alexander and the East*, Oxford, Clarendon Press, 1996. Also see his *Conquest and Empire: The Reign of Alexander the Great*, Cambridge, Cambridge University Press, 1988; Robin Lane Fox, *Alexander the Great*, London, Penguin, 1973 and Mary Renault, *The Nature of Alexander*, London, Penguin, 1983. Nietzsche denounced Alexander as 'the coarsened copy and abbreviation of Greek history'.

4   Arrian quoted in Bosworth, *Alexander*, p. 149.

5   Romila Thapar, *Ashoka and the Decline of the Mauryas*, Delhi, Oxford University Press, 2nd edn, 1997, p. 255.

6   *Ibid.*, pp. 252–3.

7   *Ibid.*, p. 339.

8   Shaku Soyen, *Sermons of a Buddhist Abbot: Addresses on Religious Subjects*, trans. D. T. Suzuki, New York, Weiser, 1971, p. 211. Also see Brian Victoria, *Zen at War*, New York, Weatherhill, 1998.

9   Friedrich Nietzsche, *The Gay Science*, trans. R. J. Hollingdale, Cambridge, Cambridge University Press, 2001, p. 242.

10   Ernst Jünger quoted in Roberto Calasso, *The Forty-Nine Steps*, trans. John Shepley, London, Pimlico, 2002. Also see Ernst Jünger, *Storm of Steel*, trans. Michael Hoffmann, London, Allen Lane, 2003.

11   Rabindranath Tagore, *Nationalism*, London, Papermac, 1991, pp. 21–2.

12   Simone Weil, *The Need for Roots*, trans. A F. Wills, London, Routledge, Kegan and Paul, 1952, p.122.

13   Friedrich Nietzsche, *Writings from the Late Notebooks*, trans. Kate Sturge, Cambridge, Cambridge University Press, 2003, p. 238. For a radical Christian critique of modern political arrangements see Reinhold Niebuhr, *Moral Man and Immoral Society: A*

Study in Ethics and Politics, 1932, rpt. Louisville, Westminster John Knox Press, 2001. For a philosophical background to the idea of the state see Ernst Cassirer, *The Myth of the State*, New Haven, Conn., Yale University Press, 1946.

14 The classic description of the rise of individualism in Europe is in Jacob Burckhardt, *The Civilization of the Renaissance in Italy*, trans. S. G. C. Middlemore, Harmondsworth, Penguin, 1990. Burckhardt had a pessimistic view of the modern individual's prospects, although he never went as far as his student, Nietzsche. See Jacob Burckhardt, *Force and Freedom: Reflections on History*, New York, Pantheon, 1943. Also see 'Burckhardt and Nietzsche' in Erich Heller, *The Disinherited Mind: Essays in Modern German Literature and Thought*, New York, Farrar, Straus and Giroux, 1957.

15 Adam Smith, *The Theory of Moral Sentiments*, Oxford, Oxford University Press, 1976. For a stimulating analysis of philosophers conceptualizing a new human being, see C. B. Macpherson, *The Political Theory of Possessive Individualism, Hobbes to Locke*, Oxford, Clarendon Press, 1962. Also see his introduction to *Leviathan*, Harmondsworth, Pelican, 1968.

16 Jean-Jacques Rousseau, *The Social Contract and Discourses*, trans. G. D. H. Cole, New York, Everyman's Library, p. 32.

17 *Ibid.*, p. 297.

18 Franz Rosenzweig, *The Star of Redemption*, trans. William W. Hallo, New York, Holt, Rinehart and Winston, 1970, p. 3.

19 Paul Valéry, 'The Crisis of the Mind' in *The Outlook for Intelligence*, trans. Denise Folliot and Jackson Mathews, Princeton, Bollingen, 1989, p. 24. Valéry was only one of the many European intellectuals forced to reconsider nineteenth-century pieties about history and progress. Also see José Ortega y Gasset, *History as System*, New York, Norton, 1962; Albert Camus, *The Rebel*, trans. Anthony Bower, Harmondsworth, Penguin, 1968; Gottfried Benn, *Primal Vision*, E. B. Ashton (ed.), New York, New Directions, 1971; E. M. Cioran, *History and Utopia*, trans. Richard Howard, Chicago, University of Chicago Press, 1998; Robert Musil, *Precision and Soul*, Burton Pike and David Luft (eds), Chicago, University of Chicago Press, 1990; Simone Weil, *Oppres-*

sion and Liberty, trans. Arthur Wills and John Petrie, London, Routledge, 2001.

20 *Sutta Nipata*, trans. as *Woven Cadences of Early Buddhists*, by E. M. Hare, Pali Text Society, London, p. 118.

21 On the fate of Buddhism in China, Tibet and South-east Asia see Holmes Welch, *Buddhism Under Mao*, Cambridge, Mass., Harvard University Press, 1972; Tsering Shakya, *Dragon in the Land of Snows: A History of Modern Tibet Since 1947*, New York, Penguin, 2000; Palden Gyatso, *Fire Under the Snow: Testimony of a Tibetan Prisoner*, London, Harvill, 1997; François Bizot, *The Gate*, New York, Knopf, 2003.

22 Nikolai Berdyaev, *The Fate of Man in the Modern World*, trans. D. Lowrie, London, Student Christian Movement Press, 1935.

23 Václav Havel, *Living in Truth*, London, Faber, 1987, p. 70.

24 *Ibid.*, pp. 154–5.

25 Nathuram Godse, *May It Please Your Honour*, Delhi, Surya Bharati Prakashan, 2000.

Western *Dharmas*

1 Friedrich Nietzsche, *Twilight of the Idols/The Anti-Christ*, trans. R. J. Hollingdale, Harmondsworth, Penguin, 1968, p. 142.

2 AN, p. 65.

3 Alexis de Tocqueville, *Democracy in America*, trans. Harvey C. Mansfield and Delba Winthrop, Chicago, University of Chicago Press, 2000, p. 512.

4 Kerouac quoted in Carole Tonkinson (ed.), *Big Sky Mind: Buddhism and the Beat Generation*, New York, Riverhead, 1995, p. 31.

5 Stephen Batchelor, *Buddhism Without Beliefs: A Contemporary Guide to Awakening*, New York, Riverhead, 1997. Also see M. Epstein, *Thoughts Without a Thinker: Psychotheraphy from a Buddhist Perspective*, New York, Basic Books, 1995.

Overcoming Nihilism

1 Friedrich Nietzsche, *The Will to Power*, trans. Walter Kauffmann and R. J. Hollingdale, New York, Viking, 1968, p. 866.

2 Nietzsche, *Anti-Christ*, p. 142.

3 For Nietzsche on Heraclitus see his little-known essay *Philosophy in the Tragic Age of the Greeks*, trans. Marianne Cowan, Illinois, Regnery, 1962. Also available on *http://www.geocities.com/thenietzschechannel/ptra.htm*.

4 Nietzsche, *Anti-Christ*, p. 142.

5 For an impressively nuanced view of interdependence in the contemporary world see Robert Wright, *Nonzero: The Logic of Human Destiny*, New York, Vintage, 2001. Also see Wright's article in the *New York Times*, 11 September 2003.

The Last Journey

1 DN, vol. 2, pp. 107–8.

2 *Ibid.*, p. 158.